11/26/88

A LASTING PEACE, VOLUME TWO

A LASTING PEACE

PEACE

Volume Two

by Daisaku Ikeda

New York · WEATHERHILL · *Tokyo*

First edition, 1987

Published by John Weatherhill, Inc., of New York and Tokyo, with editorial offices at 7–6–13 Roppongi, Minato-ku, Tokyo 106, Japan. Copyright © 1987 by Daisaku Ikeda; all rights reserved. Printed in Japan.

Library of Congress Cataloging in Publication Data: (Revised for volume 2). / Ikeda, Daisaku. / A lasting peace. / Vol. 2 lacks subtitle. / 1. Sōka Gakkai. 2. Peace—Religious aspects—Sōka Gakkai. / I. Title. / BQ8449. I384′ L37   294.3′928   81–14699 / ISBN 0–8348–0166–3 (v. 1)   ISBN 0–8348–0220–1 (v. 2)

Contents

Preface

Some years ago, Takeshi Yamazaki, vice-president of John Weatherhill, Inc., suggested that I publish a collection of the speeches and proposals I have made in various parts of the world on the subjects of peace, culture, and education. The result of that suggestion was *A Lasting Peace,* published six years ago, to which the present volume is a sequel.

Its publication this year is especially timely. To commemorate the thirtieth anniversary of the historic pronouncement against nuclear arms delivered by Josei Toda, the second president of Soka Gakkai, we have designated 1987 the Year of Peace and the Community. The publication of this book coincides nicely with the several undertakings we plan in connection with that theme.

The first volume of *A Lasting Peace* contained speeches and proposals that I delivered in Japan and overseas during the decade between 1971 and 1981. The present volume contains both material postdating that period and some earlier material that could not be included in the first volume.

For instance, "The Key to World Peace" was delivered on the occasion of the eleventh anniversary of President Toda's antinuclear pronouncement, at the Eleventh General Meeting of the Soka Gakkai Student Division, held on September 8, 1968, and marks the first time that I dealt with the China problem. Anyone who remembers what Sino-Japanese and Sino-American relations were like twenty years ago can only regard present circumstances in connection with China and her international relations as astonishing. As one person who, realizing that China holds a vital key to world peace, urged the stabilization of her international position and exerted what power I could in the name of normalization of relations and of amity between China and Japan, I am deeply gratified at the changes that have taken place since the time when this speech was made.

For the continued existence and the prosperity of humanity, no matter how much time it takes and no matter how distant the goal may seem, we must all follow the road leading to peace. But, in the face of the threat posed by nuclear weapons, we must interpret peace in a new way. We can no longer think of it in the merely relative terms of an interlude between periods of belligerence.

The French poet Paul Valéry was correct when he said that peace is the moral victory, mute and continuous, of possible forces against probable greed. Without the struggle against greed and eventual victory over it, the most ardent cries for peace are in vain.

Interestingly, Valéry's idea closely approaches the Buddhist interpretation of peace. Buddhism views greed as life's demonic aspect and the struggle against greed as the operations of life's Buddha aspect; it teaches that all living entities have both aspects, which are constantly battling against each other. The state of mental tranquility, far from static, must be the fruit of the triumph of the Buddha aspect over the demonic aspect. And building a foundation for global peace will be impossible until this triumph has been achieved in each of our individual lives. This is what Josei Toda meant when, in his antinuclear cry, he admonished us all to draw the claws of Satan from out of our own minds. Realizing the need to do this is the philosophical source of all my own approaches to peace and of the diverse antiwar and peace-promoting activities of Soka Gakkai International.

Fortunately, many of our activities are developing steadily. For example, the exhibition entitled "Nuclear Arms: A Threat to Our World," undertaken by Soka Gakkai in cooperation with the United

Nations, opened at the United Nations Headquarters in New York in 1982. It has been shown in sixteen cities of thirteen countries and, having been held in Beijing in the fall of last year, is scheduled to open in Moscow in June 1987.

I place great importance on the way in which this antinuclear exhibition has transcended national borders to bring together both East and West. There can be no doubt that someday this movement will stimulate the kind of extensive and profound awareness among all the citizens of the world that is absolutely essential to the achievement of lasting global peace. I shall be extremely happy if this book can be of some use and value to all sincere wishers for peace.

In conclusion, I should like to express my profound gratitude to the translator, Richard L. Gage; to the staff of John Weatherhill, Inc., who devoted great effort to the editorial and production work; and to all the other people who helped make this book possible.

July 1987

A LASTING PEACE, VOLUME TWO

The Key to World Peace

*Delivered at the Eleventh General Meeting of the Soka
Gakkai Student Division, held at Nihon University
Auditorium, Tokyo, September 8, 1968.*

On September 8, 1957, Josei Toda, my mentor and the second president of Soka Gakkai, sent up a cry against nuclear arms and pointed out the way to our duty when he said, "All the peoples of the world have the right to live. Anyone who would threaten that right is evil, monstrous, and satanical. Any nation that would employ nuclear arms to conquer the world is wicked. And it is the mission of young men and women from all over Japan to carry this message to the whole globe."

In contrast to the many Japanese leaders and politicians who talk glibly of peace solely for their own advantage and to pad their own popularity, Toda made this proclamation for the sake of true peace. His words, like a great sword cutting straight to the heart of the problem, represent the eternal spirit of Soka Gakkai and an imperishable guide for all humanity. We must devote ourselves entirely to living up to that spirit in a determined struggle to defeat all haughty authorities who would oppress the ordinary people.

The China Problem as the Key

We used to be told that the time would come to deal with the China problem when the Vietnam War ends. And at present some people decline to turn their attention to China, for various reasons, including conditions in Czechoslovakia. But, owing to her position, sooner or later Japan will have to come to grips with this issue, which is of essential importance to us members of Soka Gakkai, who always think in terms of all the peoples of the world.

At present, the China problem is a major bottleneck in connection with attaining world peace. Most of the misery of war that has resulted from confrontation and armed conflict between the great powers of the East and West since World War II has afflicted regions of Asia. The Korean and Vietnamese wars are cases in point. In these conflicts, the United States has represented the powers of the free world. But it has been China, not the Soviet Union, that has stood behind communist forces.

China's position in international society is most tenuous. She is not represented in the United Nations and maintains very shaky diplomatic ties with most other nations, all of whom know little of what goes on behind the Bamboo Curtain, where for that matter little is known of what goes on in the outside world. As long as China is treated as a heretic and prevented from carrying on intercourse with other nations on a footing of equity, world peace will remain unattainable. Furthermore, admission of China into the international community is an indispensable condition for the political stability and economic prosperity of such other Asian nations as Korea, Taiwan, Vietnam, Thailand, and Laos.

Into the Field of International Deliberation

The first step in achieving the desired goal is officially to recognize the government of China. The second is to give China a just seat in the United Nations. And the third is to stimulate extensive economic and cultural exchange. In terms of historical tradition, geographical location, and racial affinity the Japanese hold the most powerful keys to opening up closed China. But, at present, Japan is under the nuclear umbrella of the United States, a nation for which China entertains a great antipathy; and the Japanese government refuses to recognize or enter into diplomatic relations with its Chinese neighbor. Furthermore, what meager trade routes remain open between the two are decreasing annually.

Although the scars of war between China and Japan still linger today, twenty-three years later, the contemporary young Japanese had no direct connections with the war. Not did the young members of the Chinese Red Guard, who are now active throughout their land. It would be gravely wrong to impose the wounds of an old war on the younger generations, who must work in the vanguards of both nations. When they become the nuclei of their societies, the young people of both China and Japan must work gladly, hand in hand, to build a brighter world. When, with China and Japan as the axis of the movement, all the other nations of the region help and protect each other, the blazing sun of hope and happiness will drive the clouds of the misery and poverty of war from the face of all Asia.

I am by no means an admirer of communism and realize fully that many well-intentioned Japanese are wary of what China may do in the future. But I insist that for the sake of peace in Asia and the world all nations must cooperate in good faith. Saving humanity in an age in which nuclear weaponry threatens total annihilation depends on whether we are able to establish friendships that transcend national borders. This is precisely why I take this opportunity to discuss the China issue. Although some people may accuse me of facile thinking and criticize my lack of research into the matter, I maintain that we cannot say World War II has truly ended until we solve the China problem. Now, as conditions are developing rapidly, if we persist with the current system, convinced that it is the optimum one, and take no forward-oriented measures, Japan is doomed to fall victim to a deluge.

Raising the Living Standard is the Best Security

I know that many Japanese are afraid of Chinese aggression and strongly advocate rigid adherence to the Japanese-American Security Treaty system and feel it is better to avoid close associations with China. I take a somewhat different view.

First, I see Mao Zedong as essentially more a nationalist than a Marxist-Leninist. Furthermore, I believe that, in addition to being a materialist communist, he is heir to the oriental spiritual tradition. Chinese pride in their Chineseness is much more passionate than we can imagine. To have an idea of this, it is only necessary to remember the tears of joy shed by Taiwan and Hong Kong Chinese at the news of mainland China's first nuclear experiments and the support the Taiwan government gave mainland China in its dispute with India.

His concern with spiritual matters is evident in the way Mao Zedong stressed revolution in human ideas and the moderation of Chinese actions in the early stages of the Great Cultural Revolution. Unlike the Soviets, who, in their time, executed them on the spot, while criticizing and ridiculing supposed party enemies, the Chinese have refrained from corporal punishment. As strange as it seems to us, the Chinese apparently are attempting to bring about a revolution in awareness.

I believe that they will adopt a similar moderate attitude in their efforts to expand their influence abroad. Moreover, at their present stage of might and economic development, it is unthinkable that they should launch direct armed aggression.

As long as conditions remain stable and the Japanese people live reasonably well, I can foresee no danger of a revolution arising in Japan from deepened contacts with China. In other words, increasing the level of living of the Japanese people is a far stronger form of protection against violent revolution than being so terrified by the phantom of invasion that we increase our armaments, harden our shell against communism, and further strengthen the Security Treaty system. Of course, should China invade another nation, my way of thinking would change.

China is a vast and venerable nation with a population of seven hundred and ten million people and a history of more than three thousand years. The ways of thinking of its people are so complicated that attempting to make clear-cut judgments about them leads to dead ends. Similarly, hastily trying to gauge China on a small scale invites terrible errors. And this is why resolving all such issues as reestablishing diplomatic relations, representation in the United Nations, and Japan-China trade demands understanding of these points, plenty of background information, and persevering in negotiations with a long-range viewpoint.

Summit Conference, Now

With the treaty concluded between Japan and the government of Taiwan in 1952, Japan has assumed the position that the issue of peace with China has been settled; but this is tantamount to ignoring the existence of seven hundred and ten million people in mainland China. True normalization of relations between two nations can only have significance when it advances mutual understanding and advantage of, and mutual exchanges between, both peoples, and contributes to world peace. Since regularization of ties with China must take into consideration all the people of China, a treaty, no matter how sensible, that fails to do so is nonsense. Zhou Enlai and the other leaders of China today consider that a state of war between Japan and their nation continues to exist. And smooth relations between our countries cannot be established as long as this state of affairs persists, no matter how assiduously Japan argues that the war is over.

To solve this problem it is essential that the governments of Beijing and Tokyo confer directly with each other. The regularization of ties between the two countries entails many difficult, complex matters, including reparations for damages made by the Japanese in China during World War II and, principally, rights of claim on foreign assets in Manchuria. The solutions to these problems demand mutual understanding, profound trust, and, most of all, a shared desire for peace.

Sharp, clever diplomacy, and the inductive method of reasoning that minor problems should be solved first, and then the issue of restoration of relations dealt with, are doomed to failure. It is essential that the leaders and persons of maximum responsibility in both nations meet to ascertain their joint desire for fundamental peace; to establish basic, inclusive lines of policy; and then address themselves to the solution of smaller matters. In other words, the deductive method is the direct path to resolving the problem. Any difficulty, no matter how recalcitrant, can be solved if the leaders of both China and Japan persist in discussing it in a forward-looking manner as many times as may be required.

At present, however, the government of Prime Minister Eisaku Sato has no intention of dealing with the Chinese, who, for their part, refuse to glance in Japan's direction. Consequently, I am firmly convinced that the opposition parties, especially the Komeito, must join forces to cope with this difficult and major issue.

Considerable opposition from Taiwan and the United States can be expected to a Japanese attempt to approach China. But it must be remembered that in drawing closer to the Chinese government, we would not be breaking away from these other nations. Our major role is to serve as a bridge between the two opposed camps. I insist that Japan must accept this responsibility. If we do, far from criticizing us, in the future all parties will be grateful to us and put hope in our ability to do international good. If we perform this role, I am certain that someday all Asia will look with great gratitude on the people of Japan.

Some conscientious parties in the United States are already voicing the opinion that the roots of war cannot be severed until peaceful, amicable relations are established between their nation and China. For instance, Senator Mike Mansfield has said, regarding the Vietnam War, "Sooner or later, a temporary ceasefire may be agreed upon, as was the case with the Korean War. In my judgment, however, unless we have a frank confrontation with various problems of American-Chinese relations, no lasting peace can ever be hoped for in Korea, Vietnam or any other part of Asia."

But, I am afraid it will take a long time still before the American government and people are amicably disposed toward China. And, when we realize that the threat of war—possibly nuclear war—is too close in the offing, it becomes clear that solutions to those Sino-American difficulties must be made with the utmost dispatch. No nation is as well suited as Japan to play the intermediary between these two great nations.

Japan as Optimum Mediator

For centuries Japanese culture has developed under the influence of the great civilization of China. The sutra we Soka Gakkai members read in our devotional services is written in the Chinese language, and many of our oldest customs and traditions are actually of Chinese origin.

In the late Nara period (710–94) of Japanese history, many Chinese settled in this country, especially a place called Uzumasa, in modern Kyoto; and many place names of Chinese derivation are still to be found in that area. The great Buddhist priest Saicho (767–822) is said to have been descended from naturalized Chinese. In short, from a cultural and even a racial standpoint, friendly relations between China and Japan are part of a completely natural current of development. And it is therefore totally unnatural and irrational for Japan to turn her back on China and to stand by idle in the face of the sufferings of other Asian peoples.

A certain French critic has said that Japan holds the key to the modification of American policy in the Far East and that, to play the part of a moderator in international affairs, Japan must normalize relations with China and establish its own independent political policies with the greatest speed. I am in total agreement with his opinion. Regularization of Japan-China relations not only is to the benefit of Japan, but also is a mission imposed on us by the objective world situation.

A Place for China in the United Nations

The major difficulty of Chinese representation in the United Nations is deciding whether the representative shall be the People's Republic of China (mainland) or the Republic of China (Taiwan). Neither party will agree to establishing two seats, one for each; and both insist that their side and their side alone has the right to represent the entire Chinese nation.

The question of Chinese representation was first taken up in the fifth United Nations general assembly in 1950. After the communists triumphed in internal fighting and established a government in Beijing, the United States started giving the possibility consideration but opposed the idea after Chinese volunteer troops began taking part in the conflict in Korea. For the next decade, the United States closed the door to Chinese representation by consistently shelving the proposal.

But support for Beijing steadily grew, and, in 1960, the vote against further shelving was forty-two to thirty-four. In 1961, the issue was declared an "important question." According to article eighteen of the United Nations charter, "Decisions of the General Assembly on important questions shall be made by a two-thirds majority of the members present and voting."

America had the issue put among such matters out of fear that the assembly would approve it if it were decidable on the basis of simple majority.

The charter says, "The 'important questions' refer to such decisions as the election of the non-permanent members of the Security Council and the admission of new member-states to the Organization. Also, other problems can be decided to be 'important questions' by a majority of the seated, voting member-states."

In connection with Chinese representation, the United States took the crafty stance of claiming to be willing to recognize Beijing as representative while, at the same time, insisting that the matter be designated an important question and thus complicating the voting.

Support for Beijing steadily increased; and, at the twentieth general assembly, in 1965, the vote stood at forty-seven to forty-seven for approval. For a while thereafter, the Cultural Revolution caused a hardening of international ties and an aggravation of the emotional climate with the result that support for Beijing flagged somewhat.

Now that the tumult of that revolution is gradually subsiding, however, Pakistan and other nations, one by one, are resuming diplomatic ties with China, who once again will come to exert great influence on the international political situation.

World opinion will be generally in China's favor. Gradually, approval of the idea is gaining ground even among the industrialized nations, and people in the know say that Beijing should represent China in the United Nations in another four or five years.

Though the Liberal Democratic Party persists in servility toward the United States, since it is an independent nation with its own beliefs and ideas, Japan ought to have the right to pursue independent diplomatic policies. When we reflect on our two thousand years of profound relations with China, our position in contemporary international society, and our ideals of future peace for Asia and the world, it becomes apparent that we cannot go on following the course we pursue at present.

In the autumn of 1968, the United Nations will hold its twenty-third general assembly. At that time, Japan must cease supporting opposition from the United States and must advance the cause of recognition of Beijing as the representative of China in the United Nations. All must agree that, under existing circumstances, the effective exclusion of China—whose population amounts to one-quarter that of the entire globe—is a grave defect in the constitution of the United Nations. Solving this problem will enhance the importance of that organization and contribute greatly to world peace.

Expanding Japan-China Trade

Since trade must rest on mutual understanding, Japan cannot unilaterally ignore the demands made by China, who has in the past twice formulated a set of three general principles. The first set, issued in May 1958, after what has come to be called the so-called Nagasaki Incident, consisted of the following three fundamentally political points: (1) Japan will not adopt hostile policies toward China, (2) Japan will not participate in the plot to establish two separate Chinas, and (3) Japan will make no attempt to interfere with efforts to reestablish diplomatic relations between the two nations.

In August 1960, in connection with the possibility of reopening trade with Japan, China issued what were called three general trade principles. Instead of being direct demands, as the three political principles had been, these established three stages for the development of trade routes.

In November 1962, Liao Chengzhi from China and Tatsunosuke Takasaki from Japan exchanged memoranda on the cultivation of new Japan-China trade, which was referred to as L-T trade, from the initials of these two men. A five-year (1963–67) agreement was reached, and the Liao Chengzhi Office was set up in China while the Liaison Council for Overall Japan-China Trade was set up in Japan to sponsor trade transactions. As this term expired, further discussions were held in February of this year, instituting the so-called Japan-China memorandum trade. But this is extremely unstable since the term of agreement is only one year.

Both L-T and memorandum trade were based on government agreements. In addition to them, in December 1962, private firms signed a protocol on amicable transactions between China and Japan. In Japan, three organizations were responsible for such transactions: the Council for the Promotion of Japan-China Trade, the Japan Association for the Promotion of International Trade, and the Kansai (Western Honshu) headquarters of the second body. In China, the work was handled by the Committee for the Promotion of International Trade.

But the Japanese government, leaving such trade entirely to people in the world of finance, not only takes the negative view of a by-stander, but also firmly adheres to the idea of separation of politics and economics, an idea that China flatly rejects, and, once again servile to the United States, is imposing stringent export restrictions. Behind such steps is American hostility toward China, which the formulators of the Security Treaty system imagined to be the worst possible potential enemy.

The stance of the government of the Liberal Democratic Party clearly infringes on the spirit of the first set of three basic principles; and, quite naturally, China assumes a highly cautious position. For the past two or three years, trade with China has decreased and at present accounts for only a small percentage of the Japanese total.

The Yoshida Letter

Immediately after a visit to Taiwan in 1964, former prime minister Shigeru Yoshida sent a private letter to Chiang Kai-shek's secretary, saying that the Japanese government would not permit long-term government-fund export financing for L-T or any other trade with mainland China. This was merely a private exchange, and Yoshida is already dead. There is no reason why the letter should have any binding effect on the Japanese government. But they continue to refuse to recognize government-financed long-term deferred payment, thus strangling trade transactions. I insist that the government should proclaim its rejection of the Yoshida letter and make all efforts to expand commercial relations with China on the basis of the three trade principles.

China is still developing economically. Although great progress in some fields—like the production of nuclear weapons—can be cited, in general, the national industrial level is low. Since the severance of ties with the Soviet Union, that former source of technological assistance has been lost; and China has been pursuing an independent course. Outwardly they seem self-confident and proud; inwardly, however, I am certain that they are eager for the technology of the advanced nations. And, indeed, since the break with the Soviets, China has imported a large number of plants from Western countries.

For instance, the Chinese are building a large chemical fertilizer installation in Sichuan on the basis of a plant purchased from England. With the help of Austrian technical know-how, they are building an oxygen converter in Taiyuan. And plans are going ahead for a petrochemical combine in Lanzhou with crude-oil refineries from West Germany and a polyethylene plant from England. It is said that negotiations are underway for the purchase of extensive steel plants from West Germany.

The weight of Chinese trade, too, has shifted from the socialist to the capitalist nations. For instance, whereas in 1950, seventy percent of Chinese trade was done with the communist nations, especially the Soviet Union, in the 1960s, about seventy percent is done with capitalist countries. In the past two years, what with the Cultural Revolution and the surrounding of the British legation, trade with the West has declined somewhat. But the situation will no doubt calm down in the near future.

The French journalist Robert Guillain has said that Japan stands in the most advantageous position in relation to trade with China. Undeniably it is mutually advantageous and essential to long-term future growth for Japan to make good use of its geographical proximity and establish close connections that will make available both the immense natural resources and the huge potential market that China offers. More important still, such connections will work for the prosperity of all of Asia and for the peace of the world.

Prosperity and Peace

The heart of the misery suffered by the Asian nations, the part of the globe currently most seriously threatening the achievement of global peace, is poverty and the division of the region into the communist and free blocs. To relieve the poverty, Japan must cease turning its back on China, which represents half of all Asia, and must take positve steps to stimulate prosperity. I am confident that amicable relations between China and Japan would lessen and probably ultimately remove the antagonism between the communist and free zones of Asia.

Certainly there is much uncertainty in the region at present, and from the viewpoint of its own high-level growth only, Japan might be justified in considering its present diplomatic course the safest. I am afraid, however, that, unless changes are made, the danger of war will only deepen and could bring an end to Japanese prosperity.

At present Japan is more prosperous than ever before, with the second largest gross national product in the free world. But this prosperity is no more than a castle built on the sands of a national population with a low level of income and on the poverty of most of the rest of Asia. A certain French economist has called Japanese prosperity soulless. A noted sociologist describes the Japanese as a wealthy but emasculated people.

Our nation, our people, and our society must stop pursuing only profit and must strive to create values for the new century by adopting a broad, international viewpoint and striving for peace, prosperity, and cultural development and progress. I am certain that the most important thing in this connection is to devote all-out energy to the regularization of ties with China, support of Beijing's representation in the United Nations, and the stimulation of Japan-China trade.

No doubt some people will misinterpret my standpoint as leftist. Such an interpretation is, however, superficial. Because we base our thoughts and actions on the teachings of Buddhism and because we give precedence to humanity and to the dignity of all the peoples of the earth, it is only natural that we should hope for peace as well as for Japanese security. When this basic attitude is understood, it becomes clear that I am neither rightist nor leftist. Furthermore, I consider it a grave error to make judgments about right and left leanings on the basis of superficial appearances. All discussion that leaves out of account basic philosophy is meaningless. Our basic philosophy is the teaching that the ultimate of all reality is the oneness of the physical and the spiritual. Acting in accordance with this philosophy is to follow the Buddhist Middle Way: life is neither existence nor nonexistence but mystically partakes of both.

A New Human Culture,
of, for, and by the People

Delivered at the Thirty-fourth General Meeting of Soka Gakkai, held at the Nippon Budokan, November 2, 1971.

The Mission of Bodhisattvas of the Earth

I should like to begin with a quotation from *Ongi Kuden* (Record of the Orally Transmitted Teachings) of Nichiren Daishonin: "Now Nichiren and his disciples who chant Nam-myoho-renge-kyo are all followers of the Bodhisattvas of the Earth. The benefits of the Four Bodhisattvas are as follows: The natural function of fire is to burn things (Jogyo), that of water to purify (Jyogyo), that of wind to blow away dust and dirt (Muhengyo), and that of earth to nourish plants and trees (Anryugyo). The roles of the Four Bodhisattvas are not the same, but all of them are derived from Myoho-renge-kyo. The Four Bodhisattvas dwell underneath and Tiantai's interpretation in the *Hokke Mongu* speaks of 'underneath' as 'the ultimate depth of life, that being the absolute reality.' That the Bodhisattvas of the Earth dwell underneath means that they dwell in the truth."

In other words, all of Nichiren Daishonin's followers are like Bodhisattvas of the Earth. Just as it is the mission of fire to burn, of water to cleanse, of wind to blow away dust, and of earth to nurture plants, so it is the fundamental role of Bodhisattvas of the

16

Earth to intone Nam-myoho-renge-kyo, and constantly to exert a creative, innovating influence on daily life and society. In short, it is their inherent mission to abide by the fundamental law of Nam-myoho-renge-kyo and to work actively to make contributions to their own happiness, and the happiness of others and of all society.

The universe manifests splendid harmony. It could be likened to an orchestra filled with the limitless activities of the force of life. But the blazing sun, the orbiting and rotating Earth, the constellations, and the galaxies were not made by a creator. They are themselves creator and created. They are both director and producer of their own performances. They share one fundamental entity, which, in his enlightenment, the Buddha knew to be Nam-myoho-renge-kyo.

Just as the universe created itself from within itself, so the wisdom, activities, and dynamic movement of life within human beings emerge from within. The activities of the Bodhisattvas of the Earth, too, are the calm emergence of the force of life from the fundamental universal entity. Though the fields in which we work as Bodhisattvas of the Earth differ, all of our work is in the name of the Sutra of the Lotus of the Mystic Law.

According to Zhiyi (538–97), the founder of Tiantai (Tendai) Buddhism, the Bodhisattvas of the Earth reside in what is called "the ultimate depth of life, that being the absolute reality," which is Nam-myoho-renge-kyo. This truth is deeper still than the truths of general philosophy: it is the ultimate of the universe and of all life itself and is the meaning of Nam-myoho-renge-kyo. Tapping this fundamental, ultimate entity, which exists in the innermost depths of each individual life, makes available an abundant outpouring of the force of life and enables us to manifest our true value as human beings.

In a humble example, this might be compared to boring for hot springs. If the source lies at a depth of eight hundred meters, nothing will result from drilling no more than seven hundred. Drilling to eight hundred, on the other hand, will bring the hot spring to the surface of the ground where good use can be made of it. For human beings, to penetrate to the ultimate force of life deep within them makes available majestic power that has heretofore lain concealed. Daily faith and chanting of Daimoku are ways to achieve this goal.

Another passage in *Ongi Kuden* says, "The Bodhisattvas of the Earth were taught by the original Buddha. The word *original* refers to *kuon ganjo* which transcends the limit of *gohyaku-jintengo* and means time without beginning or end; therefore his teaching benefits all living beings eternally. These bodhisattvas possess the original law which is Nam-myoho-renge-kyo." (*Nichiren Daishonin Gosho Zenshu*, 751). In other words, Bodhisattvas of the Earth follow the course of essentially basic human life, though, from the infinite past, their actions have been sincerely in accord with the spirit of compassion since they abide by the fundamental Law, which is Nam-myoho-renge-kyo.

These quotations from *Ongi Kuden* clearly show how priceless are active, spontaneous people who bear within themselves the jewel of the force of universal life. The person whose being is founded in "the ultimate depth of life, that being the absolute reality" manifests, in the microcosm that is his body, the inner verification of the benefits without beginning and end that Bodhisattvas of the Earth have bestowed and continue to bestow on humankind. Maximum manifestation of the force of inner life in daily living and in society enables the individual to fulfill his innate mission. No life can have greater value than this.

Today it seems that there are too many passive people in society. Perhaps they reject independent thinking. Perhaps they have lost themselves in the vast mechanism of society or have become mechanized themselves. Although some of the responsibility may be laid at the door of society, I prefer to think that, on a more basic level, such people are out of contact with the force of life that could renovate and revolutionize their whole being.

We, however, must remember that we are like Bodhisattvas of the Earth, firmly born aloft on an eternal current, companions in the mission of *kosen-rufu*. The emergence from the earth of bodhisattvas of this kind, whose numbers equaled that of sixty thousand times the grains of sand of the Ganges River, symbolizes a great ceremony of life that is *kosen-rufu*. We must bear in mind our nature as a great tide of people dedicated spontaneously to our mission, and moving relentlessly to the creation of lasting peace.

Kosen-rufu as a Lifelong Mission

In the *Shoho Jisso Sho* (The True Entity of Life), there occurs this passage: "No matter what, maintain your faith as a votary of the Lotus Sutra, and forever exert yourself as Nichiren's disciple. If you are of the same mind as Nichiren, you must be a Bodhisattva of the Earth. And since you are a Bodhisattva of the Earth, there is not the slightest doubt that you have been a disciple of the Buddha from the remotest past. The *Yujutsu* chapter states, 'I have taught these people since the remotest past.' There should be no discrimination among those who propagate the five characters of Myoho-renge-kyo in the Latter Day of the Law, be they men or women. Were they not Bodhisattvas of the Earth, they could not chant the Daimoku. Only I, Nichiren, at first chanted Nam-myoho-renge-kyo, but then two, three, and a hundred followed, chanting and teaching others. Likewise, propagation will unfold this way in the future. Doesn't this signify 'emerging from the earth'? At the time of *kosen-rufu,* the entire Japanese nation will chant Nam-myoho-renge-kyo, as surely as an arrow aimed at the earth cannot miss the target. But now you must build your reputation as a votary of the Lotus Sutra and devote yourselves to it." (*The Major Writings of Nichiren Daishonin,* 1:93).

The message behind these important words is this: no matter how the times may change, people who are determined to achieve *kosen-rufu* must without fail have the inner assurance of being Bodhisattvas of the Earth.

And this assurance must remain unbroken. Again, as it says in the *Gosho,* "So long as men of wisdom do not prove my teachings to be false, I will never accept the practices of other sects" (*The Major Writings of Nichiren Daishonin,* 2:200). With this attitude, we must tread our way boldly and bravely.

In another part of the *Shoho Jisso Sho,* this passage occurs: "I cannot hold back my tears when I think of the great persecution confronting me now, or when I think of the joy of attaining Buddhahood in the future. Birds cry, but never shed tears. I, Nichiren, do not cry, but my tears flow ceaselessly. I shed my tears not for worldly affairs but solely for the sake of the Lotus Sutra. So indeed, they must be tears of *amrita* (the legendary nectar of immortality)." (*The Major Writings of Nichiren Daishonin, 1:94.*)

As is said in the Lotus Sutra, in spite of all possible criticism and bodily injury, we have no choice but to walk the path of *kosen-rufu.* People who maintain this aim as a lifetime mission are truly Bodhisattvas of the Earth.

In the *Yorimoto Chinjo,* it is said, "Wise men should remonstrate against danger to the nation and suppress the people's false views" (*Gosho Zenshu,* 1156). In other words, truly wise are people who sense danger to society and the suffering of the people as pain in the greater life force and who organize resistance movements for the fundamental solution of the problems involved. It is my hope that Soka Gakkai will produce a steady stream of people capable of making contributions to society, other people, and cultural civilization. I believe that this is where our organization's social significance lies and that this is part of our drive for *kosen-rufu.*

Our organization is the trunk of the tree, the roots of which are the philosophy of Nichiren Daishonin. The future will see what kinds of branches, leaves, flowers, and fruit we bring forth. In the next few years, we must delve more deeply into Nichiren Daishonin's Buddhist philosophy and dedicate all our energy to perfecting the organization of Soka Gakkai and cultivating capable personnel. The unprecedented building project ahead of us will demand perseverance, wisdom, and enthusiasm.

In the *Kangyo Hachiman Sho* a passage occurs that clearly sets forth the processes of flourishing and retrogression that affect peoples and civilization and shows the relation between these processes and religion.

"When a horse is only one or two years old, we do not think it sickly even though it has wobbly joints and long thin shanks and legs. By the time it reaches seven or eight, however, it grows fat with bulgy arteries and a top-heavy body on spindly legs. It looks like a tiny boat overloaded with great stones, or like a small tree burdened with heavy fruit. Many kinds of disabilities appear and the horse becomes useless to man. Moreover, it grows even weaker until it becomes clear that it does not have long to live.

"The same is true of gods; in the beginning of the aeon of growth, people were born possessed of great good fortune accumulated during previous lifetimes. And since the people did no evil, gods glowed vividly, their pure hearts shining as brightly as the sun and moon. They were as spirited as lions and elephants. Then as the aeon of growth ended and the aeon of stability arrived, the older gods declined like the waning moon. The gods next to be born had already spent most of their good fortune and the people who appeared were on the whole lacking in virtue. The Three Calamities and Seven Disasters, therefore, occurred throughout the world. The people came to know suffering as well as pleasure for the first time ever.

"This was the time of the Buddha's advent, when he provided the heavens, the people, and the gods with the medicine called Buddhism. Then, like a lamp replenished with oil or an old man given a cane to lean on, the people and the gods regained their power and influence as though it were once again the aeon of growth" (*Gosho Zenshu*, 576).

The same process is visible in races, societies, and in all human history. In the flourishing period of a race, the people are vigorous and vital, their bodies glow as the sun and the moon, and their minds are as brave as lions and elephants. But the force of life in each race tends to weaken as soon as its society enters a period of stability. People themselves deteriorate. They begin to suffer as the Three Calamities (warfare, pestilence, and famine) and the Seven Disasters —(1) extraordinary changes in the sun and moon; (2) extraordinary changes in the stars and planets; (3) fires; (4) unseasonable floods; (5) storms; (6) drought; and (7) foreign invasion and internal strife (according to the Yakushi Sutra)—begin to strike their society.

Buddhism is able to revitalize not only deteriorating races and societies, but also all living beings, just as a failing lamp bursts to new brightness when its supply of oil is replenished, or an old man walks more steadily if given a stick to lean on.

This final part of the passage shows the role religion plays in the health and therapy of societies and civilizations. One noted Japanese historian has said that all civilizations have been born around a core of religion, that religion imparts spiritual vitality to races, and civilizations develop with religion as an axis.

A Flourishing in Religion, the Demand of Our Age

The rise and fall of civilizations throughout the history of humanity demonstrate a pattern in which a people flourish when a new religion is their core element and lose their force of life, decline, and ultimately fail entirely when that religion becomes empty and formalized. India is a case in point. When Buddhism flourished there, Indian culture, under such great kings as Ashoka and Kanishka, reached a lofty peak of development and achievement. When Buddhism was lost from the land, however, India weakened to the point that it was ultimately invaded by Islam.

After being introduced there, over a period of centuries, Buddhism took root in China and resulted in the brilliant international cultures of the Sui (c. 581–618) and Tang (618–c. 907) dynasties. After the expulsion of Buddhism, Chinese civilization never again reached this high level.

The cycles of flourishing and decline may be seen in the history of Japan as well. For instance, after the introduction of Buddhism, the Japanese people developed their own distinctive Buddhist culture. Ultimately, however, this became mere empty form, and the brilliant culture of the Nara period (646–794) declined. Later, after the great priest Saicho introduced the provisional teachings of the Lotus Sutra into the country, the civilization of the Heian period (794–1181) flowered. But, as time went by, the culture became overly dominated by court aristocrats who, instead of leading, victimized the ordinary people with the result that, as the Latter Day of the Law set in, the Three Calamities and Seven Disasters struck.

But then, in the early part of that Latter Day, Nichiren Daishonin appeared to dedicate his entire life to the struggle to restore new life force to the ordinary people. The flourishing he stimulated is for not only the Latter Day of the Law, but also for eternity, and signals a dawning of the force of life for all humanity.

In another part of the *Kangyo Hachiman Sho* there occurs a passage in which the Buddhism of Shakyamuni is compared to the pale moon, rising in the west and moving eastward, and the Buddhism of Nichiren Daishonin is likened to the brilliant sun rising in the east and casting aside darkness forever.

"India is called the land of the moon, meaning a country in which the Buddha should make his advent. Japan is called the land of the sun. Certainly a sage must make his advent in this country. The moon first appears in the west and gradually casts its light toward the east, indicating the eastward propagation of the Buddhism of the land of the moon. The sun rises in the east, a sign that the Buddhism of Japan will return to India. Moonlight is comparatively dim; the people were enlightened only during the last eight years of the Buddha's life. However, the sun is truly brilliant, far surpassing the moon in brightness. This is a sign that the Buddhism of the sun will fully enlighten the long night of the fifth half-millennium. The Buddha did not have to save the slanderers of the Lotus Sutra, for there were no such people in his day. During the Latter Day of the Law, powerful enemies of the supreme teaching will abound. At such a time the practice followed by the Bodhisattva Fukyo will give benefit to them" (*Gosho Zenshu,* 588).

It has taken seven centuries for the cry of this one great sage to grow into the cry of millions of people. Modern civilization has reached an impasse. The future of humanity is dark. The life force of the people has either weakened or been diverted into wrong paths. Pollution of the natural environment is proceeding at an alarming pace.

The wise people of the world eagerly await the brilliant advent of a new religion and the creation of a new global culture to pioneer in the future of humanity. The *Genko Gosho* describes a state of decline in the human world in which the powers of the Three Poisons (greed, anger, and stupidity) dominate the human mind. As this happens human stature declines, and human life spans shorten. Conditions today suggest that, if not physically, at least spiritually, much of humankind has entered into a similar state of decline. And, as a man of religion, I am convinced that only the advent of a great new religion capable of inspiring a revolution from within can work a reversal in this trend. The creation of a truly human culture based on such a religion is our task and mission.

Humanity and Culture

Though it has evolved over the millennia as a means of protecting humanity from natural disasters and the rigors of climatic and geographic conditions, in modern times—in such unsavory manifestations as war and environmental pollution—material civilization is proving itself to be as much a threat as a blessing. In my opinion, loss of understanding of what is truly in the best human interests is the cause of this contradiction. Since humanity is the creator of civilization, it ought to reap the benefits it produces and not be threatened by it.

Soka Culture Is Human Culture

The culture we of Soka Gakkai strive to create can be aptly described by the famous words from Abraham Lincoln's Gettysburg Address: "of the people, by the people, and for the people." It is a deeply human culture. Since culture is the product of human effort, it would seem self-apparent to say that it is of and for the people. But a cool, cleareyed examination of modern civilization and its many abuses shows that this is not necessarily the case.

Josei Toda, second president of Soka Gakkai, often said that culture is wisdom converted into knowledge. By this he meant that the products of human wisdom, in the form of knowledge, are transmitted and accumulated in ways that protect human beings from the dangers of the natural environment and make possible flights of the human spirit. Extending from homely things like food, clothing, and domicile to various social organizations and the higher fields of language, ethics, art, and learning, truly human culture is an elaborate interweaving of elements that envelope man and nature in a great harmony.

Today, however, some aspects of our cultural civilization have assumed identities virtually isolated from humanity and operate on the basis of their own theoretical systems. For example, with its unrestrained development, science now threatens to crush human beings, who ought to be its masters. And, as high priests of scientific truth, scientists themselves seem to be aggravating the threat.

Politicians make power their omniscient, omnipotent deity, which they magnify at the cost of sacrificing the ordinary people. And economists, entranced by the magical power of capital, exploit the weak heartlessly and have fallen to the level of what they themselves call "economic animals." In other words, civilization has drifted away from humanity—its starting point—and the people engaged in many of its branches have become inhuman and bestial with the result that, instead of being conducive to happiness for the masses, the effects of cultural activities suppress human beings and drive them to the brink of despair. Directly or indirectly, the suffering prevalent in human society today can be traced to the loss of the idea that our civilization ought to be of, by, and for the people.

Governed by Desire

It is excessive willingness to heed the voice of various physical desires and to allow them to get the upper hand that lies at the heart of the rift between modern humanity and its civilization.

The undeniable material splendors that our civilization has generated in answer to the promptings of desires must someday fade and perish as phantoms because they are built on the sacrifice of nature for the sake of humanity, of the other for the sake of the self, and of the future for the sake of the present. Furthermore, the image of true human mental and spiritual happiness is enveloped and concealed by the smog of desire and, in this concealment, is being eroded away. For slaves of desire, happiness is like the rainbow, always just out of reach.

Certainly desires are part, but not all, of human nature. Giving in to them altogether causes us to lose sight of our most noble aspects. Desires can consume the being like flames. Learning to control them wisely and to preserve the nobility of our humanity is the starting point of such elements of spiritual culture as ethics, morality, philosophy, and religion.

In modern society, however, many people tend to regard such things as empty concepts and opt for a liberality that leads to wild excesses of license. Essentially, liberation of the desires was intended as a way of realizing the dignity of humanity. But unfortunately, in social terms, it was done before conscience and a moral sense to take the place of older moral checks on desires could be established in individual human beings. Liberation turned out to be liberation of the evil within humankind, and the outcome of this was giving perversion and desire a free hand in culture.

As our civilization advances today, it more and more vividly depicts the condition described in the *Genko Gosho*: "The intensity of greed, anger and stupidity in people's minds during the latter, impure age is beyond the power of any sage or worthy man to rectify" (*Gosho Zenshu,* 1465). Liberated and now running rampant, human desires and greed are laying waste to the natural environment and making an arid desert of our internal world.

As President Richard Nixon pointed out, in terms of its moral depravity and spiritual corruption our prosperous modern society is following in the tracks of ancient Greece and Rome, both of which crumbled from within.

After the prosperity of the age of Pericles, Athens degenerated into mob rule; it exiled and therefore lost the services of many of its best people, and finally suffered defeat at the hands of the Spartans. Then Sparta fell to Thebes, as incessant warring continued among the Greek city states until finally they all were forced under the yoke of the Macedonians from the north.

At the pinnacle of its glory, the immense Roman Empire, which swallowed up not only Macedonia, Greece, and the entire Mediterranean area, but Gaul and Britannia as well, decayed from within. The people became intoxicated with the fleeting pleasures of the moment. Morality declined, and society was swept into a whirlpool of chaos. To my mind, in their material prosperity, spiritual poverty, moral depravity, and nihilistic diffusion, the United States and the other industrialized nations are treading a very similar path.

The fall of Greece or of Rome spelled disaster for one nation or one empire; if spiritually impoverished minds put to use the immense physical forces for destruction available to us now, the collapse of modern civilization could mean the annihilation of all mankind. Our crisis is by no means fire on the opposite bank of the river. The whole world is a munitions warehouse. And averting the danger of detonating it and putting a halt to the rapidly progressing tide of spiritual decadence are the mission of all human beings. This is why we must never lag in our drive to create a culture of absolute peace.

The Essential Nature of Religious Enthusiasm

Since it is the internal psychological world of mankind that lies at the heart of the crisis, the struggle must begin with a revolution of that inner world and the establishment of new world and moral views resting on a foundation of faith in a new religion, without which individual control and suppression of desires are impossible. When such control is achieved on the basis of faith, however, human beings experience a new will toward creativity and an altruistic desire to devote themselves to the well-being of others.

Thinkers and scholars have frequently pointed out the importance of religious enthusiasm as a foundation for culture. T.S. Eliot, for instance, said, "We may ask whether any culture could come into being, or maintain itself, without a religious basis. We may go further and ask whether what we call the culture, and what we call the religion, of a people are not different aspects of the same thing: the culture being, essentially, the incarnation (so to speak) of the religion of a people" (*Notes toward the Definition of Culture*).

In his *Culture,* the Polish-born, positivist anthropologist Bronislaw Malinowsky (1884–1942) said, "This material outfit of man—his artifacts, his buildings, his sailing craft, his implements and weapons, the liturgical paraphernalia of his magic and religion are one and all the most obvious and tangible aspects of culture. They define its level and they constitute its effectiveness. The material equipment of culture is not, however, a force in itself. Knowledge is necessary in the production, management, and use of artifacts, implements, weapons, and other constructions and is essentially connected with mental and moral discipline, of which religion, laws, and ethical rules are the ultimate source" (*Encyclopedia of the Social Sciences* 4:621). Though Eliot speaks with the voice of a poet and Malinowsky with that of an anthropologist, their meaning is the same: culture is unthinkable without religion and religious faith.

The Realm of the Superrational

Aspects of religious faith fall outside the category of rationality. But this does not mean that religion is necessarily always irrational. It is true that its irrationality has cast grave doubts on European Christian theology. But total reliance on reason is not always wholesome. For instance, modern scientific rationalism has put almost fanatical faith in the ability of reason to solve all problems. And, as a consequence, when confronted with irrational but undeniably existent things like human desires, scientists can only throw up their hands and resign themselves to accept what their reason is incapable of dealing with.

People of this persuasion believe in the power of human reason as beyond question. After doubting everything else, René Descartes came to the conclusion that the only thing he could not question was his reasoning self and concluded, "*Cogito ergo sum*" (I think, therefore I am). This approach became the philosophical foundation of modern science and evolved into the deism that replaced Christianity in the minds of many at about the time of the French Revolution.

In the Christian world, God's prohibitions are supposed to regulate human desires. But God exists in a conceptual world far removed from our physical beings, where desires are real—all too real. In other words, God is dead, though the desires persist. Desire falls outside the category of reason but exists nonetheless. In the West, faith in growth and progress, adopted as a way of dealing with the discrepancy between reason and desire, has become a cultural driving force. But forgetting that, in itself, reason is neither good nor bad but neutral has subjugated rational faculties to desires, which, running wild, have contributed greatly to the evolution of the crises facing humankind today.

Reason is clearly incapable of controlling all the phenomena of the force of life. Love, hate, happiness, anger, sorrow, and joy are all beyond its control. The coolest of scholars can fall hopelessly in love. The wisest sage experiences various emotions. The eye of reason is able to see only the waves on the surface of the great sea of the universal force of life. Below lie the immense, incalculable regions of the subconscious, which is not irrational but superrational. We should not reject these regions just because they are beyond the reach of reason. It is in this superrational region that the vast energy spurring human beings to think and act is to be found.

Faith as the Source of Action

How we develop and lead that energy determines our own happiness and the well-being of society. I believe firmly that controlling this powerful source of energy is the basic meaning of faith. Buddhism, which views the whole, incalculable entity of life in terms of the doctrines of the Perfect Teaching and of *ichinen sanzen,* is the ultimate, eternal religion, opening a path of unquestionable faith that deals, not with a conceptual supernatural deity, but with life as we all know and experience it. And this faith enables us to avoid being controlled by our desires and to put our desires in their proper place within the total view of life and thus to be happy and prosperous.

In his *Zhiguan Buxing,* the great Chinese Tiantai priest Miaoluo (717–82) said, "To 'believe in the perfect teaching' means to awaken faith through doctrine and make faith the basis of practice." The truly firm faith in Buddhism rejects irrationality and agrees with reason in the judgement of those matters which reason is capable of judging. This is why we call it perfect faith. This kind of faith can become the unshakable foundation of all thought and activity. In other words, reason employed to the limits of its applicability to result in faith, which, as perfect faith, becomes the unshakable foundation of all thought and activity. In this passage, in the strictest sense, the word *practice* is used to mean Buddhist discipline. But, as is said in the *Genko Gosho* (1466), "No affairs of life or work are in any way different from the ultimate reality." In other words, *activity* should be interpreted to mean all social action, including economics and politics. In essence, this passage means that faith must be the basis of all individual practical activities and that mutual trust makes possible the smooth running of society as a whole.

Furthermore, faith must be the source of all creative cultural activities. Doubt must be eliminated, because mistrust and suspicion can only lead to rupture and destructive action. Faith must prevail and must inspire actions in real society without inspiring people to long for a remote, otherworldly paradise attainable only after death.

Nichiren Daishonin's sharp criticism of the Pure Land sect arose from its strong escapist advocacy of the Western Paradise of Amida as the goal toward which all people should strive. It is true that

Shakyamuni mentions the Western Paradise, but only as an expedient to turn people's eyes to the eternal and noble. As a hypothesis it had a certain meaning. In the Lotus Sutra, however, it is regarded only as a teaching expedient and the noble, the ideal realm, is found in the life force activating sentient beings. Ignoring this and giving preeminence in faith to Amida and the desire for rebirth in his heaven, the Pure Land sect inevitably made people reject the actual world as foul and to believe that happiness was to be found only by escaping from it. But we must live in the actual world, which is the only place where we can strive for a better society. Faith must be the foundation of this striving.

In the title of *Rissho Ankoku Ron* (On Securing the Peace of the Land through the Propagation of True Buddhism), Nichiren Daishonin uses the term *peace* in the sense of a spiritual revolution that brings tranquility to the individual human life, and to society in general, and says that the foundation of such peace must be the outcome of a valorous struggle to establish true Buddhism. This, of course, requires a groundwork of unshakable faith. The True Law is beyond all doubting. Without it there can be no peace in the land. Nichiren Daishonin left for the eternal future of the Latter Day of the Law the Dai-Gohonzon of the Three Great Secret Laws as this True Law, in which one may believe wholeheartedly and without reservation.

Today, we apostles of the Mystic Law must take the lead and accept the mission and responsibility of building a happy, prosperous civilization. The nucleus of all our practical action to this end must always be Nichiren Daishonin's great philosophy of the force of life. And ours must be a powerful religious movement carrying that philosophy to the whole world.

Harmony

The human body is a harmonious whole; and the characteristic of a society that begins and ends with genuine concern for humanity is harmony. Over the doors of the temple at Delphi is an inscription strongly indicative of typically Greek wisdom. It says, "Know thyself and do nothing in excess." The first part of the inscription turns the attention toward humanity itself. The second is a plea for harmony. I disagree with the widely held opinion that the injunction to do nothing in excess and the very word *harmony* are negative and nonprogressive in connotation. I look upon both as highly creative and forward-looking.

If concern with humanity is wanting in modern civilization, so is overall harmony. Each of the aspects of our culture enjoys considerable autonomy, but there are imbalance and discord among them. In the West, each of these fields of endeavor has been unchained and allowed to run berserk because of the prevailing belief that human beings need only work for development in their own lines of endeavor since harmony, provided by the grace of God, will take care of itself.

Of course efforts must be made in individual fields, but no less effort must be expended on harmonizing the whole and determining the effects that technological advances—no matter how brilliant—have on economics, education, and human spiritual life. Shameful tardiness in dealing with this issue is attested to by such problems as the threat of nuclear weapons, the dangers of environmental pollution, disregard for human dignity in the face of the great speed and efficiency of computers, drug abuse, harmful additives in foods, and so on.

For the sake of all-important harmony, human beings must attempt to define in philosophical terms their own position with relation to the whole system, including civilization, nature, and the cosmos. But, at the most fundamental level, a great religion is absolutely essential.

The harmony of which I speak must of course be created by an enlightened populace and not be the outcome of interference on the part of people in positions of power and authority. But human beings are afflicted by the Three Poisons of greed, anger, and folly, which are a major hindrance in the generation and preservation of widespread harmony. That is why to make the majority of the populace wise and enlightened demands a great religion capable of stimulating a fundamental human revolution. I believe that the Buddhism of Nichiren Daishonin is that great religion.

In considering the necessary basis for a civilization in which the interests of humanity take first precedence, thought must be given to harmony in a wide range of relations other than those of material production and human beings alone. Some of these relations are between the ordinary masses and people in authority; problems related to occupation and social class; the relations between the city and rural areas; relations between producer and consumer; relations between the individual and society; relations between humanity and the natural environment; and so on.

Although touching on all aspects of modern society, the question of overall harmony is too big to be dealt with in detail here, I should like to say that the perfect, flawless philosophy of Nichiren Daishonin —the life-force teaching of the oneness of mind and body and the great doctrine of *ichinen sanzen*—is a philosophy of magnificent harmony. It provides the fundamental doctrines for the harmony required in the construction of a new civilization. In putting it into actual practice in society and in applying and developing it we are taking part in the construction of ideal harmony, or the total revolution that we call *kosen-rufu*.

Global Civilization as the Key to Lasting Peace

I insist that the key to success in establishing lasting peace throughout the world lies in the ability of all peoples, while continuing to work for the development of their own local cultures, to create a global civilization on the most basic level of our common humanity.

In the past, as such examples as the empire of Alexander the Great, the Roman Empire, the development of the United States, and the expansion of Russia illustrate, the establishment of unity and peace in major areas of the world has always involved force and military power. At the present time, from the standpoints of the threat of nuclear war, densely interwoven economic systems, and environmental pollution and destruction, global unity is of the most pressing importance. But it is no longer possible, as it has been in times gone by, to bring about union with armed might, because today the friction generated by an attempt to achieve such a goal could spell the annihilation of all humankind.

The only way to create global unity now is to build a world civilization linking together all humanity which, while preserving and making positive use of local traditions, at the same time, is a truly international culture. Doing this will demand delving deeper than the racial and national—plumbing to the level of our common humanity. The foundation of this world civilization will be the new global religion: Nichiren Daishonin's great Buddhism of the Three Great Secret Laws. I am firmly convinced that when a splendid new civilization blossoms on the basis of this Buddhism, the hearts of all peoples all over the globe will be united in unity and ideal peace.

Contributors to the building of this civilization must come from all peoples and all social classes. At present, raising our voices, advancing in the vanguard, and holding the flag of culture high, our organization is boldly confronting the dark clouds of these confused times.

The Significance of Regional Activity

The longest journey starts with the first step. For that reason, we must all devote sincere attention to *kosen-rufu* activities in our local societies and regions. Though it seems inconspicuous work, converting small local districts into true Buddha-lands of light and tranquility through *kosen-rufu* activities is the sure way to take true Buddhism to the entire world. In all times and places, *kosen-rufu* has welled up from the people, starting with individuals and spreading through regional societies to reach entire nations and the world. In his own time, for instance, Nichiren Daishonin entrusted *kosen-rufu* work on the northern island of Sado to a man named Abutsu-bo (*Gosho,* 1304) and similar work in the vicinity of what is today the city of Fuji to a lay priest named Takahashi (*Gosho,* 1467).

Winning the Trust of the People Is the First Step

Nichiren Daishonin made Kamakura, the political capital of Japan at the time, the home ground of his work for *kosen-rufu.* When he nearly lost his life at the hands of government executioners at a place called Tatsunokuchi near Kamakura, he said that this location, where he was prepared to lay down his life, was in no way inferior to a Buddha-land. Similarly, those places where we devote our lives to spreading faith in the Mystical Law are precious Buddha-lands of tranquility and light. Nikko Shonin (1246–1333), the second high priest of Nichiren Shoshu and founder of the head temple Taiseki-ji, followed in the tradition established by Nichiren Daishonin during his lifetime of centering his *shakubuku* efforts on the region in the vicinity of Fuji, where, indeed, the head temple is located.

We too must carry on in the same tradition by placing great emphasis on our own local regions but working to create new cultural movements in all other regions. Founded in a sense of shared humanity, such movements will be concentrations of thought and strength that can gradually expand beyond the bonds of authority-bound nationalism to contribute to the building of the global international culture that I have already said is of the utmost importance to the world today.

In Japan at present, however, regional society is still subjugated to the state government. It is time for people in these regions to decide whether they wish to remain in feudal submission to those in high places or are willing to work together to make the conversion into an autonomous governmental organization in which they participate directly and which can be called a democracy of the universal force of life.

Recent emergence of what could be called the power of the ordinary people in attempts to deal with such problems as environmental pollution seems to represent concerted strivings to restructure society on the basis of shared human emotions. From the standpoint of the current of the times and from that of the optimum nature of society, we must take the lead in this movement and must root our actions deeply in regional society and become one with local populations. This is why I consider local regions the fundamental unit of our practical action in the name of *kosen-rufu*. To utilize it to the fullest, we have made organizational revisions in our structure to concentrate on regional blocks that will be places where our leaders can actually become one with local members and assist them in creating with their own hands a new movement—a true power of the ordinary people—for happiness and prosperity in their regions. Though working for themselves, their families, and their friends throughout their local districts, all of these people must maintain the heart of faith as their nucleus, for without it, they will inevitably disperse like smoke.

In the *Ueno-ama Gozen Gohenji* (Reply to Ueno-ama Gozen), Nichiren Daishonin explains that the reason the lotus and not some other flower is used as a symbol in the title of the Sutra of the Lotus of the Mystic Law is that this plant bears blossom and fruit simultaneously. And its teaching is one of simultaneous unity of cause and effect. In other, lower-level scriptures, cause precedes effect; that is, merits accrue only after the roots of goodness have been planted in the individual. In contrast to this, however, the Lotus Sutra teaches that the hand that takes up the scripture and the mouth that recites it are at once the hand and mouth of a Buddha. A quintessential teaching, this means that the religion founded on the Lotus Sutra does not seek something distant from the actual world or pursue ideals alone. It is instead a lofty religion of great power seeking the ideal and the ultimate in the thoughts and actions of everyday life. It does not pursue vanity or empty concepts. It is not a philosophy of rejecting actuality. It is not intoxicated with self-indulgence or fantasy. A philosophy courageously facing the facts of life and a religion truly of the people, it alone can bring comfort and relief to the hearts of human beings living in this age of spiritual aridity and lack of faith, and in this way become a great driving force in the creation of a splendid new culture of the people.

Faith and Fortitude

Delivered at the Soka Gakkai Young Men's and Student Division Summer Seminar, held at Taiseki-ji, Fujinomiya, July 31, 1972.

Freedom of faith must be eternally protected as the core of humankind's fundamental rights. As I have said on several other occasions, it is the fountainhead of all other freedoms, including those of thought, conscience, speech, and assembly; the right to form organizations; the right to select one's own place of residence and occupation; and freedom of education.

History shows that throughout the long struggle to establish basic human rights in the West, freedom of religion has always been the starting point for ensuring other freedoms. The fight for freedom of religion is fundamentally related to human spiritual freedom. When this has been established, freedom of thought and conscience emerge, and finally lead to freedom of expression and the right to form organizations, which are the foundation of democracy. As this brief resumé shows, freedom of religion is the point of origin of modern democracy and remains today the most basic of all the other democratically ensured human rights. And it is the duty of all people of religion to guard and protect this freedom diligently now and in the future.

History has another lesson to teach in connection with faith. As Schopenhauer said, enforcing religion evokes skepticism. People in power behave very foolishly when they try to force those subject to them to accept a certain religion, since this blocks up the vital, natural flow of faith. Religion is characteristically a supplier of inner spiritual energy, and it is the social duty and responsibility of all believers constantly to protect this inner world from incursions by political or any other exterior authority. Part of the struggle to protect the inner world is the creation of an environment, like an oasis in the surrounding deserts of pressure from without, where people can talk and express themselves freely and openly on religion, the force of life, and other similar topics.

Our *shakubuku* activities provide a chance for the creation of such an environment since they are opportunities for human beings to come into close spiritual contact in circumstances in which the great universal force of life in them is awakened. *Shakubuku* is a way for people to come together to share and discuss their sufferings and to strive to find a better way to live. In other words, *shakubuku* has a stimulating spiritual effect on the self and the other as well. The Mystic Law, the heart of our *shakubuku* work, is the source of the inner human revolution that has this awakening effect. Our mission is to guard the Mystic Law like a precious jewel while we work to take its philosophy to others and, in this way, contribute to the establishment of true peace for mankind.

Doubt

Nichiren Daishonin's *Kanjin no Honzon Sho* (The True Object of Worship) says, "That common mortals born in the Latter Day of the Law can believe in the Lotus Sutra is due to the fact that the world of Buddhahood is present in the world of Humanity" (*The Major Writings of Nichiren Daishonin,* 1:53). This shows how important— especially in connection with other aspects of our philosophy such as the mutual possession of the Ten Worlds and the doctrine of *ichinen sanzen* ("a single life-moment possesses three thousand realms")— faith is. But young people tend to have doubts, and Josei Toda, second president of Soka Gakkai, used to encourage them to question.

Though doubt runs counter to faith, this does not mean that one should not doubt. Faith is made deeper and stronger by being subjected to questioning. René Descartes started by doubting everything until he found one thing he could not doubt: his own doubting self. From this conclusion he laid the foundation of modern rationalism.

Our faith does not reject doubt. But we insist that doubt must not stop at doubt. As Descartes doubted in the name of his search for truth, so we may doubt for the sake of building firm faith. Straying from this path will not lead to enlightenment. The German novelist Herman Hesse said that faith and doubt mutually reinforce each other and that there can be no true faith without doubt. The important point is whether the individual loses to doubt or employs it as a starting point for the building of firmer faith and a greater way of life.

People of True Strength

In times of pastoral tranquility, achievement and success may depend on lineage and education. In the troubled seas of our times—especially the seventies and no doubt into the eighties as well—ready-made standards of this kind will not ensure a safe voyage. Nor can the authority of an establishment be relied on. In our times, to ride the storm through and carry the lamp of peace into the future, we require people of perseverance and strength.

Knowledge and learning alone will not impart the kind of strength necessary. Nor can it be acquired as a consequence of power, fame, or economic might. Faith is essential to its cultivation. This strength becomes possible only when the free and magnanimous force of the universal life force as manifest in such writings of Nichiren Daishonin as *Kanjin no Honzon Sho* imparts to the personality sincerity, a vigorous sense of responsibility, strong powers of action, health, psychological flexibility, and reliability. Once these traits have been cultivated, it is necessary to go out into actual society to learn technical skills and knowledge and to acquire powers of observation. Young people who make the effort to develop in this way are certain to be outstanding in any age, environment, or field of endeavor.

A Firm Foundation

Youth is the time to don working clothes and sweat and struggle in the building of a strong, firm foundation on which the remainder of the individual human life must rest. In the mud and sweat, young people must build for themselves a foundation that will not crumble and that will withstand the trials life in society will inflict on it. With such a foundation, those young lives cannot fail to achieve excellent things.

Of course a firm foundation is essential in connection with faith too. And it is my wish that all our young people will persevere and advance courageously toward the peaks where they have set their goals.

There may be setbacks and frustrations along the way. But these can be overcome as long as unfaltering faith and the Soka Gakkai spirit remain alive and vibrant in the heart. And, in middle and later life, the frustrations of youth will be seen as the bitter doses needed to work a cure. Winston Churchill, and Charles de Gaulle, too, suffered setbacks in their youths. For instance, as a young boy, Churchill disliked his studies and was a poor student. Later, however, it was his rugged fortitude, indomitable courage, and determination to go ahead at all costs that enabled him, together with the English people, to save their nation in the hour of darkest crisis. During World War II, de Gaulle, who had once been acclaimed by the people before the Arc de Triomphe, was forced to take refuge in England, where, in spite of trials and frustrations, he remained certain that his people were waiting for him. Watching carefully for the right time to realize his aims, he moved forward a step or halted as circumstances required but nonetheless advanced steadily.

As the examples of these two great leaders illustrate, life has its ups and downs. But the universal Mystic Law is our unfailing guide in life. If we have an indefatigable spirit and firm faith and move courageously toward the achievement of *kosen-rufu,* we will without fail someday smile in fulfilled knowledge of triumph. No matter what their environment, our youth must challenge each new day, completely confident that eventually they will wave the glorious banner of victory.

Humanity and Learning

*Delivered at the Second Summer Seminar of Soka University,
held in Hachioji, Tokyo, August 22, 1974.*

Since I am no specialist in the field, I am unable to present an ordered treatment representing the fruits of research into the topic of humanity and learning but ask your indulgence as I casually relate, in a fragmentary way, some of my thoughts and impressions on the subject.

I believe that, generally speaking, to one extent or another, though they may not realize it, most human beings are scientists, philosophers, and economists. Without a considerable amount of scientific knowledge and without abiding by scientific proceedings it would be impossible to live and work day by day in sophisticated modern civilization.

Similarly, every day, within our information-filled society, each person must select the data required by his circumstances and, after considerable reflection, work this data into his own view of life and system of thought, a processes demanding philosophical abilities of no mean quality. All of the decisions that we must make on our own if we want to live and act to good advantage demand correct knowledge of all kinds of things. Acquiring this knowledge means that the relation between human beings and learning is by no means limited to a strictly academic situation. Furthermore, many people do think philosophically about their acts, and therefore make skillful decisions daily to meet life's changing circumstances.

Philosophically speaking, the intellectual activity of acquiring knowledge about things is related to being (*sein*) and the objective field of awareness, whereas making decisions about what actions to undertake belongs in the field of obligation (*sollen*), or the subjective self-conscious. Without *sein,* there can be no *sollen,* and without *sollen, sein* is worthless. The relation between *sein* and *sollen* has long been, and will always remain, a central philosophical issue.

Practice and Study

People who are outstanding in objective matters are often called talented geniuses, great intellects, and sages; those of excellence in dealing with subjective matters are referred to as men of high character and virtue, saviors, teachers, Buddhas, and bodhisattvas. For a good and happy life, we ordinary mortals must attempt to develop ourselves as much as possible in both fields.

Nichiren Daishonin said, "Without practice and study, there can be no Buddhism. You must not only persevere yourself; you must also teach others" (*The Major Writings of Nichiren Daishonin,* 1:95). His words *practice* and *study* correspond precisely with my categories of *sein* and *sollen.*

A life lived without both practice and study is gray and flat. For richness and color, both elements are essential. Another great truth fitting into the same context is found in the sutra and in the *Gosho,* the collected written works of Nichiren Daishonin: "To have a profound knowledge of the world is in itself Buddhism" (*The Major Writings of Nichiren Daishonin,* 1:75).

Since the relation between objective knowledge and subjective judgment has an amplifying effect on life, though it is difficult, we should all strive for equal growth in and balance between them. In my own view, Socrates and Plato were outstanding in the realm of *sollen,* and Aristotle in that of *sein.* Whereas the people of Japan have been strong in the subjective zone, the peoples of the West have excelled in the objective one.

Objective awareness begins to develop as soon as an individual is conscious of the things around him and proceeds vigorously during early youth, a time when subjective awareness is retarded. In young adulthood, however, the relation reverses. And from then until full maturity, growth in subjective awareness is stronger. In old age, increases in objective knowledge virtually cease, whereas subjective development continues. It is probably in the early forties that the pace of growth in the two achieves equilibrium. The Japanese saying that it is impossible to trust a man under forty reflects the feeling that at such an age, weaknesses mar the development of both the objective and subjective aspects of personality, and that persisting immaturity of thought entails an element of risk. Teachers usually grow more brilliant and achieve greatness as they grow older. There is a good reason for this.

It is my belief that Christianity suffers greatly because its founder died young and that it would have been a very different kind of religion if Christ had lived into his fifties or sixties. But his death in his early thirties, before balance is achieved between the objective and subjective facets of the personality, spelled tragedy for the religion he founded. I have the greatest respect for the elderly, who are at the stage in life when this balance has been reached. And that is why I strongly advocate a system of adult education extending into their age bracket.

Clear Distinction between Knowledge and Ignorance

The greatest enemy of true knowledge is failure, or proud refusal, to admit what one does not know. Confucian thought says that true knowledge is knowing what one knows and realizing what one does not know. In other words, it is essential to make a clear distinction between one's knowledge and ignorance. When this distinction has been made, using knowledge as a tool, it is possible to move into the realm of the unknown. This process of elucidating what has been concealed in ignorance is called learning and results in knowledge. In Buddhist terminology, it is represented by such statements as "ignorance is knowledge" and "delusion and enlightenment are one."

Learning begins with the observation of the studied object. From this observation arises information, which, through the mediation of the all-important manipulation of words, becomes an object of contemplative thought. The correct use of words is of the utmost importance to the establishment of learning. The situation can be compared to the use of the automobile, which, if properly driven, is highly convenient but which, if misused, can lead to possibly fatal accidents.

Though less important in the loose verbal usage of conversation, in the acquistion of learning, logic must govern the use of words. For instance, the theme of investigation must be specified, its contents explained, its terms defined, and the context in which they are used clarified. The isolated passage "The mind of faith is limited to the Lotus" is ambiguous and difficult to understand unless the terms are defined. "The Lotus" might refer to the Lotus Sutra as interpreted by any of various Buddhist sects including Tendai (Tiantai), Nichiren Shoshu, Nichiren Shu, or Butsuryu. But if this point is clarified, the passage will convey the same clear meaning to anyone who reads it. Logically used, words are the tool that make the known of the unknown or, in Buddhist terms, "convert illusion into the essential nature of the Law."

The Buddhist View and Modern Science and Philosophy

In the modern world, we are surrounded by a daunting number of things and events that we should like to and must understand if we are to make sense of life and to ensure our own psychological stability. Since the early part of this century, learned opinion has debated the question of whether our world is made of entirely physical matter or entirely of energy; that is, of things or of events. We all know what matter is and all experience things that fall outside the category that can accurately be called matter: energy, sound, light, society, humanity, numbers, love, positional relations, relations in time and space, the spirit, rules, and so on. As to the establishment of precedence, in recent years, scientific thought has been tending to give nonmaterial entities first place in importance over material ones and to consider the universe as an aggregation of processes or events.

Matter is only a short-term, limited part of a longer process. I can illustrate my meaning in this way. The manuscript I hold is made of the kind of matter called paper. But in the long-term view, that paper is only part of a process whereby sunlight and rain fall on the ground, making a tree grow. Human beings cut down the tree, process it into paper, use it, then burn and discard it when they have no further employment for it. After the dissolution of the ash to which it is reduced by flame, the paper continues, part of a still continuing process. For the purpose of speculative thought, insistence on the concept of one small part of the process—the thing that is for temporary linguistic convenience called matter (paper)—leads nowhere. In early stages, insistence on the concept of matter is acceptable, but in later stages, beyond knowledge, objective human thinking (what I call the *sein* mode) ceases. When this happens, subjective judgment too slows down, resulting in unbalanced words and deeds.

Buddhism interprets the world as the temporary coming together of what are called the Five Skandhas, or Five Components of Life (form, perception, conception, volition, and consciousness). I am profoundly interested by the similarity between this view and recent scientific and philosophical ones to the effect that our universe is not matter, but an aggregation of processes.

Compassionate Healers
Embracing the Mystic Law

Delivered at the Third General Meeting of the Soka Gakkai Doctors' Division, held at the Soka Gakkai Headquarters, Tokyo, September 15, 1975.

Such flowers of evil of modern civilization as environmental pollution, mental illness, and stress, plus a whole complex of more subtle issues, threaten the health of peoples all over the globe. And the pitiable human wish to ensure or preserve good physical condition finds expression in current trends to resort to ancient Chinese medicinal herbs and fungi—about the efficacy of which learned opinion is divided.

Men of medicine attempt to promote good health by objectively discovering the causes of illness and applying therapeutic methods to remove them. The relation between their approach and Buddhism is interesting. Buddhism seeks the basic sources of illness in the fundamental force of life and strives to eliminate them by means of a revolutionary process. The Buddhist approach is especially important in treating the various sicknesses of the present times and the emotional instability associated with them.

The illnesses characteristic of our times arise from the basic force of life because of the nature of the age, and can be cured only by something that affects that force—in other words Buddhism. In the *Fahua Wenju,* a commentary on the Lotus Sutra by Great Teacher

Tiantai (538–97), there occurs this passage: "The age is defiled when the Four Defilements arise at once and in great abundance. A great increase in anger causes warfare; a great increase in greed causes famine; and a great increase in stupidity causes pestilence. Due to these Three Disasters people's earthly desires grow terribly intense, and distorted views abound" (*Gosho Zenshu*, 718). The Four Defilements are those of delusion, the people, thought, and life itself. When they are rife, the minds of men grow wrathful, and conflict ensues. Greed then leads to famine. And stupidity—that is, dulled mental operations generating irrationality—produces pestilence and other kinds of illness. Because of the Three Disasters, delusion increases in a vicious circle, aggravating the situation until all human values become confused.

In other words, the Four Defilements represent distortion and madness permeating all of society, as they do today. This in turn compels the life force to adhere to defilements, resulting in mental and physical illness and social disorder.

Another passage in the *Gosho* says, "The illnesses of human beings may be divided into two general categories, the first of which is illness of the body. Physical diseases comprise one hundred and one disorders of the earth element, one hundred and one imbalances of the water element, one hundred and one disturbances of the fire element, and one hundred and one disharmonies of the wind element; a total of four hundred and four maladies. These illnesses can be cured with the medicines prescribed by skilled physicians such as Jisui, Rusui, Jivaka, and Bian Que.

"The second category is illness of the mind. These illnesses arise from the three poisons of greed, anger, and stupidity, and are of eighty-four thousand kinds. Only a Buddha can cure them; thus they are beyond the healing powers of the two Brahman deities and the three ascetics, not to mention those of Shen Nong and Huang Di" (*Gosho Zenshu*, 1178).

The illnesses of our time are of the spirit—or of the fundamental force of life—and can be cured only by true Buddhism. A restoration of the best of which human nature is capable is the key to the solution of the many problems inherent in modern society; and, if it is to be truly effective, all discussion in this connection must deal with a concrete examination of the basic meaning of human nature and with actual ways of effecting such a restoration.

Instead of remaining at their mercy—as we tend to do now—we must become the masters of the complex social structure, vast and excessively developed scientific-technological civilization, and immense flood of information that characterize our world. To do this, we require tough spiritual natures and sound bodies. Furthermore, to return ourselves to the master's seat, we must come openly to grips with the egoism that lies behind our slavery to the pursuit of profit and leads us to the folly of warfare.

Throughout the ages, however, overcoming egoism has been a very difficult matter. As history shows, far from being universally effective, moral codes have sometimes been twisted into rhetorical justifications for such things as nationalism and armed intervention. Putting any code into practice demands a tough spirit and tremendous practicality. The word *gentleness* has a kind and warm ring. But being gentle demands the most intense practical activity. Gentleness means concern for others and eagerness to rid them of their suffering. But, no matter how much a person may entertain sympathetic concern and the idea of assisting someone, unless that person possesses the resolve and energy to take practical steps, he leaves himself open to criticism as cold and unfeeling. In brief, gentleness emerges only when a potentially gentle person manifests abundant justness, a life force brimming with energy, and the readiness to undergo hardships if necessary to be of help to others.

The restoration of the best of which human nature is capable demands good mental and physical health. A sickly and weary person may have clever thoughts but is unlikely to produce forward-looking, constructive ideas. From experience I know that ideas filled with the will to challenge the problems of modern society are born only of minds and bodies overflowing with the energy of the life force.

In "On Prolonging Life," there occurs this passage: "Life is the most precious of all treasures. Even one extra day of life is worth more than ten million *ryo* (an old Japanese monetary unit) of gold. The Lotus Sutra surpasses all other teachings because of the *Juryo* chapter. The greatest prince in the world would be of less consequence than a blade of grass if he died in childhood. If he died young, even a man whose wisdom shone as brightly as the sun would be less than a living dog" (*The Major Writings of Nichiren Daishonin*, 1:230).

I think this passage expresses more than just the wish to extend life. It means that, in addition to being long, life must be filled with energy and imbued with vitality. Furthermore, since physical and mental debility can cause retrogressive and vain thought, even a sage as bright as the orb of the sun can manifest his brilliance in society only if he is sound in mind and body.

Understanding the Causes

The *Gosho* says that therapy performed by a person ignorant of the causes does no more than make the illness worse (*The Major Writings of Nichiren Daishonin*, 1:193). It is my belief that only doctors who base their judgments on an understanding of the life-force philosophy of Buddhism are capable of delving to the deep, ultimate causes of the many illnesses afflicting man in modern society.

The *Moho Zhiguan* (*Maka Shikan* in Japanese), a guide to Tiantai meditation, written by Great Teacher Tiantai, sets forth the following causes of illness: "There are six causes of illness: (1) disharmony of the four elements—earth, water, fire, and wind, which the ancient Indians believed to constitute all matter; (2) immoderate eating or drinking; (3) poor posture; (4) an attack of demons from without; (5) the work of devils from within; (6) the effects of karma" (*The Major Writings of Nichiren Daishonin*, 2:247).

The first three causes are commonly recognized origins of illness, such as unhealthy climactic conditions, lack of moderation, or disruption of the rhythms of daily life. By "an attack of demons from without" is meant causes arising from influences of the nonsentient environment (*Eho* in Japanese) on both the physical and psychological being. Illnesses produced in this way may result from viruses and bacteria or from emotional stimulations provided by ideas or external conditions. The fifth (devils from within) and sixth (karma) causes are actually various aspects of the subjective environment (*Shoho*). In other words, influences from the deepest regions of the force of life cause diverse sufferings. Distortions, warpings, and other tendencies in the force of life itself are the causes indicated by the term *karma*. Whereas modern medical science is capable of understanding both the physiological and psychological causes of illness as covered in the first four of Tiantai's causes, undeniably, much of the sickness occurring in modern society is caused by categories five and six. And the tendency for this to be true is growing stronger.

Physicians in the Mystic Law

As I have already indicated, it is clearly the mission of all members of the medical profession who are believers in the true Buddhism of Nichiren Daishonin to apply the philosophy of life force to the therapy of the mental and bodily illnesses of modern man, and in the wider operation of discovering and eliminating the causes of the social malaises of our time. In other words, I hope they will all become doctors in the Mystic Law helping human beings revolutionize their inner forces of life. Basing your thought and actions on the philosophy of life force, you can move beyond the province of curing illness and maintaining health to tackle such new themes as the prevention of illness and the improvement of health. In this way you can contribute to the creation of a society filled with happy, healthy people and blessed with a natural environment. We must always remember the importance of going beyond curing and ensuring good health for individuals and of striving to create the conditions requisite to health and happiness for all society.

Though the task may seem dauntingly big, it can be achieved through sincere, persevering application of the life-force philosophy to all daily activities. After all, the longest journey starts with the first step. And even small, apparently insignificant acts done in the name of the good of humanity can join and swell into a great tide rolling toward the twenty-first century.

As encouragement to doctors in their vital task of restoring and maintaining good health in their many patients, I offer the following quotation from "The Three Kinds of Treasure": "More valuable than treasures in the storehouses are the treasures of the body, and the treasures of the heart are the most valuable of all. From the time you read this letter on, strive to accumulate the treasures of the heart!" (*The Major Writings of Nichiren Daishonin*, 2:279).

The spirit of this quotation, which must be the foundation upon which all physicians carry out their mission, should be instilled in all patients as well. People must be brought to realize that the "treasure of the heart," or good spiritual health, lends tremendous power for physical recovery. When the spirit is in sound condition and improving still further and when the person is filled with courage, hope, and the desire to live, physical health will, on its own, follow the same course. This is true because a person who has become aware of the precious nature of life and of being alive will no longer be content with simply fighting illness but will take the initiative in programs to increase health and vitality to the maximum.

From the physician's viewpoint, technical skill and knowledge suffice for fighting disease. But to inspire a program to actively promote health, a doctor must be able to instruct his patients in philosophy and lifestyle. Through close contacts, he must transmit to his patients respect for the dignity of humanity and the immense value of life. To do this, the doctor must understand Buddhist philosophy and possess the wisdom of the Mystic Law. Physicians of this kind are therefore of the greatest significance for the present and in the building of the future on the basis of respect for humanity because, in their daily work, they practice the Buddhist spirit of reverence for the dignity of life and humankind.

Become International-minded

Delivered at the Eighth Matriculation Ceremony of Soka University held in Hachioji, Tokyo, April 10, 1978.

Tradition is not built in a day; it takes many, many years. Soka University is still very young, and I hope that you will pursue your studies, develop your minds and bodies, and evolve a worthy school tradition.

I am sure that you are all burning with hope and ambition, but the conditions in society are not so tolerant as to allow indiscriminately the realization of all your ambitions. In spite of such conditions, however, I hope you will live out your lives in such a way as to leave worthy proof of your having lived.

The evaluation of Soka University by society depends on your behavior and activities, and those of its graduates. Lofty theoretical dissertations alone cannot convince people. What matters is how you act; the weight of this truth is very great. In that respect, I hope you will develop your potential to the fullest extent during your four years at this university.

Indomitable Spirit

The future of Japanese society seems very bleak, and the path before you is undoubtedly thorny. The university must feel the full brunt of the storms of society.

But you are still young. It is the potential and prerogative of youth to meet whatever severe circumstances they face with boundless energy and hope and with a sense of idealism.

I hope you will all develop the "fighting spirit." An indomitable spirit inevitably develops into attributes of leadership, and strong leadership invariably influences the trend of the time.

Outside of Classrooms

Whenever I think about methods of teaching and learning, I always recall what I have read about the Greek philosopher Aristotle and his pupils. As you may know, the school of Aristotle was known as the Peripatetics ("Men of the Peripatos"). The name was derived from the Greek word "Peripatos," meaning "covered walk." In other words, Aristotle taught his philosophy to his pupils while they took a walk in the Peripatos of the Lyceum in ancient Athens.

Aristotle's philosophy is very difficult to comprehend, and I cannot help being amazed that a difficult philosophy was discussed and taught while taking a walk.

I do not intend to comment on teaching and learning methods in general from Aristotle's example, but from my experience, it seems that the thinking faculty generates new ideas in the process of moving around.

What I would like to say is that although classroom studies are basic, I hope you will promote your relations with your teachers and friends through lively discussions on the human plane outside of class hours.

According to one's frame of mind, everything encountered can teach you something; everything encountered can become a springboard for your own development. I look forward eagerly to the day when the entire campus of Soka University will become a place for heart-to-heart communication, a place filled with laughter.

Along the same line, I would like to mention an episode concerning Dr. Robert Koch, the German physician who identified the tuberculosis germ and the cholera bacillus.

It was the time when sleeping sickness was prevalent in Africa. A huge amount of money was spent and many scientists tried to find the cause of the disease, but in vain. Koch also was discouraged at not making any headway in his research.

One day he took a walk and came to a place where two paths converged by a river. Along one path came stretcher after stretcher carrying patients with sleeping sickness. Along the other path came none. Feeling that this was strange, he asked one of the natives what there was in one path and not in the other. The native answered: "Crocodiles!" It flashed in Koch's mind: "Crocodiles, the cause?"

Upon investigation, he found out that the cause of the disease was the Trypanosomia carried by tsetse flies that swarmed about the crocodiles.

When Dr. Koch came to Japan in 1908, he confided that if he had confined himself in the research laboratory, he might not have been able to discover the cause of the disease. He said that one must always look out the window.

When I read about the episode, I was greatly impressed. Whether it be humanities, sociology, natural sciences, or other fields of study, living knowledge is born when the student links his studies with the people and society and is fully engaged with that reality. Studies cannot be alienated from society if knowledge is to become practical.

Cultivate Cultural Interests

Your turn to act will come in the twenty-first century, and your stage will be the world. When that time comes, the manner in which you spend the next four years could well influence your ability to act.

A journalist with whom I am acquainted recently wrote a book. This journalist, a veteran in international reporting, says that the decisive difference between the top-class people in Japan and those in America and Europe is that the latter have a broad and deep cultural knowledge. He says that at dinner or at tea, their discussion is very lively and interesting, and does not in the least tire out the other party. The Japanese may have the handicap of the language barrier, but even at that, he says, the Japanese are always overwhelmed by the other party.

He mentions that the late President Pompidou of France entertained a state guest by reciting a poem by Jean Nicholas [Arthur] Rimbaud, and that British Prime Minister Heath is famous for conducting an orchestra playing a Beethoven symphony.

The journalist also says that apart from those in leading positions, the Japanese youths who will shoulder the future conspicuously lack cultural knowledge and interests. From the observations gained from my several trips abroad, I tend to agree with him.

International-mindedness

In that connection, I earnestly hope that you will acquire a broad sense of international-mindedness. Fortunately, we have many students from other countries at this university, and there are also many Japanese students who have opportunities to study abroad.

The important thing is to develop proficiency in foreign languages. Still more important is to ascertain, not from the standpoint of superiority or inferiority, that the cultures of various countries have common human features but different traditions and customs. It is essential to know that there are various ways of life, not just your own. I hope that you will realize that reality and develop a sense of understanding and warm-heartedness toward others.

At any rate, the duty and objective of students lie in the pursuit of learning. You must not forget that objective and be swayed by insignificant matters.

A Ten-Point Proposal
for Nuclear Disarmament

A Proposal for the First Special Session of the United Nations General Assembly on Disarmament, May 22, 1978.

Even today I vividly recall words spoken by the late Zhou Enlai, in December 1974: "The last twenty-five years of the twentieth century will be a period of the greatest importance for the whole world." None of us can afford to be indifferent to the fate of the coming generations, and in this context the most important pending question is the reduction of nuclear weapons.

The First Special Session of the United Nations General Assembly on Disarmament is the object of the attention and hope of peoples everywhere. I should like to express my respect for the efforts of the many persons who have worked to make this conference possible. At the same time, I want to state my deep hope that the representatives who come together at this historic meeting will approach their deliberations on the future of humanity with the greatest seriousness.

Less than a quarter of the present century remains. In the past, mankind has experienced various crises, but none has been of the scale and difficulty of the one we face at present. In discussing peace, the most cherished dream of all peoples, I hope the members of this conference will go beyond issues of political interest and ideology and will move surely and firmly, step by step, toward solutions to larger problems.

Voice of the People

I am not a specialist in nuclear matters. But, like many others, I believe that the voice of the ordinary people of the earth should be heard at this United Nations conference. Therefore, as one of the ordinary people, all of whom long for peace, I should like to offer my opinions on the subject.

I have been blessed with many opportunities to meet and discuss the future of mankind with political, cultural, and scholarly leaders from many parts of the earth. As a result of these meetings, I have gained the impression that, given the opportunity to come together mind to mind, with no concealment of any kind, these men would be filled with willingness to transcend political maneuvering and prejudice in open dialogue.

My fondest hope for the discussions in which I participated with the late Arnold J. Toynbee was that what we were saying at the time would provide hints for solutions to some of the problems facing mankind. Today, though Mr. Toynbee is no longer with us, I still recall the strength in his voice when he replied to my summons by saying, "Let us go on. Let us continue our discussions for the sake of the people of the twenty-first century."

Aurelio Peccei, a leader of the Club of Rome and a man who has persistently warned of the dangers of the future, made a profound impression on me by explaining his almost religious viewpoint.

He insists that the industrial, scientific, and ideological revolutions that man has experienced in the past century have all been external and that the only way to overcome the dangers and confusions that they have brought is for human beings to experience an inner revolution.

Toynbee and Peccei are only two of the many intellectuals and philosophers who have shared with me their deep concern over the future of man. And the time has come when each of us must make a courageous choice on the subject.

One of the things that stimulated me to offer my modest proposal in connection with nuclear weapons reduction was a remark you [Mr. Kurt Waldheim, then secretary-general of the United Nations] made three years ago. At the conclusion of our interview, I asked what you consider to be the most serious obstacle to world peace. You replied, "Lack of mutual trust." This answer, given without the slightest hesitation, struck me as a clear indication of the real efforts for peace that you, the most responsible member of the United Nations, are making.

People from all over the world have gathered at the United Nations to discuss arms reduction. Though I am by nature neither a pessimist nor an optimist, I pray from the bottom of my heart that these representatives will apply intellect and reason to the utmost for the sake of lasting and significant results.

Man's battle against nuclear weapons began at 8:15 on the morning of August 6, 1945, in Hiroshima. The moment of the first atomic bombing has passed into history, but its importance has only increased as the years have gone by. What will this conference do to eliminate the danger of holocausts still worse than any that have occurred in the past?

To a nonspecialist like me, the world already seems to have moved into the final phases of atomic and hydrogen weaponry. And now there is ominous, frightening talk of the production of the demonic neutron bomb. This bomb is described as more humane than other nuclear weapons because, by eliminating the heat and blast that accompany nuclear explosions, it directs its force toward the destruction of military personnel only. This is the point on which attempts to justify its development are based.

But no weapon can be humane and moral. And to speak of this fiendish device in such terms indicates frightening spiritual decay.

According to the figures published by the Stockholm International Peace Research Institute in April 1977, nuclear-armed nations at that time possessed weapons equivalent to approximately one million bombs of the kind dropped on Hiroshima. The figure staggers the imagination. The Hiroshima bomb—nicknamed "Little Boy" in shocking contrast to its destructive power—took more than 200,000 human lives. Should the weapons currently at man's disposal ever be put to use, they could, as a simple calculation shows, take the lives of more than two hundred billion human beings. What could be greater "overkill" than this? With such death-dealing weaponry already on hand, we must not permit the production of the neutron bomb.

I fully realize that the path to total disarmament is thorny and steep. In addition, I deeply respect the sincere and diligent efforts of many people and of the United Nations to make headway in this direction, as well as the long and well-intentioned strivings of the scientists who participated in the Pugwash conferences, which developed from the Russel-Einstein Declaration. In spite of all this effort, however, the arsenals of the nuclear-armed nations have altered little. As you pointed out last year, at the thirty-third general session of the United Nations, the small results achieved since World War II have taken the form, not of arms reductions, but of alterations and adjustments of armed preparedness. Instead of reducing their important arms systems, the big powers have limited mutual competition and have stopped developments in apparently unpromising weapons categories. Furthermore, technical advances have outstripped the pace of arms-reductions negotiations.

Goethe once said that, regrettably, no nation has ever had a mighty armed force and a perfect defense system and maintained them to the last. Goethe's words ring like a dismal omen in my ears now, over a century later, when the destructive and killing powers of man's armaments have grown drastically.

In 1976, Japan finally ratified the Nuclear Non-Proliferation Treaty, first promulgated in 1970. While realizing that the treaty is imperfect and in some respects unequal, I nonetheless hoped that it would be a valuable positive step toward nuclear-arms reduction on a global scale. (The famous Japanese scientist and international champion of global peace, Hideki Yukawa, aptly termed the treaty "positive feedback.") But presently, such openly nuclear nations as France and China and other covertly nuclear nations have not signed the treaty. Their reluctance may stem from intransigence but is more probably the outcome of a virtual monopoly of nuclear weapons on the parts of the United States and the Soviet Union.

The Strategic Arms Limitations Talks (SALT) between these two nations symbolize this state of affairs. SALT is the focus of the current arms-reduction scene. Furthermore, it is an important chance for negotiations between the two giant countries. But the talks have dragged on since they first began in 1969, and it is difficult to regard them as a steady movement toward complete disarmament. Since the start of SALT, the nuclear arsenals of both the United States and the Soviet Union have only grown, and the arms race has become more heated. Furthermore, both nations have weakened SALT by setting up a gray zone of development of new arms systems that can be used either tactically or strategically. The American Cruise missile and mobile ICBMs and the Russian Backfire bomber are some of the results of research in this gray zone. An even more recent development is the use of killer satellites to destroy enemy reconnaissance satellites. Clearly, as you point out, the tendency for technological development to outstrip negotiations has not slackened.

False Doctrine

Today, as at no other time, it is vitally important to shed the light of truth on the false, wicked doctrine of deterrent power. A product of fear, this doctrine claims that deterrent power prevents an enemy's belligerence by instilling in him the fear of retaliation. But a balance of fear spawns an unlimited arms race. And, when fear is given the tangible form of nuclear weapons, the monstrous outcome can be the annihilation of the human race and the destruction of the planet. The wicked doctrine of deterrent force regards human beings as no more than ciphers or physical objects. If the enemy kills millions of our people, we can retaliate by killing millions of the enemy. How can such a doctrine prevent war? Like the unfortunate victims of the ancient Greek bandit Procrustes, man today must be stretched or hacked to fit a set of arbitrary dimensions; in this case, the dimensions of the arbitrary Procrustean bed of deterrence are nuclear weapons. Procrustes was finally killed on his own bed by the hero Theseus. We must be heroic in our times so that we can prevent the current over-saturation of nuclear arms from ending in the destruction of life on earth.

Today humanity is on a disaster course that will lead to holocaust unless some effective method of altering it is found. The path is long, but we must make the first bold step, while keeping an eye firmly fixed on the actual difficulties of our undertaking. The ideal is prohibition of the production, testing, and use of nuclear weapons and, ultimately, the elimination of all such weapons from the face of the earth. If we do not join forces and muster courage to attain this ideal, we may face the fires of hell; and the twenty-first century may never be.

To prevent this, we must carefully investigate the reasons why nuclear weapons have become larger and more numerous and why arms reduction makes no progress.

Lack of Trust

The first reason for both of these phenomena is the lack of trust among nations, and especially, among the nuclear-armed nations that you mentioned. The deep rift between the United States and the Soviet Union is an excellent example. During the period of the Cold War following World War II, mutual fear and mistrust inspired both nations to repeated arms expansion. Then a thaw set in, and today both nations are apparently guided by a policy of détente and peaceful coexistence. A closer look at the situation, however, shows that the roots of distrust have not been severed and that the two parties are still deeply suspicious of each other.

This is true because détente arises from fear of nuclear-arms expansion and the self-preservation instinct. Interpreting it as an attempt on the part of the Soviet Union or the United States to dominate the world, other nations might well react strongly against détente.

The Nuclear Non-Proliferation Treaty does not improve the situation. While imposing strict limits on nonnuclear nations—that is, restricting the horizontal spread of nuclear weapons—the treaty is riddled with escape holes on the subject of the development of nuclear devices by nations already possessing them; that is, it is much less severely restrictive of the vertical diffusion of nuclear arms.

I am not rejecting the idea of détente. I consider it a step forward and an improvement over the Cold War. Nonetheless, unless we realize the distrust at its root, détente can do nothing for the attainment of true world peace.

In the cases both of individual human beings and of nations, distrust breeds mutual isolation. An isolated nation probably has no choice but to regard other nations with suspicion and to devote itself to strengthening and expanding its own arms system. But this means relying on force and military strength only, in other words, on principles of opposition and dominance, not of coexistence and reciprocity. The French philosopher Henri Bergson divided human society into two major categories: open societies and closed societies. Our society today is an example of the latter. Within this closed society, nations regard each other with a distrust and suspicion that greatly hinder progress in disarmament.

National Egoism

The issue of national egoism is the second factor hindering progress in arms reduction. And the most chronic and harmful case of such egoism is that of large nuclear nations who, while restricting diffusion of nuclear weapons among nuclear nations or potentially nuclear nations, continue to refine and expand their own systems, which are already capable of destroying mankind tens of times over. Egoism is evil. To attempt to control evil by means of evil inevitably sets up a vicious cycle of wickedness. The irony of the current situation is vividly underscored by national leaders who have sent congratulatory telegrams—"Hurrah! Today we become one of the great nations!"—to laboratories conducting successful nuclear experiments.

With so many nations wanting to join the nuclear club, it should be evident that the protective nuclear umbrella is now torn. It is no longer possible to rely on national prestige or egoism now that we already know that nuclear weapons can be stolen or that, using readily available materials, private individuals can produce nuclear bombs. And, if the nuclear nations persist in using nuclear weapons as a vehicle of power-and-prestige egoism, the responsibility for having destroyed the morality of disarmament will have to be laid at their doors.

Remaining silent in the face of evil is tantamount to complicity in evil. Rampant superpower egoism played havoc with the seventeenth Pugwash conference, at the conclusion of which the sole silent protest is said to have been words written on a blackboard: "For the devil to prosper it is sufficient if good people remain inactive." We must not allow the devil to prosper. I insist that we must persevere until nuclear weapons have been completely eliminated.

Indifference to Nuclear Threat

Apathy to the nuclear threat is the third factor working against successful arms reduction. Japan is often criticized for having a nuclear allergy. But, in my opinion, such an allergy ought to be considered the normal condition everywhere. Indifference in the face of the threat of nuclear weapons is the greatest enemy to peace. And criticism of the so-called nuclear allergy amounts to a wicked attempt to inspire such indifference.

I am perfectly aware of the inconsistency in the Japanese attitude of seeking shelter under the American nuclear umbrella by means of the mutual security treaty while theoretically manifesting a nuclear allergy. And in this connection, I unashamedly express my profound dissatisfaction with the Japanese government.

I should like to make it clear, however, that the nuclear allergy of the general Japanese public has a very deep source: the loss of hundreds of thousands of our countrymen and the continued suffering today of many others inflicted with nuclear-related sickness. The cry, "Never a third atomic bomb!" springs from the very lifeblood of the only people on earth ever to have suffered a nuclear attack.

It seems to me that, with limited exceptions, the people of the world have been excessively deaf to the threat. I wish that awareness of the danger—to the extent of allergy—would spread throughout the whole world.

Everyone must become firmly convinced that nuclear weapons are an absolute evil. In 1957, just before his death, my mentor and the second president of Soka Gakkai, Josei Toda, issued to the younger generations his Proclamation on Nuclear Weapons. In this document, he said, "The use of nuclear weapons on any pretext must never be countenanced. The very idea that nuclear weapons have positive value is mistaken. Nuclear weapons are an absolute evil, a product of the devil." On the basis of the philosophy of Buddhism, Soka Gakkai actively promotes peace and cultural development. It is only natural that we should be deeply concerned about nuclear weapons. And I too have resolved to expound to the utmost limits of my strength the philosophy of no more nuclear weapons.

Expansion of Atomic-energy Use

The fourth element hindering progress in arms reduction is the fact that it is no longer possible to overlook the vast and virtually irreversible expansion of nonmilitary atomic-energy resources and research facilities, and the related bureaucracies of the nuclear superpowers. In the noncommunist world in particular, the military industrial complex with its huge labor and research forces has usually joined hands with military authorities in the blind development of new weapons. Today such cooperation has given rise to a virtual commercial war in the field of atomic energy. As is well known, the industrially advanced nations sell plants to other nations complete with nuclear furnaces and facilities for recycling and nuclear enrichment. Although done under the banner of peaceful use of atomic power, this process can increase the number of nations capable of producing nuclear weapons. Individual national conditions and social systems are closely related to these merchant-of-death structural economic problems. But, for the sake of progress in arms reduction, some solution must be found to this overall problem. Nothing is as tragic as human beings so bewitched by lust for gold that they are willing to sacrifice priceless human lives for their own aggrandizement.

Lack of trust, national egoism, indifference to the danger, and expansion of nonmilitary use of atomic energy— these are the four elements that I believe hinder arms reduction. To make matters worse, the intensity of the present arms race makes many feel helpless about their predicament. As you have pointed out, the history of negotiations for arms reduction is one of much hard work and few concrete results. It almost seems as if the huge nuclear-weapons systems have broken free of human control, to walk about as they wish and to reproduce themselves on their own.

Man Must Act

I am convinced that we must rise up with faith and courage in the defense of the precious cultural heritage that man has created over many thousands of years. The basic issue is actually surprisingly simple. "Even Solomon in all his glory was not arrayed like one of these [lilies of the field]," it is said. In other words all of Solomon's artificially created glory had less impact on people than the beauty of a single flower. All nuclear-weapons systems, no matter how vast, are the products of the human intellect—a force for both good and evil. The political powers that control those systems are also created by the human mind. There is no reason why that mind cannot find a way to get the upper hand over both.

Man has played the leading role in the creation of his own history. Remembering this, we must move bravely and steadily along our difficult path. But we must keep our eyes fixed always on the future and not on the past.

Over the ages, man has experienced recurring cycles of schism and unification. Unification always contained the seeds of further schism, and, after each schism, people invariably groped for new unification. The advent of nuclear weapons has altered this pattern, since a serious schism today threatens imminent and total destruction.

Of course, mankind faces many other problems: environmental pollution, shortages of natural resources, population explosion, and food scarcity. Each of these issues requires speedy and far-reaching solutions. Nonetheless, as Albert Einstein said, the problem of avoiding global disaster takes precedence over all others. His words carry more weight than any other warning man has known.

Priority to Humanity

If consensus can be achieved on the nuclear question, the effect is certain to be great. It may become possible to break free of the doubt that has plagued human history in the past. The direction in which we will move then will not be the old one of schism followed by superficial unification. From sincere dialogues will emerge a deep union that will in turn give birth to the creation of a new way to the future. The resulting liberation from the old bonds of human history will constitute a dramatic change. In my opinion, this is the only way for humanity to continue playing the leading role in the creation of its own history.

If this kind of deep union is achieved, the significance of the United Nations will alter drastically. Today, nation-states and their interests play the leading role in the United Nations. You and the other leaders and representatives work very hard for the sake of mutual security and adjustments of advantages and disadvantages among various nations. I greatly respect your efforts. But I feel that, in the future, the United Nations will have to expand its scope. On the wider stage on which it must operate, humanity in general, and not nation-states, must take the lead.

To use the diplomatic channels of single nations as an example, I believe that the narrow path of communications among national representatives (foreign ministries) and their overseas organizations will gradually decrease in importance. In their place, as means of transportation become more convenient, direct encounters between government leaders—like Richard Nixon's trip to China—and among private individuals and private groups will increase. This will make it possible to establish much more intimate, human-level exchanges of opinion than was practical through older diplomatic channels. In my own frequent travels around the world as a private individual, I have been deeply impressed by the slow but certain growth in the circle of international citizens liberated from the old bonds of nationalism. I sense a historic change in which the ordinary human being, long in the shadow of government organizations, is advancing to take the major role in world affairs. It is my wish that the United Nations will make full use of its organizations and authority to stimulate this trend and to provide a place for close exchanges among people. And, with this in mind, I should like to make a few proposals to this conference.

In the past, I have made various suggestions for the elimination of nuclear weapons and the reduction of conventional weapons. In addition, with only the limited strength of one man of religion, I have taken some practical steps in this direction. Here, however, I should like to make the following suggestions, which are a more concrete version of general ideas included in the petition that I submitted to you when I visited the headquarters of the United Nations on January 10, 1975.

In the earlier paper, I touched on what I consider the duties and my own expectations of the United Nations. In addition, I made some proposals about the major problems facing the world today: nuclear arms, food shortages, and the population explosion. Finally, I expressed my hopes for the United Nations University and proposed the establishment of an organization to realize these hopes. This organization I tentatively named the Council of World Citizens for the Protection of the United Nations. My proposal for the total abolition of nuclear arms, included in my earlier suggestions, remains an unchanging part of my philosophy and beliefs as a man of religion. I here repeat that proposal in a more detailed and expanded form.

Summit Conference

My first proposal is for the immediate summoning of a meeting of top leaders from all nations, both those that possess and those that do not possess nuclear arms. I realize that this may require several stages to achieve; nonetheless, it is necessary. The United Nations itself must take the initiative in calling the conference and must have power to express its views and to assume leadership in all actions, from the initial controls to be put on the production of nuclear weapons to their eventual destruction.

The current Special Session of the United Nations General Assembly on Disarmament is one opportunity to advance toward the summit meeting that I advocate. But this conference involves only representatives with lower levels of responsibility. I feel that you and the United Nations must call a meeting of the top leaders—the people who promote nuclear policies and military expansion in the nations possessing nuclear weapons, and those intending to possess them in the future. Furthermore, as United Nations secretary-general and organizer of the meeting, you should press for a nuclear ban and a reduction in conventional weapons and should see that debate on these matters continues until some definite conclusion has been reached.

The vitally important nuclear weapons issue requires a coming together of the top leaders because such a conference is certain to be more meaningful than a meeting of lower-level representatives acting under suggestions given them by their superiors at home.

Safe Controls

My second proposal is that, as a move toward total abolition of both nuclear weapons and reduction of conventional weapons, the United Nations must take the initiative in an attempt to find ways of ensuring safe control of atomic energy.

As I have already pointed out, the amount of destructive power contained in weapons currently possessed by such nuclear superpowers as the United States and the Soviet Union is terrifying. A foolish move, an error, or a sudden fit of madness could instantly plunge the world into disaster. Furthermore, nuclear waste from atomic reactors has accumulated to such an extent that individual nations are no longer able to deal with it. Natural disasters like earthquakes or the stealing of nuclear materials could unleash horrifying danger. The first step in expanding control is to allow the United Nations to set up a supervisory organization to which all nations must entrust the control of nuclear waste. The second step is for nations with stocks of nuclear weapons to entrust them, in stages, to the United Nations. Hopefully, at some date in the future, the United Nations can assume responsibility for ensuring the safety of all such weapons. The third step is that, when they are under United Nations control, in accordance with the will of the peace-loving peoples of the world, all nuclear weapons will be dismantled and destroyed.

Though my proposal may sound idealistic, I am convinced that, in the face of the rapidly growing threat of total disaster, we must take some definite step toward the total destruction of nuclear weapons. And that step must be taken at once. In the hope of finding a way, I shall make more detailed proposals in the following pages. What I say pertains to conventional as well as nuclear weapons.

My third proposal is that the United Nations should enjoin all nations, whether or not they possess nuclear weapons, to a statement promising not to use them. I realize that this would have little immediate effect in deterring the nuclear or potential nuclear nations from their weapons race. Nonetheless, by consolidating the will of the non-nuclear nations and by forbidding resort to these weapons, the agreement could be a step in the direction of total prohibition. As their numbers grow, signatories to the agreement will become able to apply greater moral pressure against the use of such weapons. The content of the agreement should be an important topic of debate at the meeting that I proposed of top national leaders. At the very least, however, the agreement must demand that nations possessing nuclear weapons promise not to use them first and not to employ the threat of their use. I have heard that the current special session devoted to disarmament is to be concluded with a general statement. This document will be more significant if it is compiled in the name of all humanity and if it bears the signatures of the leaders of all nations, signifying willingness to cooperate. With the passing of time, such a declaration can degenerate into mere words. Making this one truly effective will require ceaseless efforts. The signatures of the national leaders will serve as a symbol of the need for such efforts.

Nuclear-free Zones

My fourth proposal is that the United Nations set up and attempt to expand nuclear-free zones, perhaps in the following way. First, those nations that have signed the statement to restrain themselves from using nuclear weapons should individually or in groups seek to establish zones into which they would forbid the introduction of nuclear weapons. They would remove quickly any such weapons held within the zone and so make themselves secure from nuclear attack from without. The United Nations could then work for the expansion of such zones until the entire globe was free of nuclear weapons.

An Actual Plan

I realize that one problem in this proposal is the likelihood that the People's Republic of China and France, on the basis of the stances they have taken in the past, would be recalcitrant. But I believe that my fifth proposal would make possible both their cooperation and that of other nations currently preparing to produce their own nuclear weapons.

The idea for this proposal came from remarks made at the thirty-second general session of the United Nations in 1977 by President Jimmy Carter, who said that the time has come to end nuclear devices, both peaceful and military, and mentioned the willingness of the United States to reduce its nuclear arms by ten, twenty, or fifty percent. Since this remark was made in the very headquarters of the United Nations, you should call on the United States to submit to the UN an actual plan to bring about such an arms reduction. With such a plan, you could call on the Soviet Union to submit the same kind of plan. And finally, through compromises on both sides, it would be possible to actually reduce devices in stages from ten to twenty to fifty percent. No doubt, on the basis of this achievement, if diligent in its mediations, the United Nations could bring China and France to a meeting of leaders for nuclear-arms reduction. And, if these four nations began sincerely working for such disarmament, nuclear nations like England and India and potential nuclear nations like Japan, West Germany, Italy, and Canada would work out their own plans to the same end.

Prohibition of New Arms

My sixth proposal is for the United Nations to urge countries to halt development of such new weapons as the neutron bomb and Cruise missiles and then to take the initiative in drawing up an international agreement to forbid them. Highly difficult, reduction of nuclear arms cannot ensure global disarmament. Indeed, given the nature of power politics inherent in the distrust characteristic of modern international society, as nuclear reduction takes place, military preparedness in terms of conventional weapons is likely to increase in geometric progression. Unless the United States and the Soviet Union call a halt to their competition in the development of new weapons, France, China, and other nations will be stimulated to increase their efforts in the production of both nuclear and conventional weaponry.

Therefore, for the sake of disarmament on a worldwide scale, the United Nations must create a situation in which it can recommend that the United States and the Soviet Union cease producing all new weapons.

Military-status Reports

My seventh proposal is closely related to and a completion of the fifth and sixth proposals: starting with 1978, the year of this Special Session of the United Nations, each nation should be required to submit to the United Nations an annual report on its military status, including weaponry, military manpower, and facilities. These reports must be treated as confidential, but the United Nations must have the right to conduct investigations of actual conditions on the spot. If reports are discovered to be false, the fact must be made public to the whole world. Further, the United Nations must issue warnings to all nations that work to increase nuclear preparedness or develop new-model weapons, and should inform the world of such activities.

To enforce this, a special organization—which might tentatively be called the United Nations arms-reduction organization—should be established and run by a special committee and empowered to investigate the armament conditions of all nations. Furthermore, this organization should ensure the implementation of all of the foregoing proposals and serve as the central body for enforcing arms reduction and investigating conditions. In addition, it must serve as an information center enlightening the world on the fearsomeness of nuclear arms and the need for arms reduction. If such an organization should come into being, as a private individual, I should be happy to cooperate in its work.

Information Center

My eighth proposal calls for the United Nations to make an appeal for research, debate, advertising, and publication activities directed toward total and complete disarmament. Though, when established, the United Nations arms-reduction organization should handle these duties, until that time, such existing organs as the United Nations University could play a role. In other words, something like an arms-reduction research information center should be attached to the United Nations University.

This center would collect information at the private level on arms reduction in all nations and then disperse this information throughout the world to make known the threat of nuclear weapons and the need for total disarmament. Since the headquarters of the United Nations University is in Tokyo, it is entirely practical to set up the information center in Hiroshima or Nagasaki.

By bringing the truth of the cruelty of war and the horror of nuclear weapons to the widest possible audience, it will be possible to create a popularly based movement and international public opinion for the abolition of war, nuclear weapons, and other weapons of intense destructive power.

Encourage Anti-war Exhibits

To this end, the United Nations must do two things. First, it must establish at its headquarters a museum, which might be called the United Nations Peace Center, where the general public could have access to documents, photographs, motion pictures, videotapes, and paintings showing the horrors of war, the destructive power of nuclear weapons, Hiroshima and Nagasaki as they were after the bombings, and current conditions in nuclear weaponry. The center could collect and display materials and make them available for people visiting the United Nations and for anyone in the world who expressed a need.

Second, it must encourage anti-war and pro-disarmament exhibitions all over the world. This movement could be based on activities like those of the Soka Gakkai Youth Division, which has arranged an anti-war and anti-nuclear arms exhibition that, in its travel throughout Japan, has aroused especially strong response among the younger generations. I believe that this exhibition has had at least a small part to play in educating the young to the misery and suffering of war. And, by keeping the memory alive and inspiring them to maintain an anti-war spirit, it can contribute to the building of a lasting peace. Efforts on the part of the United Nations to conduct similar exhibitions on a long-term, global scale would be highly effective in creating international public opinion in favor of disarmament. And this might inspire all nations to establish their own permanent peace centers.

Though my eighth and ninth proposals are not directly related to concrete negotiations for arms reduction, they are important in connection with the future role of the United Nations. Last year, in Japan, the generations born after World War II—that is, the generations who have never known warfare—came to account for the majority of the population. In all nations, people who have experienced war pass on their memories to the young. But nothing they say can do justice to the facts. Anyone who has lived through war hates it. The thing that must be done is to garner the emotions and recollections of the ordinary victims of war and to preserve them for the younger generations.

In comparison with the large numbers of motion pictures made in the West about the cruelties of the Nazis in Europe, the horror of the atomic bombings is still comparatively little known. In publicizing them, there is no need to make distinctions between the inflicters and the sufferers. The aim must be to disseminate knowledge about the threat of the weapons themselves. Any style, from documentary to science fiction, will do, as long as people come to know and as long as a contribution is made to world public opinion. A broad-base petition movement could serve as excellent education and publicity against development, testing, and use of nuclear weapons. Furthermore, activities of this kind would allow public opinion to reflect more deeply on the United Nations and would make the United Nations a place for more open debate.

Economic Transformation

My tenth and final proposal is to provide the economic conditions that will make feasible my nine other proposals and thereby make arms reduction possible. It will be necessary to break up the traditional war economy and move to an economic structure that can preserve peace. In this way the vast sums now spent on nuclear development and armament expansion can be diverted to the uses of peace and prosperity.

During the current General Assembly devoted to disarmament, there should be discussion on the establishment of a planning committee on economic transformation for the sake of arms reduction. When this committee has finally been set up, it must study and debate ideas for a new international economic order founded on disarmament and must then compile a concrete program for the realization of this order. The program will have to include economic adjustments needed by all nations for its implementation, together with advice on the transfer of resources, labor forces, and technology from military to peaceful uses. It should reveal the various economic factors involved in peaceful utilization of atomic energy and should prepare an economic plan for development of new energy sources to replace nuclear ones.

At present twenty-five percent of the world's scientists and forty percent of the world's research expenditures are devoted to military purposes. It is essential that the United Nations take the lead in pioneering a way to disarmament with the greatest speed and thus make this expenditure of talent and research meaningless. The funds and energy liberated by the changeover must be used for the support of peace, and it is to be hoped that the scientists of the world will employ such funds with wisdom in producing a program for the sake of the continued survival of the human race.

All of the above depends on a strengthening of the United Nations initiatives for disarmament, which in turn depends on two points. First is the organization's financial basis, an issue of long-standing concern. In my modest opinion, one possibility is that part of the funds spent on military activities could be diverted to the United Nations. The mass media suggest that the French are contemplating a tax on military over-preparation beyond certain fixed limits. Money from such taxation should be used for management and control of disarmament programs and to assist developing nations. This last is a subject fully deserving of consideration. By no means should the tax be considered a permit fee that, once paid, allows for increased armament, and checks should be made to make certain this does not take place.

We must expand our viewpoint until we see that it is better to spend money for the sake of the entire human race than to spend it for the good of a single nation-state. The time has come to think from this standpoint. And, if we do not, we may—as the Japanese proverb has it—trim the horn and kill the cow.

Impartiality of UN Officials

As the United Nations comes to fulfill more important functions, demand for its political impartiality will grow stronger. The United Nations must not allow itself to be a place for power struggles among the large powers or a place for behind-the-scenes negotiations. The significance and weight of nations must not be judged by the size of the financial contributions they make. The structure of the Security Council and other elements complicate the matter, but I think to make the United Nations as politically impartial as it must be, the secretary-general and all other leaders ought to consider making a declaration of complete political nonalignment.

Oneness with the Environment

A Proposal Commemorating the Forty-eighth Anniversary
of the Founding of Soka Gakkai,
November 10, 1978.

The problems faced by humanity spring from three sources: first, dealing with one's own interior world; second, establishing relations with other people; and, third, dealing with the natural environment. All problems can be traced to this triad of relations with the self, with others, and with the environment. Obviously, environmental problems arise directly from relations of the third category. But actually the three are inseparable, for a person whose inner world is disturbed and unbalanced will constantly sow seeds of discord to subjugate and destroy the natural environment.

Quite naturally, industrialization on a vast scale comes to mind at the first mention of environmental pollution, but I think we ought to bear in mind the desolation that war has wrought and always wreaks on nature. At the United Nations environmental conference, held in Stockholm in 1972, the United States' use of napalm bombs and defoliants in the Vietnam War was criticized as massive, egoistic destruction of the ecological system. The damage done by such weapons was so great that it can justly be called ecological murder.

As is stated in the UNESCO charter, war begins in the heart of man. In all ages, destruction of the external environment has been inseparably linked with imbalance in the human interior environment. But it has only been since the 1960s that mankind has turned serious attention to environmental problems. Modern scientific technological progress, beginning with the Industrial Revolution of the eighteenth century, continued on an upward line to approach a peak in the decade of the 1960s. The progress made in that relatively short period was great and rapid, but its negative aspects—especially pollution—grew just as rapidly, ultimately to come to full light and to capture the attention of many people.

Modern Europe was the place where scientific progress based on rationalistic thought originated, and where its basic patterns were established. The energy generating such progress, however, creates distortion as long as it is based on egoism, the lack of harmony and balance in the human ego—that is, as long as its source is a polluted interior environment. In concrete terms, energy traveling along such a distorted course has produced colonialism in relations among human beings and destruction and pollution in relations between human beings and their natural environment. Concentration on nothing but the needs and desires of human beings has led us to the predicament in which we find ourselves today. I believe that we have reached the point where the only way out is the oriental philosophy of the central importance of nature and of harmony and cooperation between human beings and the nonhuman elements of their environment. I further contend that recognition of the dignity of each living entity on the basis of Buddhist teachings—the paramount wisdom of the Orient—is the only way to solve and eradicate environmental problems.

Ecological Geography: the Oriental View of Nature

The Buddhist doctrine of *esho funi* (the indivisibility of the subjective entity and its environment) seems to answer the needs of our time.

According to the doctrine of *esho funi,* which is based on the Buddhist teaching of *ichinen sanzen,* the interior environment of the individual and the exterior environment are one indivisible entity. The teaching includes the idea that the subjective individual is, in fact, created by the environment. Furthermore, it advocates splendid interrelations and harmony since it maintains that a revolution for the betterment of the interior environment can have a revolutionary, ameliorating effect on the exterior environment as well. In the past, mankind has pursued a one-way course of subjugating and exploiting nature. But following the Buddhist teaching of *esho funi* and thereby establishing mutual correspondence makes receptivity to messages from the world of nature possible and, through exchanges with nature, makes it possible to build a spiritually rich and sensitive culture.

This teaching would enable us to abandon the policy of invasion and subjugation of nature in favor of a policy of unity and common interest. The valuable views on nature set forth in *Jinsei Chirigaku* (The Geography of Human Life) by Tsunesaburo Makiguchi, first president of our organization and a devout believer in the Buddhism of Nichiren Daishonin, are currently the object of re-evaluation and possible application by many intelligent thinkers. While ranging far and wide in the learning of both East and West, the book is permeated with the Oriental view of nature and describes in detail how it is possible to lead a receptive human life in the rich setting of the natural environment. It is undoubtedly Oriental philosophy and the Oriental view of nature expressed in it that attracts the attention of intellectuals. For instance, *Jinsei Chirigaku* explains how people can cultivate a sense of beauty and subdue ferocity within themselves by coming into contact with plants, and how courage, affection, and receptivity to beauty can be developed and intensified by exchanges with animals and with such inorganic environmental elements as mountains and rivers. In addition, the book penetrates into essential matters by explaining how by being part of the mystical actions of the great world of nature, people can not only cultivate enthusiasm for art and truth, but also generate a spirit of religion by opening their hearts to the rhythms of the universe.

There are places on earth where not a tree or a blade of grass now grows, though relics of past civilizations tell that life once flourished there. Some historians claim that at one time such places were lush and green but that human beings and other animals destroyed the vegetable cover.

About two hundred years ago, beginning in England and spreading throughout Europe, a movement got underway to make the natural environment a garden. It took root in Germany from the eighteenth into the nineteenth century. Although it was forgotten for a while in the heat of industrialization, it came to life again in the late nineteenth century and continues in effect to the present day. In my travels through Europe, I have been impressed by the spacious parks in cities and the beauty of the greenery in rural landscapes. I realize now that this beauty is the outcome of the unflagging efforts of the local citizenry over a long period.

More than two thousand years ago, the Indian king Ashoka of the Mauryans, a devout Buddhist, decreed in his Fourteen Articles (a kind of constitution) that trees should be planted along all the streets of the nation. When I visited India some years ago I saw rows of thick-trunked trees lining streets everywhere and realized, first, how much people rely on greenery in severe climates and, second, how generation after generation of Indians for thousands of years have attempted to protect and care for their trees.

Here I have cited only a few examples of my meaning, but *Jinsei Chirigaku* is a detailed explanation of the importance of the natural environment as the great womb from which springs human life, not only in physical terms, but also in relation to the spiritual elements that are the source of prosperity in cultures and civilizations.

Pollution and destruction of the natural environment lead directly to the downfall and extinction of humanity. In reverse terms, however, maintaining and stimulating the abundant rhythms of nature are the most important keys to lasting human prosperity.

In the world of nature there are no national boundaries or man-made marine zones. The fish and animals of the world pay no attention to delineations of this kind; only man has established boundaries as a consequence of his narrow-mindedness. The atmosphere and the waters of the seas move and act on a global scale. The fish swimming in the Arctic Ocean have no concern with boundaries. Pollutants dumped into the Rhine in Germany do not stop at the border but flow along with the water to do damage in the Netherlands. The seas are spacious; it is man who tries to narrow them by dividing them into parcels.

Dr. Gerhard Olschowy, professor at Bonn University, has said that high-level human cultures are possible only in places where the land is fertile and that the histories of certain peoples demonstrate that this is true. He proceeds to substantiate his point by referring to the rise and fall of a number of civilizations. All of his illustrations prove the connection between the prosperity of cultures and the wealth of their natural environments. A people that desolates its land is doomed to fail and ultimately to disappear from the stage of history.

Today we have reached the point where all human culture is one, where people from East and West and from other parts of the world are adopting the civilization of modern scientific technology. In such circumstances, the desolation of our natural environment means the downfall, not of a single nation, but of all humankind. The global pollution taking place at the present time threatens our very survival powers and those of our civilization.

A way to do something about the dilemma was advanced at the United Nations Conference on Deserts, where it was suggested that, in order to halt further desertification of the globe, the industrialized nations, including Japan, should use their economic powers in a program of irrigation and reforestation. If Japan were to take part in such a program, it might alter the Japanese way of thinking that has branded us among the industrializing nations as exporters of pollution. I further propose that, in order to enable people everywhere to continue living and to prosper, all nations must pool their brain power in study and research for the development of concrete policies to solve these difficulties.

Possibly I shall be criticized as too idealistic for saying this, but the only way to find solutions to these problems is to transcend national boundaries and racial barriers and to think on a global scale. It is my hope that repeated efforts, dialogues, and agreements in this direction will be the foundation for something which would have to be called the United Nations for the Environment, a place where discussions and decisions can be held on a worldwide basis. The UNEP (United Nations Environmental Plan), which was evolved by the United Nations Conference on the Human Environment in 1972, and the HABITAT (United Nations Conference on Human Settlements) of 1976 could serve as a basis for the organization, which would have to fit into the existing structure of the United Nations. Giving it great weight would improve the functioning of the United Nations and enable it to work better for stability and peace. As a Buddhist, I sincerely hope that such an organization will come into being and will be a foundation for wholesome, international agreements on environmental issues.

Essential to the creation of the United Nations for the Environment is close attention to worldwide harmony, especially between the industrialized North and the developing South. Consideration of this issue was a focal point in the United Nations Conference on the Human Environment. Like the nuclear arms issue, the environment problem is global and obviously has been brought on by so-called progress employing modern science. The whole world is threatened by the negative aspects of pollution produced by scientific technology, but the positive aspects—increased wealth and flourishing economies—are limited to the industrialized nations. The developing nations enjoy none of the blessings of technology and continue to face poverty and hunger. It is true that pollution is a negative aspect of industrialization that afflicts the whole world. Nonetheless, it is egoistic of the industrialized nations to overlook the needs for scientific growth and progress of the developing nations and to attempt to limit their industrialization in order to solve the pollution problem. Cries from the developing nations participating in the United Nations Conference on the Human Environment to the effect that poverty is the world's greatest pollutant were scarcely surprising.

The major key to the creation of a United Nations for the Environment must be the devising of ways to ensure not only harmony between man and nature, but also harmony, coexistence, and coprosperity among the nations of the world—especially between those of the North and the South. All nations who have built their own prosperity on sacrifices, large or small, on the part of developing nations must pay for what they have done. I include Japan among the industrialized nations to whom I strongly address a plea for reparation.

In addition to balance among nations and between the North and the South, the industrialized nations must strive to maintain a domestic balance between their own economic growth and environmental conservation. Scientific technology and economic prosperity are essential to the building of a bright human future since they are vital physical bases for the survival of mankind. But the blind pursuit of scientific culture alone is fated to upset the rhythms of nature and to fracture the ecological system. For the sake of the people of the twenty-first century, wherever a conflict arises between domestic economic growth and the environment, first precedence must unhesitatingly be given to environmental conservation and the restoration of the natural system.

It is gratifying to know that scholars and specialists in ecology are gradually clarifying the tolerances of the natural environment. It is to be hoped that the knowledge they gain will be included in attempts to restore and stimulate natural environmental functions in places where they have been upset. Our leaders must now take measures to ensure low-level economic growth that does not exceed the environment's powers of recovery.

But it would be too optimistic to think that measures of this kind alone are enough to solve environmental problems, for at the base of conservationist movements must be broad support from the people in general. Only when people accept oneness with the world of nature as a matter of profound faith can a movement of this kind go steadily ahead.

When the situation is viewed in this light, it is obvious that the major responsibility for balance between North and South, for balance between the environment and economic growth, and for all the other environmental problems rests with the industrialized nations, who have "progressed" without thinking of the welfare of other nations and have regarded the sacrifice of the natural world as a matter of course. In this way they have built the current culture of mass consumption. The process whereby this culture has been developed has been one of unrestrained human greed.

The repayment that the industrialized nations must make is the imposition of restraint on greed. I realize that human nature finds it difficult to control something that has expanded to the extent that greed has reached today, but I want to believe that humanity is wise enough to prefer to make reparations, even in this difficult way, than to allow the current drive toward global destruction to continue. But, for the cultivation of the kind of wisdom that is needed, humanity requires a philosophy or a religion. We must shift emphasis from material things to spiritual values. We must stop being materialists and become "life-ists." As the *Gosho* says (p. 273), the body is more important than wealth in the treasury, and the heart is the most valuable of all. Never before in history has this criterion of value been more needed than it is today. I believe that when mankind embraces this value system, all problems, no matter how severe the trials they entail, will be unraveled, and ways will be found to solutions. Just as pollution of the internal human environment is related directly to the destruction of the external, natural environment, so harmony in the internal environment evokes harmony in the external one.

Hope for a Second Renaissance: a Pacific Culture

Only a few years ago, the future looked rosy. Today the outlook is thick and black. People seem to be petrified with hopelessness and joylessness. Ruptures between man and wife and between parent and child are common. Social problems, notably matters related to the elderly, are aggravated. Crime is increasing and growing increasingly violent. In Japan, one reads of the suicides of middle-school and elementary-school children. I am sure that I am not the only person who is gravely upset by these developments.

Not only individuals, but all society is sick as well. Nations everywhere face such mountainous problems as nuclear arms, depletion of natural resources, and food shortages. In reflecting on these difficulties, I have come to believe that men have lost the basis for living and that we are now at a turning point in history where we must seek a new basis. The repeated attention the mass-communications media pay to the possibility of a restoration of philosophy to a leading position in human life, and to the importance of cultural matters, convinces me that people today are looking for a new way of life. After all, in the final analysis, culture and philosophy are ways of life and examinations of those ways.

The Renaissance, which took place in Europe in the fourteenth and fifteenth centuries, had the revolutionary effect of bringing God down from his position of absolute ruler of everything and of enthroning him in the inner world of the individual human being. But after this, in developments contrary to human dignity, exterior authority assumed power and people came to put their faith in a series of externals including progress, the establishment of capital, and finally, nuclear power. Yet today none of these things maintains its value. Though they required centuries to erect, all systems based on them have collapsed, leaving a vacuum that people are now beginning to recognize.

The ideal of the future must originate from religious faith deep in the human heart. The time has come to take first priority away from exterior authority and give it to the revolution that must occur in the heart of each human being. This must be the age of a second Renaissance in which the ordinary individual human being must play the leading role. The battle he must fight is the struggle to transform his own life from within.

The Buddhism of Nichiren Daishonin can make this possible. In his writings, Nichiren Daishonin says that one person must be the model, on the basis of which all sentient beings are equally capable of attaining Buddhahood. Nichiren Daishonin's Buddhism delves to the profoundest depths of life to establish the true dignity of the individual, and its teachings are great enough to save all sentient beings.

In 1970, I held a total of ten hours of discussion with the late Count Richard Coudenhove-Kalergi, who is sometimes called the father of the European Economic Community. At that time, I was especially impressed with the forceful way in which he insisted that Japan has grave responsibilities to fulfill. First, he said that our nation must exert every effort in the name of peace. Second, Japan must take the leadership in the creation of the new civilization of the Pacific. He said that we are currently in a period of transition away from the Atlantic civilization of Europe and America and toward a civilization based on the Pacific. He added that Japan must play the major role in that civilization.

Count Coudenhove-Kalergi went on to say that Japan ought to export more than material goods. The time has come for the Japanese to introduce to other peoples the great life-respecting Buddhist philosophy that, born in India, passed through China and developed finally in Japan.

Others have said similar things. The late Arnold J. Toynbee, whose historical perspicacity was great, said to me that the time has come for the emergence of a Pacific civilization. Many members of the intelligentsia are predicting that the twenty-first century will be a century of oriental civilization. The journal *The Economist* has stressed this point and has carried an article in which a specialist on America reported that Henry Kissinger, former United States secretary of state, said that signs already indicate history's move from Europe in the direction of the Pacific. The same article said that Mike Mansfield, United States ambassador to Japan, is of the same opinion. I have met all of these leaders and have had direct experience of their ways of thinking and feeling. Deep in my heart I entertain a special emotion in connection with them for a different reason. What they say indicates that Nichiren Daishonin's confident proclamation is about to come to pass: "I say that, without fail, Buddhism shall arise and flow forth from the east, from the land of Japan" (*The Major Writings of Nichiren Daishonin,* 1:115), and "The sun rises in the east and casts its rays to the west. The same is true of Buddhism" (*The Major Writings of Nichiren Daishonin* 1:114).

On the basis of Buddhist teachings, we must contribute to peace and the creation of the new culture. We have entered an age that is like a great river. The twenty-first century will be the age of a great sea, in which the teachings of true Buddhism will flow throughout the world.

Hope and Courage for
the Twenty-first Century

*Delivered at the Headquarters Leaders' Meeting, held at
the Arakawa Cultural Center, Tokyo, November 18, 1978.*

The Goal of Faith

Clearly, the ultimate aims of our faith are the attainment of Buddhahood in this life and the achievement of the universal propagation of the faith in True Buddhism, or *kosen-rufu*. And for the sake of fulfilling these aims, Josei Toda, second president of Soka Gakkai, left as our eternal guide the following three goals: (1) Faith for harmony and happiness in the family, (2) Faith for the happiness of the individual, and (3) Faith to overcome hardships. We should bear these three firmly in mind constantly, since they are all profoundly connected with the way we conduct our lives.

Human life is invariably accompanied by deep suffering—which, in Buddhist terms, is described as birth, old age, sickness, and death; or the need to associate with the loathed and part from the beloved; or being constantly thrown into contact with the detested and made to encounter suffering. No political or economic system, science, learning, or morality can do anything about such suffering. The only way to solve the problems associated with it is through the help of a true religion.

In contrast to many other religions, which posit escapist paradises as a post-mortem answer to suffering, the Buddhism of Nichiren Daishonin faces the actuality of the situation straight on and, by means of the Dai-Gohonzon, opens the way to a state of Buddhahood characterized by the four virtues (eternity, happiness, the self, and purity).

The *Gosho* says, "The four faces of the Treasure Tower mean birth, old age, sickness, and death. These four aspects give solemnity to the individual tower of life. By chanting Nam-myoho-renge-kyo through birth, old age, sickness, and death, we send forth the fragrance of the four virtues of eternity, happiness, true self, and purity" (*Gosho Zenshu*, 740).

What a wonderful teaching this is! Many people undergo all the greater pain by attempting to flee from suffering. We, on the other hand, find that suffering becomes the ornament of our lives.

Proverbs say that without hope nothing can be accomplished, and that despair is the conclusion to which fools come. We are certain in the hope of faith. For that reason, we are able to live in the Mystic Law, the highest and most hope-filled way of all, and can be certain that our philosophy of the eternal nature of the force of life enables us to live in a world of happiness.

Personnel Development

The harmonious organization called Soka Gakkai is a vitally important element for our ultimate goal of *kosen-rufu*. But, like all organizations, it begins and ends with individual human beings. A truly valuable organization depends on the powerful faith of its constituent members and on the good relations binding them together. Without these things, an organization can become a source, not of good, but of evil. And this is why we must place the greatest emphasis on cultivating, on all levels, the kind of personnel needed to ensure that Soka Gakkai remains a harmonious body eternally dedicated to the mission of achieving *kosen-rufu*.

With great wisdom, Nichiren Daishonin says, "One who wishes to study Buddhism must first learn the time" (*The Major Writings of Nichiren Daishonin*, 3:79). Historically, Soka Gakkai has now completed one stage of its development. Furthermore, the confusion of the first three decades of the period following World War II has now ceased, and society has entered an era of order and stability. To avoid becoming isolated from society, as Nichiren Daishonin enjoins, we must hereafter devote our attention to creating a firm foundation that conforms to the needs and nature of our times. The way to perpetuate social stability is for each individual to examine and attempt to improve his own way of life. We must avoid narrow interpretations of people as mere means to facilitate organizational operations and take a wide, all-inclusive view. The most fundamental element in cultivating the kind of personnel we need is realizing that each person has his own approach to faith and to the kind of lifestyle consistent with the achievement of *kosen-rufu*. We can be proud that, in our regional societies, a very wide variety of different kinds of people are busy working for the fulfillment of our mission.

In addition, we must give consideration to our attitudes toward the elderly. The *Gosho* has the following comment to make on this subject: "King Wen of the Zhou dynasty cherished his elders and was victorious in battle. Though there were periods of misgovernment during the eight hundred and thirty-seven transitions in reign, the Zhou dynasty as a whole prospered due to the virtue of its founder" (*Gosho Zenshu*, 1250). This suggests how valuable the elderly are. Experience of all aspects of life has refined and molded them. Having them with us gives us relief, security, confidence, and courage to carry out our task of achieving *kosen-rufu*. Furthermore, the elderly can offer great assistance in the cultivation of younger people strong and wise enough to shoulder the responsibilities of the future.

Unbroken Harmony between Priesthood and Laity

Throughout human society, actual ways of harmonizing tradition and modernization and the relations between the weight of history and progress have always been important issues. Development without models, progress without stability, and modernization without tradition are shallow and cannot be expected to last long. This is why, in our work to carry Buddhism to our age and society and to the whole world, we must always base our thoughts and actions in the true teachings of Nichiren Shoshu. In addition, unless we maintain constant and perfect harmony between the laity and the priesthood we cannot hope to achieve *kosen-rufu*. Protecting the priesthood from without must always be the policy of Soka Gakkai.

Five-year Plans Oriented toward the Twenty-first Century

The year 2000 will mark the seventieth anniversary of the founding of Soka Gakkai and the centennial of the birth of Josei Toda.

Mr. Toda made a vow that the membership of our organization would reach seven hundred and fifty thousand during his lifetime. When it did in fact reach that number, the high priest Nichijun said that he knew from where Toda had taken the figures five and seven in his goal: the seven from the seven characters used to write the Daimoku—Nam-myoho-renge-kyo—and the five from the five characters needed to write the name of the Lotus Sutra itself—Myoho-renge-kyo.

Until recently we have continued using the seven in connection with a series of seven-year stages of growth. Starting in 1980, however, we shall divide our development into five-year stages. The use of this shorter period should not, however, make anyone think that we are in a hurry or acting hastily. During the first stage I want us to concentrate more deeply and on a wider scale on the cultivation and education of personnel who, putting faith first, are nonetheless well-rounded in all respects. We must never forget that personnel development is so closely related to the achievement of *kosen-rufu* that the latter is unthinkable without the former. People of the kind I have in mind are treasures. They represent strength. Nothing is more important. I hope that we will be able to send such personnel out to bear witness to the truth of Buddhist teachings in all fields of society.

The year 1990, the end of the second of our five-year phases, marks the seven-hundredth anniversary of the founding of Taiseki-ji, our head temple, and the thirty-third anniversary of the death of President Toda. The five years terminated by these two occasions will provide us with a chance to demonstrate stability and majestic power for peace in society, as we attempt to carry out President Toda's behest to rid the world of nuclear weapons.

I believe that the third period—between 1990 and 1995—will be the final stage of preparation for the achievement of *kosen-rufu* both at home and abroad. Right now our members of middle-school and elementary-school age are already setting in motion the current that, at this time, when they are in their twenties, will swell into the millions of members who will make up the second and third generations of Soka Gakkai. The fourth of our stages will end in 2000.

Then, the year 2001 will witness the start of the second of our Seven-bell programs; and 2002 will mark the seven hundred and fiftieth anniversary of the founding of Nichiren Shoshu. Though, by this time, many aspects of society will no doubt have changed drastically, it is my hope that, as a symbol of the conclusion of our four five-year stages and of our work for *kosen-rufu* in this century, we will erect a *kosen-rufu* tower in a significant location and on the basis of consultation with the whole membership. As we walk together toward a brilliant new dawn, I hope all members of our organization will do everything with deliberation and careful preparation, always remembering that daily life must be a manifestation of faith.

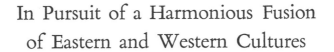

In Pursuit of a Harmonious Fusion
of Eastern and Western Cultures

Delivered at Sofia University, Bulgaria, May 21, 1981.

I have visited many countries throughout the world as founder of Soka University and as president of Soka Gakkai International, which promotes exchanges of goodwill, culture, and education based on true Buddhism.

At the kind invitation of the Bulgarian government, I am now able to be here on Balkan soil, which I have long pictured in my mind. I am overwhelmed with deep emotion.

I received an honorary Ph.D. from your time-honored university at the very beginning of my most memorable stay in Bulgaria. First, I would like to extend my sincere gratitude to Rector Ilcho Dimitrov and others who gave me this opportunity to speak. I would also like to express my appreciation to all the professors and students who have taken time to attend my lecture today. I will try to repay your favor.

Before coming to Bulgaria, I visited the Soviet Union for the third time after a six-year absence. When I met with Premier Nikolai A. Tikhonov, I strongly emphasized the significance of cultural exchanges. There is no way other than through cultural exchanges for one people to know the true heart of another.

I stayed in Moscow about one week, during which time I began a dialogue with Dr. A. Logunov, rector of Moscow State University. Our dialogue concerned the future of mankind; its contents will be published sometime in the future. So far, the educational exchange between Soka University and Moscow State University has been steadfast, through the mutual dispatch of students and the exchange of professors. On this trip, the Ginrei (Silver Summit) Chorus, representing the students of Soka University, visited Moscow State University to hold a Japan-Soviet Student Friendship Festival. The Ginrei Chorus and a chorus from Moscow State University (the Science Academy Chorus) sang together, and they sounded even better together. Their voices beautifully transcended the boundaries of the two nations.

I understand that in Bulgaria choruses are very popular. Your country has even been called "a kingdom of choruses." I have heard that they maintain a high reputation, even on an international level.

In the past, three of the chorus groups which your country takes great pride in visited Japan. These concert tours were made possible through the sponsorship of the Min-On Concert Association, which I founded. They were the Men's Chamber Choir of Bulgarian Radio and Television, the Tolbuhin Children's Choir, and the Svetoslav Obretenov Bulgarian Capella Choir. They performed a total of 117 times throughout Japan and impressed the Japanese people very much. The Bulgarian folk songs especially touched their hearts.

My sincere desire is to dedicate myself as a common citizen to broadening and eternalizing this type of spiritual rainbow that bridges the hearts of different peoples.

Until today, I have lectured at various universities: at the University of California at Los Angeles in the United States, with the theme, "Toward the Twenty-first Century"; at Moscow State University in the Soviet Union, on "A New Road to East-West Cultural Exchanges"; at Beijing University in China, on "Personal Observations on China"; and at the University of Guadalajara in Mexico, on "Thoughts on the Mexican Poetic Spirit." And today, praying for the further cultivation of friendship between your country and Japan, I would like to talk about your country under the title, "In Pursuit of a Harmonious Fusion of Eastern and Western Cultures." In doing so,

I would like to recall the great magnanimity of the Slavic and Balkan peoples—a nature which is familiar to the Japanese people.

Twice in the past, I had the opportunity to speak with your country's ambassadors to Japan. The first ambassador was Mr. Rumen Serbesov, whom I met six years ago. Then last year I met Mr. Todor Dichev, the present ambassador to Japan. When I visited Mexico last March, I also met with your minister of culture, Miss Lyudmila Zhivkova, who was on an official visit there, and we developed a friendship through amiable conversation. Because of these encounters, I believe that I have deepened my understanding of your country, whose culture is perhaps not very well known in Japan.

In July 1975, when I met Ambassador Serbesov for the first time in Tokyo, I frankly related my impression of your country. I said that it seems to me Bulgaria is a very young country, and the image of the rising sun aptly describes the future of this nation. My feeling has not changed since. Rather, it has deepened each time my attention was drawn to some cultural achievement of your country.

I read Ivan Minchov Vazov's *Under the Yoke,* which is widely regarded as a masterpiece throughout the world and has been translated into thirty-two languages as a representative of Bulgarian literature. Now that I have read this book, I have become all the more keenly aware of the Bulgarian people's youthfulness. I read through this work which depicts the "April Revolt" of 1876, when the spirit of the Bulgarian people rose up valiantly, as they tried to free themselves from the yoke of the Ottoman Empire, which they were forced to endure for so long. The steadfast human love depicted vividly in this book reminded me of Victor Hugo's *Les Misérables,* which was one of my favorite books during my youth. As is well known, Hugo was one of those intellectuals who strenuously protested the Ottoman Empire's cruel oppression during the "April Revolt."

The revolt failed, but Vazov has the book's protagonist, Ogun-yanov, say: "It is sad, but it is not shameful." This statement is indeed full of pride and courage, and it helped me, like a ray of light, to understand the hearts of the Bulgarian people, of whom I had only a vague knowledge. Pride or courage is perhaps another name for true youth. Vazov himself says that even if the revolt should be branded as a thoughtless attempt, or even if it should be criticized by historians, "Poetic mind alone permitted this revolt and gave it the crown laureate of the hero . . . in respect for the spirit which drove the wooden cannons and the usually quiet tailors of Anatolia to the sacred heights, Sredna Gora . . . . It was, so to speak, poetic madness, because a young race is poetic, just like young people."

Of course, even if I say you are a young culture, I know very well, on the other hand, that Bulgaria has its own history and traditions which may be the oldest within Slavic civilization. The first Bulgarian Empire blossomed into one of the greatest cultures in the world during the reign of King Simeon (893–927) in the ninth and tenth centuries. The vestiges of the second Bulgarian Empire, which emerged at the end of the twelfth century, are still somewhat alive in the old city of Turnovo. Such a glorious tradition has kept within itself tremendous energy, just like the magma of a volcano, throughout its thirteen-hundred-year history. Unfortunately, for five hundred years during the history of your country, you were in the dark ages, governed by the Ottoman Empire. During this bitter period, however, Bulgaria was never like a dead volcano; rather, she was like a dormant one. In the bottom of the Bulgarian soul, the magma of your people's spirit whirled about vehemently seeking a way out. In this vein, the Bulgarian Renaissance of the nineteenth century can be compared to a spectacular eruption of magma which has long been quietly waiting in a dormant volcano.

Because your youthful nation has such a splendid history and tradition, I am strongly attracted to the spirit of the Bulgarian people. I would like to place special emphasis on the fact that geographically, historically, and spiritually, your country has often found itself at the crossroads between East and West, where the two were fused while at the same time confronting and clashing with each other. The reason I decided on the topic "In Pursuit of a Harmonious Fusion of Eastern and Western Cultures" is that I feel the Balkan Peninsula has the potential for playing a key role in constructing a new human society where East and West can be ideally fused.

Talking about the fusion between East and West may seem easy, but it is a vast subject with many complex and diverse aspects. For this reason, I would like to focus on just one aspect, and try to expand on my thoughts on the basis of it. What I am referring to is the characteristic and intrinsic nature of the Eastern Orthodox church, which is deeply related to the history of Bulgaria.

Frankly speaking, I am a Buddhist and my religious tenets differ from those of the Eastern Orthodox church. In my opinion, whether Eastern or Western, Christianity is monotheistic in a strict sense. Therefore, in the eyes of Christian believers, Buddhism may seem rather atheistic because it is based on a law rather than a god.

Setting aside any discussion of religious tenets, I can say that the role the Bulgarian Orthodox church played in preserving the spirit of the people and in contributing to their freedom and independence is by no means insignificant. Rather, I believe it should be highly regarded.

True, there were a number of problems within the Eastern Orthodox church, including pressure from the Greek Orthodox church, which bowed to the authority of the Ottoman Empire. As symbolized by the courageous action of Father Paisii, a monk who wrote *The History of Bulgarian Kings, Biographies of Saints,* and other works toward the end of the eighteenth century, and who later was regarded as the father of culture in your country, the people of the Bulgarian Orthodox church continued to protect the integrity of the people even during the five centuries of rule under the Ottoman Empire. Their achievements, in fact, were hailed during a ceremony to commemorate the one thousandth anniversary of the establishment of the Rila Monastery, during which Georgi Dimitrov said: "Our Orthodox church should be honored for its great historic undertaking of protecting the Bulgarians' national consciousness and their lives."

In this regard, I am compelled to pay attention to the role religion has played in the formation of history. To roughly sum up my own impression of the Eastern Orthodox church, I would say that the relationship between God and human beings seems much closer within this church than in other Western churches, such as the Roman Catholic church. That God and human beings are closer means that there are no unnecessary intermediaries between them. As long as a religion is monotheistic, it naturally draws a clear distinction between God and human beings. In the case of the Western church, however, it seems to me that the distance between God and human beings became remarkably wider because of the pyramid-like hierarchy which centered around the Pope, who represents God, towering over the people imposingly. In contrast, such intermediaries are fewer in number within the Eastern Orthodox church.

Creating a distance between God and human beings naturally means creating a disparity between the clergy and laity, or divine powers and secular powers. Throughout the history of the Middle Ages and modern times in Western Europe, there was a succession of conflicts between the divine and secular authorities. As a result, politics and religion became antagonistic to each other, and this situation remains basically unchanged even in these contemporary times.

Jean Jacques Rousseau (1712–78), considered somewhat of a heretic in Western Christian society, once said, "This double power and conflict of jurisdiction have made all good polity impossible in Christian states; and men have never succeeded in finding out whether they were bound to obey the master or the priest."

However, the circumstances are fairly different in the world of the Eastern Orthodox church, which is originally derived from the same source of Christianity. I strongly feel that it is necessary to approach, from a somewhat different angle, the subject of the "divine right of kings." Of course, without a doubt it had a negative aspect. It resulted in the subjugation of the religious powers to the secular powers. This led to the misuse of religion by the political authorities. My close friend, the late Arnold J. Toynbee, called this practice the "idolization of an institution" and cited it as the foremost reason for the short life span of the Byzantine Empire.

Despite this historical reality, I think that its positive aspect is that the principle of divine right has created, in a broad sense, an intimacy between politics and religion that cannot be overlooked.

In the world of Roman Catholicism, there was always only one choice: either "politics for the sake of religion" or "religion for the sake of politics." In contrast, what I would like to point out now is that politics and religion should try to commit themselves jointly to a common concern, and that concern should be none other than the human being. Needless to say, both politics and religion can fulfill their own original roles only when they uncompromisingly maintain their total dedication to the human being, not to their own interests. I see this possibility in the Eastern Orthodox church, which tries to bridge the gap and create a closeness between God and human beings, the clergy and lay believers, the divine and secular powers.

Of course, this is merely like the sprouting of a bud, and I doubt that this principle of closeness has been truly realized, for I see many negative aspects in the Greek and Russian Orthodox churches: they have been deeply intertwined with the authoritative dictates of the Ottoman Empire. If I see any positive aspects or potential in these churches at all, I see them in Bulgaria, which has long been under suppressive rule.

I am also drawn to Leo Tolstoy's view of religion. As you may know, he was excommunicated as a heretic from the Russian Orthodox church. In the latter part of his life he made the assertion that "the country of God is within yourself." He also stated, "God can be perceived only within ourselves. Unless you discover God within yourself, you will discover God nowhere." It is no exaggeration to say that in Tolstoy's view God and human beings are so close that there is almost no separation between the two.

The poem, "My Prayer," written by Khristo Botev (1848–76), a revolutionary poet of your country, captures my attention: "Oh! My God! My right God! It is not the God which dwells above in heaven! It is the God living within myself. It is the God within my heart and soul."

You may find it a little strange that I discuss on the same level a revolutionary poet who took up arms and died at a young age after being shot by the enemy and an old man of literature who martyred himself for his philosophy of love, urging, "Do not protest against evil." However, these were the cries of two souls that were deeply rooted in the soil of Slavic and Balkan traditions.

The God cherished in the hearts of Tolstoy and Botev seemed to reach the soil of human life from the pinnacle of heaven, as if to liberate people from the chains of all kinds of authority. It was like a cry of love for mankind, similar to the sunshine which pours down on oppressed farmers and common people. Though different in form, in no way does such humanitarian love oppose the ideal of socialistic humanism which your country pursues. Moreover, such a humanistic love even reminds me of the Buddhist view of the human being—

the view of the ultimately inherent condition of Buddhahood which exists within the life of each individual.

In this sense, it is meaningless to merely discuss the God cherished by Tolstoy or Botev in terms of religious doctrines. The point they were trying to make at the risk of their lives was that everything, including religion, exists "for the human being." To put it another way, they insisted that once this pivotal point is forgotten, any doctrine or ideology swiftly falls down the slope of corruption.

Pointing to the "April Revolt" of 1876, Vazov said, "The national spirit of Bulgaria had never before been enhanced this much. It will never be enhanced this much again in the future." I believe that the national spirit of Bulgaria soared during the "April Revolt" because of an irresistible urge to protect the dignity of human beings at any cost.

Whether or not such an enhancement of your national spirit will ever take place again will depend upon your wise judgment. However, so long as this banner of humanity is proudly kept waving over Bulgaria, a path will surely be opened toward a global humanistic society in the twenty-first century, transcending any national barrier. I believe it will be a vast lush field where the Eastern and Western cultures will fuse, and the flowers of peace and culture will bloom.

Lastly, I have heard that the lion is the symbol of your country. The lion has been regarded as having deep meaning in Buddhism as well. You may be aware of King Ashoka of ancient India whose peaceful rule was based upon the spirit of Buddhism. King Ashoka constructed a pillar whose top was decorated with four lions looking out over Sarnath, near Benares, where Shakyamuni Buddha expounded the Law (Dharma) for the first time.

The voice of Shakyamuni, who first preached there, standing up for the happiness of all people, is symbolized by the lions on the top of this pillar. This is profoundly significant, I think, because I believe the teachings of Shakyamuni were as penetrating as a voice which can overpower any other voice and instantly move people's hearts. In this sense, his teachings were just like the roar of the lion, the king of animals. This spirit was later taken up by Nichiren Daishonin as the founder of Nichiren Shoshu Buddhism. I myself am determined to travel throughout the world as a Buddhist who believes in the

Daishonin's teachings. I would like to conclude my lecture by sincerely praying that you will continue to wave the banner of human liberty, peace, and dignity, dauntlessly and bravely like a lion king forever.

Buddhism, a Sun to Light the Twenty-first Century

Delivered at the Second General Meeting of Soka Gakkai International, held at the Neal Blaisdell Center, Honolulu, August 24, 1981.

Goethe once said that animosity among peoples occurs most violently at low levels of cultural development, but that there is another region where, transcending national interests, people regard the happiness and unhappiness of their neighbors as their own. This is the region that Goethe said was most compatible with his own personality. And I concur with him entirely. Furthermore, I am convinced that Buddhism—and specifically the Buddhism of Nichiren Daishonin, which is the core of all others—is the foundation on which to create a region of that kind.

It is a fact that all civilizations that have brought peace and cultural advancement to humankind have been rooted in philosophy or religion. This is as it must be: a tree without roots withers and perishes. Today, however, in the face of shifting value criteria and radical diversification, many of the established religions and ideologies are fading and no longer have the power to offer firm leadership and control. The result is that, lacking such guidance, human beings fall prey to evil desires and egoism. At best, such religions are like the moon. What light they give cannot resuscitate humanity and provide reliable guideposts for future thought and action.

In contrast, the Buddhism of Nichiren Daishonin is like the sun (the characters with which the name Nichiren is written mean sun and lotus). With a seven-century tradition and with firm, contradiction-free views of human existence, the ultimate force of life, society, and the universe, Nichiren Shoshu Buddhism sets forth the doctrine of cause and effect, and in this way is capable of being the mainstay of humanity in the twenty-first century.

Furthermore, the Buddhism of Nichiren Daishonin inspires the firm faith that is essential if the new century is to be one of peace. By this time, all humankind knows fully the horror and cruelty of war. There is no one who does not want to spend his life peacefully pursuing and contributing to cultural improvement and civilization. But peace is not born of concepts alone. To achieve it, each human being must become aware of the need to take practical action always rooted in faith and profound respect for the force of life. Action of this kind, not mere concepts and slogans, is essential.

One field in which the vital importance of such action is especially apparent is that of nuclear arms. Until not very long ago, people talked of these weapons as deterrents only—weapons that would never be used. In more recent times, however, discussion has often shifted to what is called offensive containment. In strategy of this kind, nuclear arms would no longer be mere deterrents but would come into actual use.

The very idea of nuclear weapons as a deterrent for the sake of peace is a foolish myth resting on the distrust, hatred, and fear that are the basic causes of war. With the advent of the idea of offensive containment, however, the myth has crumbled; nuclear weapons have revealed their demoniacal countenance with full clarity as the idea of putting them to actual use gains open currency. A further development of the same psychology—one that causes all peace-loving people intense anxiety—is talk of neutron bombs that, while sparing buildings, kill the human beings inhabiting them. At no time in history has it been more essential to uproot the distrust, hatred, and fear causing our present dilemma.

Buddhism finds the ultimate cause of these things in fundamental ignorance. And, in our age, we must work and strive to eliminate this ignorance by carrying out the revolution on the fundamental level of the universal life force without which peace, or even continued human civilization, cannot be expected. In other words, the time has come for us to convert fundamental ignorance into the innate Buddha nature. It is unthinkable that we can ever live in peace and happiness without a great labor of faith based on lofty Buddhist wisdom. Consequently, the Soka Gakkai movement of faith will inevitably increase in significance in the twenty-first century.

In the *Sado Gosho,* Nichiren Daishonin reveals, as he does in all his writings, the profound humanitarianism and pacifist nature of his teachings when he says, "The most dreadful things in the world are the pains of fire, the flashing of swords, and the shadow of death" (*The Major Writings of Nichiren Daishonin,* 1:33). By "the flashing of swords" is meant war, in which many are called to suffer death, the most dreadful of all things in men's minds.

Today, our most imperative task is to bend all our wisdom, effort, and perseverance to the total cessation of war. All peoples, leaders, and groups face this same fate. And for us to attempt to evade it risks the danger of global destruction.

Deeper, broader cultural ties are one way we can help all mankind to live together in tranquility and joy. And such ties can be formed in spite of often deep-rooted, ancient animosities. The most moving scene in the splendid First World Peace Culture Festival, held in the presence of twenty thousand of our members and many distinguished guests in Chicago, on June 28, 1981, was the shaking of hands and embracing, in friendship, of individuals from Arab nations and Israel.

The mission of Soka Gakkai International is to advance along a broad road leading to peace, cultural growth, and education, founding all thought and action on the Buddhism of Nichiren Daishonin. Part of our work must be to apply all the effort of our enlightened movement to supporting the United Nations in its efforts to bring lasting peace to the world. In addition, I intend to go on with my international travels and discussions with political, educational, and cultural leaders. In doing this, attempting to overcome all obstacles, I hope to carry True Buddhism and its eternal, immutable Law of Cause and Effect to as many people as possible.

Persecution as
a Source of Strength

Delivered at the Eleventh Soka University Festival, held in Hachioji, Tokyo, October 31, 1981.

Hardship Changes Destiny

Today, on the occasion of our annual Soka University Festival, I should like to share with you some thoughts I have been mulling over recently concerning individuals in history who faced persecution and the ways in which they courageously endured and overcame it. My theme might be summed up in the title "Persecution in the Life of the Individual."

In my teens I was very greatly struck by the following axiom from Western philosophy: "Every time the wave encounters an obstacle, it becomes that much more powerful." It could be said that I have made that axiom a fundamental part of my life and have lived in its light.

In order to carry out an important and meaningful undertaking in the course of the long journey of a lifetime, one inevitably faces periods of frustration and disappointment and encounters many formidable obstacles. But one should never forget that it is precisely such periods of hardship that serve to train and toughen us and make us stronger individuals.

The famous Austrian writer Stefan Zweig (1881–1942), who produced many fine works, put it this way: "Has anyone ever written a hymn in praise of exile? Exile, that in the midst of the storm serves to ennoble the individual, that through its severely enforced loneliness refreshes the power of the wearied spirit and focuses it upon the creation of a new order, that, in a word, brings forth power to create a new destiny—has anyone written a hymn in praise of such exile? The rhythm of nature desires this kind of enforced break in the life of the individual. Because only a person who has known the depths of Hell can understand life in its totality. Only when a person has been abandoned and cast out does he acquire the power to forge ahead with all the strength that is in him."

Zweig goes on to discuss such religious leaders as Shakyamuni, Moses, Christ, Mohammed, and Luther and such artists as Dante, Milton, Cervantes, and Beethoven. He then describes how exile or persecution served to nurture their creative genius. Hardship is truly capable of changing the life and destiny of the individual, dramatically reversing its course, turning it away from darkness, chaos, and destruction, and redirecting it toward light, order, and constructiveness. In the time available to me today, I should like to examine in brief the lives of a few individuals in Eastern and Western history and suggest ways in which persecution and exile influenced them.

Japanese Figures

Let us turn first to Japanese history and the famous scholar and literary artist Sugawara no Michizane (845–903). His father, grandfather, and great-grandfather had all been distinguished scholars, and early in life he himself displayed remarkable talent. In time he entered the bureaucracy and rose to the extraordinarily high position of Udaijin, or Minister of the Right. He lived at a time when the bureaucracy was dominated by members of the Fujiwara family, and it was a mark of great distinction for anyone outside that family to rise high in court circles. The only person who surpassed him in rank was Fujiwara no Tokihira, who held the post of Sadaijin, or Minister of the Left.

Just as it appeared that Michizane might be destined for an even higher position, however, he suddenly fell from power and was exiled to Dazaifu, a government office in Kyushu. His downfall had clearly been brought about by Fujiwara no Tokihira, who slanderously accused him of treason. Thus he fell victim to the device that the Fujiwaras so often employed when they wished to dispose of a rival to power. He was fifty-seven at the time.

His journey into exile in Kyushu was no doubt a long and bitter one, since the provinces through which he passed were forbidden to provide him with food or horses along the way. When he left the capital, he addressed the plum trees at his home in the following famous *waka* poem:

> When east winds blow,
> send out your fragrance,
> plum flowers—
> though masterless,
> do not forget the spring!

He had no way to clear himself of the false charges against him and died at his place of exile at the age of fifty-nine.

The injustice he suffered caused his name to be honored and remembered ages afterward. In contrast to the tragic circumstances of his closing years, after his death his scholarship and literary ability won him fame that only grew with the passing years. Because of his outstanding poetry in Chinese and Japanese, his calligraphy, and his accomplishments as a scholar and historian, he was looked upon as the patron saint of literature and learning, and in the Edo period (seventeenth to nineteenth centuries) his name was known to school children throughout the country. A well-known children's song, *Toryanse,* deals with a visit to a shrine dedicated to his memory.

During the Middle Ages, Michizane was referred to as one of the three gods of Japanese poetry, the other two being the eighth-century poets Kakinomoto no Hitomaro and Yamabe no Akahito. The scholar Takeshi Umehara has recently put forward a new, extremely interesting theory concerning Hitomaro, one of the most famous and admired of early Japanese poets whose works are preserved in the anthology entitled *Man'yoshu.* Professor Umehara suggests that, in his late years, Hitomaro was banished to the province of Iwami in present-day Shimane Prefecture and died there in disgrace. He lived at a time when the so-called *ritsuryo* system of centralized bureaucratic government was being established and Japan was being transformed into a society regulated by a strict code of laws. Persons who failed to conduct themselves as men in authority believed they should were summarily banished one after another. According to this theory, Hitomaro was among those who suffered such a fate, ending his days in Iwami as a condemmed criminal. Hitomaro has been called the greatest poet in all Japanese literature, and his solemn and majestic works are regarded as prime examples of the masculine style in Japanese poetry. Sad as it is to contemplate, even such a man of genius, if the Umehara theory is correct, could be rejected and driven into exile by the authorities of his time.

Now I should like to talk about two men who lived in Japan in the nineteenth century: Rai San'yo (1780–1832) and Yoshida Shoin (1830–59).

A hundred years ago, practically everyone would have named Rai San'yo as the greatest writer in Japan. He is especially remembered for his poems in Chinese, many on historical themes, and for lines such as these describing the military leader Uesugi Kenshin (1530–78) in his protracted battles at Kawanakajima:

> The crack of his whip sounds sharp and clear
>   across the night river;
> what regret—ten years sharpening
>   his single sword!

But San'yo's most influential work was the *Nihon Gaishi,* or *Unofficial History of Japan,* in twenty-two chapters, which stresses the theme of loyalty to the imperial institution and which played a role in the movement that led to the overthrow of the Tokugawa shogunate and the restoration of power to the emperor in what is called the Meiji Restoration.

This book, which helped to inflame the generation of young Japanese who carried out the revolution, was begun by San'yo when, twenty-one years of age, he was confined to his room for a period of three years as a penalty for having left the feudal domain where he lived without official permission. The *Nihon Gaishi,* which begins with the period of the Taira and Minamoto clans and describes in clear and sonorous language the history of the great military families that held power down to the founding of the Tokugawa shogunate, was, in other words, a product of years spent in prisonlike confinement. Perhaps because deprivation of liberty and confinement within a narrow space give a person opportunity to ponder the meaning of life, the circumstances seem to have spurred San'yo on in his literary activity.

In his closing years, when he spat blood and was confined by illness to his bed, he mobilized his disciples and worked furiously to carry on his literary activities and finish the book he was writing. For a person like Rai San'yo, such hardships as confinement—even the devils of sickness and death—served only to stimulate him to greater effort. He appears never to have looked on them as obstacles at all.

Yoshida Shoin, another thinker and revolutionary, who lived at approximately the same time, had to contend with repeated persecution and adversity while attempting to put his beliefs into practice and opening a new path for his country. Shoin's short life came to a close before he had reached the age of thirty, after his revolutionary activities aroused the ire of shogunate officials. Like so many other young patriots of the time, he fell victim to the Great Persecution of the Ansei Era and was put to death in prison in Edo (modern Tokyo). But, before the end came, he had been daring enough to pass on his ideas to a number of devoted disciples, who carried them on.

The scholarly habits Shoin developed in his youth were maintained and further ingrained in him by years of imprisonment and house arrest. The record he kept of the reading he did while in prison indicates that, during a fourteen-month period of imprisonment, he read a total of six hundred books. Nor did he merely read through them: he carefully copied out passages that impressed him and recorded his thoughts concerning them.

Shoin, who constantly confronted the problems of his time and in the end died in the search for a solution to them, set for his disciples a striking example of how a man should live. Even today, in the city of Hagi in Yamaguchi Prefecture, where he lived, the site of the prison where he was confined is pointed out. It is said that while in prison he exercised a great influence over the other eleven prisoners in the jail, holding discussions with them, lecturing and reading to them, and gradually lifting them out of their despair. He seems to have been the kind of man who radiates an air of humanity and concern for his fellow men. It is reported that even the jailer and his son would come and stand in the corridor outside the room in order to listen to Shoin's lectures.

One can imagine the wrath and outrage Shoin's disciples must have felt when they learned of the monstrous injustice inflicted on their teacher by shogunate officials in Edo. Takasugi Shinsaku, one of Shoin's two most outstanding followers, wrote of his determination to avenge his master's death, saying, "Because I and the others were bound to him by the ties of master and disciple, we can never rest until we have taken vengeance on his enemies!" And Shoin's other leading disciple, Kusaka Genzui, wrote, "It is pointless to mourn the untimeliness of our master's death. The important thing is not to betray his hopes!" These young disciples of Yoshida Shoin did in fact rise up in anger to carry on their master's cause, playing a leading role in the struggle that overthrew the shogunate and initiated the Meiji Restoration.

Chinese Personalities

I would like to leave Japan now and speak of China and one of the most famous poets in Chinese literature, Chu Yuan, who lived in the state of Chu in about 300 B.C., during the Warring States Period. According to his biography in Sima Qian's *Shi Ji,* or *Records of the Historian,* he served as an aide to King Huai of Chu (reigned 328–299 B.C.) and was "possessed of wide learning and a strong will . . . , wise in affairs of government and skilled in the use of words."

China at this time was broken up into a number of feudal states that were engaged in a protracted struggle to swallow up weaker neighbors and extend their own spheres of dominance. The chief rival of the state of Chu, which was situated along the middle reaches of the Yangtze River, was the powerful state of Qin in the northwest. In order to counter the constant threat posed to Chu by the existence of Qin, Chu Yuan urged the ruler to establish friendly ties with Qi, another powerful state that was situated northeast of Chu. In this way he hoped to insure the future safety of the state, but his advice went unheeded. Indeed, the ruler of Chu took steps to enter into closer relations with the state of Qin. Moreover, flatterers and syco-phants at court succeeded in slandering Chu Yuan and in turning King Huai so strongly against him that, in time, he was driven from power.

But, unable to rid himself of fears for the safety of his ruler and his country, Chu Yuan wrote a long poem entitled *Li Sao,* or *En-countering Sorrow,* in which he poured out his anguish for posterity. What Chu Yuan said in the poem was that "To subdue the heart, bridle the will, endure the punishment of exile, suffer disgrace, guard one's purity and integrity, and face death for what is right and just— this indeed is the way taught us by the sages of antiquity."

Chu Yuan's fears proved justified, for King Huai was in time tricked into making a journey to the state of Qin, where he died in captivity. His son and successor, King Qing Xiang (298–269 B.C.), was equally indifferent to Chu Yuan's loyal advice, treating him with hostility and banishing him to the south. Driven from his homeland and frus-trated in his efforts to serve an enlightened sovereign, Chu Yuan predicted the coming downfall of the state of Chu and in despair drowned himself in a river. As he had foreseen, less than five years after this poet-prophet had died for his convictions, the state of Qin marched south with a large army and destroyed the Chu capital.

> What my heart tells me is right—
> though I die nine deaths for it,
> I will have no regret!

Such are the words of this patriot and poet Chu Yuan. He believed that he had been banished because of what he believed to be right and was determined that, as long as he continued to defend that right, he would have no regrets regardless of what harm and affliction might be imposed upon him.

Sima Qian (145?–90? B.C.), the author of *Records of the Historian,* mentioned earlier, and one of the first and greatest of China's historians, is another example of a man who, though faced with severe adversity, remained true to his principles and to the course he had set himself.

During the reign of Emperor Wu of the Former Han dynasty (206 B.C.–A.D. 8), he was appointed to the post of Grand Historian, a post that his father held before him and that entailed handling of astronomical matters and keeping records. At this time, China was frequently troubled by invasions of the Xiong Nu, a nomadic people living in the desert lands north of China, and from time to time the Han rulers sent military expeditions against them. On one such expedition, in spite of brave efforts on the field of battle, a Chinese general by the name of Li Ling found himself cut off without reinforcements, and was forced to surrender to the enemy. When news of this reached the Chinese court, courtiers and officials who earlier had outdone each other in praising Li Ling's military exploits now joined in speaking ill of him.

In spite of this sudden change of opinion in the Han court, Sima Qian dared to speak out in Li Ling's defense. He pointed out the great boldness Li Ling had shown in leading a small force of men against the huge army of the Xiong Nu, and stated the opinion that Li Ling had allowed himself to be taken alive only because he hoped in time to escape and make his way back to China. Unfortunately, Sima Qian's defense aroused the wrath of Emperor Wu, who had him thrown into prison and castrated.

Castration represented the highest degree of disgrace a man could suffer. Writing to a friend some years later, Sima Qian said, "I should probably have committed suicide. But I chose to suffer disgrace and go on living so that I could complete the task I had undertaken." The "task" he speaks of was writing the *Records of the Historian,* a monumental history of China that had been begun by his father, who on his deathbed begged his son to complete it. True to his father's entreaty, Sima Qian spent the remainder of his years completing the work in 120 chapters, which is recognized as one of the masterpieces of Chinese historiography.

In a famous passage at the beginning of the biographical section of his history, viewing a world where right seems to fail perpetually and wrong to prevail, Sima Qian asks in perplexity, "Is this so-called Way of Heaven right or wrong?" Earlier writers had asserted that it was Heaven's way to aid the good man, but Sima Qian was led to question whether that was in fact what Heaven did. Nevertheless, instead of spending his time mourning over them, he used his doubts as a spring-board to propel himself into the task of writing his history. And it should be noted that, unlike most other Chinese historical works, the *Records of the Historian* demonstrates great sympathy and under-standing for persons who failed in their undertakings or otherwise lived tragic lives. This, I cannot help believing, was because the historian himself had experienced severe hardship. In the words of Zweig, he had "known the depths of Hell" and could therefore see deeply into the sufferings of others.

Indian History

The figure to demand attention in Indian history is Mahatma Gandhi (1869–1948), known as the father of Indian independence, a man whose whole life was marked by persecution and struggle. A famous advocate of nonviolence, Mohandas K. Gandhi called upon his fol-lowers to practice neither resistance nor submission. He chose this policy as the most conscientious means of carrying out his struggle to break the harsh chains of British colonialism that enslaved his country.

His life was an endless round of arrests, imprisonments, and hunger strikes, through which he sought to bring pressure upon his foes. When he first initiated his struggle, he announced that "non-coopera-tion is a religious, and in a strict sense, a moral movement, but its aim is the overthrow of the government." With such a goal, it was inevi-table that Gandhi should meet with pressure and persecution at the hands of the British Raj, as he was fully aware. Undoubtedly he believed that persecution offered him the best possible opportunity to strengthen and refine his beliefs.

Gandhi was in the habit of saying that "Goodness moves at a snail's pace," a remark that I have always been very fond of. Because he had faith in the power of the human spirit, he rejected any recourse to military action, any attempt to force a precipitate solution, and in-stead relied upon the patient and persevering efforts of the people. Gandhi's movement did indeed proceed at a snail's pace, and to many observers no doubt seemed a very roundabout way to try to reach the goal. But I am sure he understood it was the best way.

That is probably the reason why this man, who had suffered every kind of persecution without flinching, was unable to remain at rest even after independence had been achieved. He did not even attend celebrations marking the establishment of independence but chose to live out his last days in the slums of Calcutta, where clashes between Hindu and Islam believers continued unabated. In other words, he continued to devote his life, which had been tempered and refined through repeated subjection to persecution and struggle, to the liberation of his people from trials and hardships, never allowing himself to rest. Albert Einstein spoke of Gandhi's existence as "a miracle of the twentieth century," and I heartily echo his words.

French Figures

In France too, over the centuries, resistance against tyranny has produced many outstanding historical figures. Victor Hugo was a writer whose works are still read throughout the world and who is known as a "poet of the people." He was a man of indomitable spirit who refused to surrender in the face of repeated persecution, a man of uncompromising integrity who devoted his life to singing the praises of the common people and of humankind as a whole.

At the age of twenty, Hugo was acknowledged as the leader of the Romantic movement. At the time of the revolution of February 1848, which dethroned King Louis Philippe, he was forty-six. That year he ceased writing poetry and fiction to devote all his energy to political activities, speaking out eloquently and fighting in the movement to free the French people from poverty and insure the independence of education and the rights of the citizens. His activities are still recalled today in the French Senate, and a gold plaque bearing his engraved portrait in profile marks the place where he sat.

But Hugo's ideals and methods of action clashed with those of more seasoned politicians, and he became increasingly isolated. His speech in the Senate in 1851, denouncing Napoleon III, was his last political act. Thereafter he was forced into exile. Writing in a poem that "joy is the fruit borne on the tree of suffering," he was obliged to spend nineteen long years as a political exile before being allowed to return to Paris.

Hugo's fighting spirit, however, was in no way dampened by hardship. On the contrary, substituting the written for the spoken word, he worked with greater vigor in his place of exile. More than half of his literary works date from the years of his exile, including the fierce satire on and condemnation of the oppression of Napoleon III's regime entitled *Napoleon le petit,* the collection of poems entitled *Châtiments,* and the world-famous novel *Les Misérables.* The plot of his last work, *Quatrevingt-treize* was worked out during this period too.

Hugo, who declared that "life is a voyage," surmounted surge after surge of its heavy seas, moving majestically forward, pushing on and on without stopping. After his death, he was extolled by the populace and treated as a national hero, and his remains rest in the Pantheon. True to his name, he was a man of victory.

If Hugo's character was marked by stout-heartedness, Jean Jacques Rousseau (1712–78), who was persecuted and forced into exile, strikes me as gentle in nature. Rousseau's philosophy has been called "a prediction of the twentieth century." Because of his foresight, he greatly surpassed all the other thinkers, philosophers, and scholars of his time and has even been called the father of the French Revolution. I like to think that, underlying his farseeing intelligence, running through his character like an underground stream, was concern and sympathy for human beings, particularly for the weak.

His writing on education and politics and his works of literature have assumed the stature of classics and, two hundred years after their appearance, continue to shine with the light of genius. *Emile* and *The Social Contract* (both published in 1762) reveal a profound understanding of nature and humanity and of relationships between them. And, probably because of the gentleness of his nature, he was critical of the harsh dogmatism of Christian theology and became increasingly acute in his attacks on the church and the political forces of his day. As a result of the publication of *Emile* and *The Social Contract,* a warrant was issued for Rousseau's arrest, and he was forced to undergo five years of flight and exile. Moreover, the administrative council of his beloved Geneva, of which he was a citizen, went so far as to ban these two publications in an attempt to keep their ideas from spreading. Rousseau's late years were shadowed by ill fortune, as he was hounded from one place to another by church and political authorities. But such is the path all pioneers are destined to travel, a path glorious yet beset with storms. After the outbreak of the revolution, Rousseau was hailed as a hero of the French nation. His remains were exhumed and reburied in the Pantheon, where Hugo was later to rest.

Paul Cézanne (1839–1906), the man who has been called the father of modern art, looms as a major figure in the history of Western painting. Yet during most of his lifetime his work was met with incomprehension and derision.

He was born in the city of Aix-en-Provence in the south of France. In time, he made his way to Paris, where he cast about for a style of painting that suited him. At the time, Paris was the scene of a new movement in art that sought to challenge the academicism of officially approved painters. Finding himself in sympathy with their thinking about the proper approach to art, Cézanne made friends with such men as Monet, Pissarro, and Renoir, who later were to become leaders of the Impressionist school.

In 1874, Cézanne exhibited three works in the first exhibition of Impressionist works. But his pictures were greeted with severe derision by the critics, who described them as "paintings by a madman whose senses are deranged." Three years later, he exhibited fifteen works in the show that was later to be recognized as the high point of the Impressionist movement. But public reaction to the work of the group continued to be highly critical. Cézanne's paintings met with even greater scorn than before. One of his portraits was described derisively as "a madman's painting of a madman."

Highly sensitive by nature, Cézanne was deeply wounded by such criticism and returned to his home in southern France in disappointment. There he determined that, though he might live a humdrum existence as "a painter of Aix," he would pursue his own artistic ideals, no matter what the world might say. He died there in 1906 at the age of sixty-seven, having devoted the remainder of his years to his art. Death came to him as a result of a collapse he suffered while, characteristically, he was painting outdoors in the rain.

After his death, true recognition of his work came when Picasso and other painters of the Cubist movement, who were deeply influenced by Cézanne, gained worldwide attention because of their striking artistic innovations. In time, Cézanne came to be hailed as the forerunner of modern art. In June of this year I visited his birthplace, the city of Aix-en-Provence. As I gazed, morning and evening, at Sainte Victoire, the mountain that Cézanne painted assiduously, I imagined I could see him at his work, enduring the laughter and jeers of the world and continuing undaunted to paint in the way he believed was right. Once again it struck me how difficult it is to pursue one's ideals and beliefs unperturbed and without faltering in the face of all the hardships and storms that may beset one.

Lenin's Influence

To close my remarks, I must say something about the man who played a decisive role in determining the shape of the world as we know it today, the Russian revolutionary leader Nikolai Ulyanov, older brother of Vladimir Ulyanov, or Vladimir Lenin (1870–1924). Just at the time when Nikolai was executed on charges of attempting to assassinate Tsar Alexander III, Vladimir Ulyanov had entered the University of Kazan, founded in the early years of the nineteenth century in the city of Kazan on the Volga River. But because of his relationship to his condemned older brother, he was dismissed from school and denied permission to reenter. Though his adult years began disappointingly, without hope for future advancement, he refused to be defeated, and set about reading voraciously on his own from morning to night.

Later he engaged in revolutionary activity and was arrested, spending a year and two months in prison in Saint Petersburg, the present-day Leningrad. In February of 1897, he was sent to Siberia for a three-year exile that lasted until January 1900. During this period, he studied the Russian economy and wrote *The Development of Capitalism in Russia*. The eminent historian and sociologist Kovalevsky was amazed at this book's display of Lenin's talent as a historian.

In time, Lenin realized his goal of carrying out a revolution in Russia, but in its wake he had to struggle with domestic strife caused by counterattacks of conservative forces and foreign intervention. These years proved to be the most difficult of his life. Beginning with industry and agriculture, the entire nation was in a state of general collapse. Anxiety mounted as the people began to view the future development of the country with alarm.

But undismayed, Lenin called upon the young people for support, reminding them that "In one's youthful years the most important thing is to study." This, it seems to me, reveals the true greatness of Lenin as a person. In the darkest days after the revolution, he entrusted everything to the youth of the nation, putting all his hopes in them and repeatedly urging them to study.

The epoch-making accomplishments all these men made in the midst of persecution were not achieved in easy or ordinary ways. These men pushed ahead in the face of hardship and trial, half-resigned to such conditions as an inevitable part of their destiny. Later, as they looked back on their lives, they found they had accomplished deeds surpassing the imagination. They had in fact bequeathed miracles to posterity.

Nietzsche, in his youth, denounced the evils and obstacles that beset people who would accomplish feats worthy of memory by saying, "Stupid habits, petty things, coarse and mean things fill every corner of the world, create an oppressive atmosphere on the earth, hang over and enshroud all those who are great, placing themselves squarely in the path that the great man must travel to reach immortality, blocking his way, deceiving him, taking away his breath, choking him."

Rooted in the Populace

I am fully aware that the great deeds of history are never carried out by solitary heroes or geniuses. Naturally, the great doers require the support and help of countless ordinary, now anonymous people.

No matter what famous personage is associated with the great undertakings of history, they are all firmly rooted in the populace as a whole. For that very reason, men in power, the elite, who have gained dominance at the expense of the people, are inflamed by jealousy and envy born of ambitions and instincts for self-preservation. Whatever their rank or position, the true nature—the real selves—of such enviers has sunk to the level that Goethe referred to when he said, "When human beings become truly base, their only interest lies in rejoicing over the misfortunes and failures of others." It is only natural to expect that storms of persecution will rise up to confront leaders who emerge from the populace. A certain proverb says, "Review the old so as to understand the new." In this brief survey of the history of persecution I can discern a hard and fast rule of human history applicable equally to past and present.

As a Buddhist believer and a member of the common people, I have been repeatedly subjected to groundless slander and persecution. I believe this survey suggests that persecution can be a supreme source of pride and glory.

I have no doubt that you young students, in the course of the long years ahead of you, will at times find yourselves facing vexing hardships and storms of one kind or another. If at such a time you find some comfort in recalling the remarks I have made today, I will feel extremely gratified.

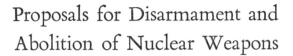

Proposals for Disarmament and Abolition of Nuclear Weapons

A Proposal for the Second Special Session of the United Nations General Assembly on Disarmament, June 5, 1982.

On several occasions, I have had opportunities to talk with Dr. Aurelio Peccei, one of the most active and influential members of the Club of Rome. He is deeply involved in that organization's unceasing efforts to foresee and resolve problems and crises of the future. Each time I see him, he returns to the same topic: Is humankind plunging headlong into ever more difficult situations and increasingly complex problems, with no idea of how to cope with them, or of what to do when it is too late to reflect?

Even without Dr. Peccei's warnings, few people remain unaware of the ever-present realities of the crises—potential or ongoing—that surround us. The most awesome of them is the possibility of nuclear war. And this is why it is impossible to convey the gratitude, relief, expectation, and hope with which I, together with millions of other Japanese citizens, greet the Second Special Session of the United Nations General Assembly on Disarmament. Let me express my most profound thanks to everyone whose efforts made this session possible. Realizing the urgency of our situation is no more than practical realism. If we fail to avert nuclear war, we may face the virtual extinction of the human race.

People all over the world are anxiously watching the special session, for their hopes lie in the outcome. If the aggregate wisdom of all people can be concentrated in this meeting and if human needs are given first priority, a path toward disarmament will surely be found. I am no expert on nuclear disarmament and am unqualified to discuss its technical aspects. It is out of religious beliefs and commitments that, on this occasion, as at the time of the first special session, I feel compelled to offer proposals for nuclear disarmament and abolition of nuclear weapons. And I hope that in doing so, I can express the dread that the very idea of possible annihilation of the human race inspires in me. For the sake of humanity, I want to share my awareness of the crisis with you in the hope that a solution can be found.

Tensions between the United States and the Soviet Union in connection with nuclear armament have risen palpably since the first special session, four years ago. It is has now become commonplace to regard nuclear weapons as having actual applicability in combat. Originally considered unthinkably destructive and therefore virtually unusable, they were designed as retaliatory deterrents. But recent advances and improvements have created faster, more deadly and accurate weapons that have worked a fundamental change in strategic thought.

Nuclear weapons are now looked on as a counterforce with strategic potential for attack and destruction to be directed, not at enemy cities, but at missile bases. This approach to the matter encourages the very dangerous notion that a nuclear war can be won by the party that uses nuclear weapons first. When such thinking dominates strategic planning, the idea that their deterrent value makes nuclear weapons tolerable becomes senseless.

One day very soon I hope all people will see that nuclear weapons represent absolute evil and will cooperate in removing them from the face of the earth.

But the pushing of a button to launch a nuclear attack before such a consensus has been achieved could doom major parts of Europe. And behind the repeated mass campaigns of protest against nuclear weapons that have taken place since last year in Western Europe and in the United States lies the fear that just such a thing might happen.

We must face the objective truth that an escalation of nuclear armaments is taking place and must realize that the balance that barely keeps the situation in check is being steadily eroded. But we must not be pessimistic about the future of the human race. If the deeply motivated movement for the abolition of nuclear weapons that has grown in Europe spreads to all the peoples of the world and if we mobilize our wisdom and the best of which human nature is capable, we can eliminate the horrible threat. Symbolically, the rallying cry "No More Hiroshima!" transformed into "No Euro-shima!" became the most powerful slogan in the European anti-nuclear campaign. Our task now is to inspire all people with the righteous wrath felt by the Europeans, and to thus stimulate the world to rise up against these weapons. Humankind created them, and humankind can destroy them.

Four years ago, in my proposal to the first special session, I pointed out the following four major factors hindering disarmament. The first is mutual distrust among nations, particularly between the United States and the Soviet Union, the two greatest nuclear powers. Instead of improving, the basic pattern of arms escalation stimulated by fear and distrust has grown graver since that time.

The second factor is national egoism. The old malaise that has consistently confounded disarmament attempts, egoism, impels the nuclear powers to continue sharpening their own nuclear swords while denying such weapons to others. By this stage, the figurative swords of the nuclear powers are powerful enough to wipe humanity out several times over.

Widespread apathy among most people to the threat of nuclear weapons is the third factor impeding disarmament.

Fourth, and finally, is the huge investment of capital in nuclear weapons. Organizations for nuclear research and the associated bureaucratic structure have grown so gigantic in the nuclear superpower nations that dismantling them would require enormous displacements and painful adjustments. Nonetheless, to arrest the escalation of nuclear armament and encourage disarmament, we must remove these obstacles one by one. This is possible if the peoples of the nuclear nations unite their voices in demanding peace and thereby destroy the national egoism blinding their governments. In other words, a truly motivated citizenry is the crucial factor in dismantling the structure behind arms expansion.

I strongly believe that nongovernmental organizations (NGOs), whose goals and characters are transnational, can be instrumental in bringing disarmament about. As will be recalled, nonaligned nations and NGOs motivated the first Special Session of the United Nations General Assembly on Disarmament. On that memorable occasion, about thirteen thousand NGO representatives gathered to seek ways to bring about world peace and disarmament in a popular solidarity completely transcending national boundaries. On the final day of the session, Secretary-General Kurt Waldheim personally endorsed the activities of NGOs and their contributions to the cause of peace. I believe NGO contributions will be even more important in the second special session.

At present, an estimated ten thousand NGOs are grappling with such universal problems as war and peace, pollution, ecology, and so on. Our organization, Soka Gakkai, a nongovernmental organization formally registered in the Information Bureau of the United Nations, has a membership of more than ten million in Japan alone and hundreds of thousands of members in more than ninety other lands. All of these people are energetically working for peace.

In Japan, the Young Men's and Young Women's divisions of Soka Gakkai have been working for six and one half years on two anti-war publication series, one of fifty-nine volumes and one of three volumes. Some of the books have been published in English-language translations. They have all been generally well received in Japan and abroad, and their publication symbolizes an unprecedented, large movement conducted by people of generations who have never experienced war. Both series record the terror and misery remembered by the older people from their lives during World War II in order that these experiences will be preserved for posterity. In addition to publications of this kind, Soka Gakkai encourages determination for peace among the Japanese people by holding anti-war and anti-nuclear exhibitions all over the country.

I ceaselessly urge people—ordinary citizens and world leaders, Japanese or non-Japanese—to support the United Nations in its work for peace. For instance, in January 1975, I gave Secretary-General Waldheim a petition for ridding the earth of nuclear weapons. The petition bore ten million signatures collected by our Young Men's Division. In addition to petition campaigns of this kind, the Young Men's Division has conducted fund-raising programs for refugees from Indochina and for the peoples of Africa and has sponsored in Japan exhibitions and lectures on the United Nations. To strengthen the solidarity of people who realize that, more than citizens of national states, they are citizens of the world, I have encouraged what is called the World Citizens Association to Support the United Nations. I believe that the support of such organizations as this can assist the United Nations in making peace and disarmament realities for our world.

Because they are in a position to transcend national interests and act on behalf of all peoples, NGOs are extremely valuable in the search for peace and universal human welfare. Up to this point, the nation-state has maintained its position as the basic unit of the international order. But that order is becoming too expensive to maintain. As long as the doctrine of the priority of national interests remains unaltered, the current international order poses too many unsolvable problems.

Working separately, people cannot find a solution to the overall problem. The system of separate nations only undermines attempts to fulfill requirements for global peace. Whether this special session produces positive results depends both on whether it is able to transcend differences, frictions, and competition among nations and on how strongly worldwide sentiment against nuclear weapons and arms expansion is represented.

In the past, I fear, the sentiments of many of the world's peoples have been inadequately represented in the United Nations, which, perhaps for historical reasons, has been compelled to emphasize the functions of the Security Council. The use of the veto in conflicts involving the big powers has blocked effective action and eroded confidence in the authority of the United Nations. Restoring world trust in the United Nations—one of the tasks facing this special session—is enormously significant but difficult. Its successful fulfillment hinges on whether the United States and the Soviet Union make firm commitments to the preparation of a concrete nuclear disarmament program. As things stand today, it is doubtful that they will make such a commitment.

So far, none of the many nuclear disarmament plans presented and discussed at international conferences has borne fruit. The two nations that count most in such matters, the United States and the Soviet Union, greet all such plans with ambivalence or downright hostility; and, in the end, all have been frustrated because of the priorities of national interests. No matter what plans other nations formulate or encourage, disarmament will remain impossible until the United States and the Soviet Union demonstrate a serious interest in making meaningful efforts. And, unless we can overcome this greatest obstacle, there is no hope of dealing successfully with all the others connected with nuclear disarmament and therefore, perhaps, no hope for the world.

Brandishing their nuclear weapons in the face of a horrified world citizenry, the United States and the Soviet Union are poised for confrontation. Unless they pull back a little and understand that mutual concessions offer the only way to a breakthrough, both the Security Council and the General Assembly are shackled. For example, when, at the thirty-fifth general assembly, in 1980, an overwhelming majority approved two bills calling for a comprehensive treaty banning nuclear tests, the five nuclear powers either voted against them or abstained. As a consequence, continuing nuclear tests still expose populations of the world to danger.

The concrete, ten-point proposal for nuclear disarmament and the abolition of nuclear weapons that I presented at the first special session of the General Assembly specified an agreement to refrain from the use of such weapons and an international agreement prohibiting the development of new types of nuclear arms.

I once again urge consideration of these measures. The menace of nuclear war makes the older people feel desperate and turns young people into cynics who wonder how they have deserved being robbed of their time for dreams. We can restore peace of mind to both groups if the United States, the Soviet Union, and all other nuclear powers pledge never to launch an initial attack. The most important task before this special session is achieving a consensus among nonnuclear nations and passing a resolution requiring nuclear nations to make this pledge. This is crucial because in no other way is it possible to prevent the currently entertained, dangerous notion of limited nuclear war from corroding the human psyche till it leads to utter destruction. At the very least, the nonnuclear nations must demand that nuclear armaments be frozen at their present level until concrete programs for reduction can be prepared and effected.

Nonnuclear nations face still another task: they must evolve a plan for ridding the world of nuclear arms. This plan must be one they can implement by themselves, independent of American or Russian intentions. Once determined, such a plan could compensate for the weakness of the United Nations in its present state. In the past, I have suggested that the authority of the United Nations and its peace-keeping functions need to be strengthened, that this organization can provide a platform from which to seek a new world order, and that power-politics must not be permitted to influence the nature of that order.

In addition, I have urged that the independence and autonomy of national regions and districts be respected and that all peoples be accorded the dignity and justice to which they are entitled. This is both a practical consideration and a human imperative since stable world peace must be built on a truly universal, democratic basis. A premise of regional independence and autonomy and the dignity of each nation is essential to disarmament and to the reinforcement of the peacekeeping function of the United Nations.

The fourth item in my earlier proposal was the establishment, under United Nations initiatives, of nuclear-free peace zones, which should gradually be expanded in scope. Signatories to nuclear-nonuse agreements should set up such zones in ways and under conditions that could be determined through consultation and discussion. All nuclear weapons existing in these zones would be removed at once, and further introduction of such weapons should be permanently barred to eliminate a possible cause for attack by countries outside the zone. The United Nations could strive to expand these zones until, finally, they encompass all regions of the Earth.

Recently the idea of the nuclear-free zone, included in the final communique of the first special session, has been receiving more attention. Indeed, creating such a zone was one of the major goals of the anti-nuclear movements that started in Europe last year and in the United States this year. This trend indicates the beginnings of a shift away from theory toward actual implementation.

Of the several plans for making Europe a nonnuclear zone, the one prepared by Alva Myrdal, former Swedish minister of disarmament, attracts me most. Her plan is unique in that it envisions creating nonnuclear zones in stages and making adjustments to accommodate the particular situation of each nation. Myrdal suggests that, in the first stage, Sweden, Finland, Yugoslavia, Austria, and Switzerland—none of whom belongs to either NATO or the Warsaw Pact—become core nonnuclear zones, later expanding to include first Denmark and Norway, and then such central European countries as East and West Germany, Poland, Czechoslovakia, the Netherlands, Belgium, and Romania. The group would later be joined by such southern European countries as Italy and Greece and then by Turkey.

My own plan, which is basically similar to Myrdal's, posits a nonnuclear zone proceeding in stages ultimately to embrace Europe, Asia, the South Pacific, Africa, the Middle East, and all other regions.

The idea of the nonnuclear zone was codified for the first time in the Treaty of Tlatelolco, concluded in Mexico City in 1967. This treaty, the formal title of which is the "Treaty for the Prohibition of Nuclear Weapons in Latin America," consists of a preamble and thirty-one articles. The first article prohibits Latin American countries from receiving, storing, or deploying nuclear arms or to possess them in any form, and bans testing, use, manufacture, production, and acquisition of nuclear arms by any means whatsoever.

Two protocols were attached to the treaty. The first consists of three articles, the first of which stipulates that non-Latin American signatories may bring no nuclear arms into the nonnuclear zone established by the treaty. The third of the five articles of the second protocol prohibits non-Latin American nations to use or threaten to use nuclear weapons against Latin American nations. Encouragingly, the United States, the Soviet Union, England, France, and China—the five major nuclear powers—signed both protocols.

As of April 1979, twenty-five nations, including Mexico, Brazil, El Salvador, and Venezuela, have signed the protocols, which have been ratified by twenty-four nations. I hope this is indicative of a growing trend and look forward to the day when all peoples will make nonnuclear declarations and will demand that their governments ban production, possession, and introduction of nuclear arms into their lands.

A resolution presented to the United Nations General Assembly calls on the nuclear powers to promise to refrain from such crimes against humanity as nuclear attack on countries not possessing nuclear arms or countries where such arms are not deployed, and to never threaten such countries with the use of nuclear arms in violation of the United Nations charter. Now that this resolution has been approved by one hundred and twenty-one nations, it is time for the nuclear powers to make a declaration against all use of nuclear weapons. A total, loophole-free commitment to non-use would represent great progress toward acceptance of the principle of banning production, possession, and introduction of nuclear weapons.

In England, and elsewhere too, local communities are increasingly declaring their cities, towns, and villages nuclear free. Such communities as South Yorkshire, the first to declare itself a nuclear-free autonomous district, are dedicated to forbidding storage of nuclear weapons within and even the passage of vehicles conveying such weapons through their boundaries. According to reports, more than one thousand two hundred cities, towns, and villages throughout England are preparing to make similar declarations. The emergence of such a movement in England demonstrates the possibility of nuclear-free zones even in a nation possessing nuclear weapons.

In my previous proposal, I had a reason for speaking of nuclear-free *peace* zones, not merely nuclear-free zones. The removal of nuclear weapons alone is insufficient. Even after all such arms have been eliminated from a given region, it is still possible that conflict entailing the use of conventional weapons could escalate into nuclear war. Since, in such a contingency, the words *nuclear-free* would be meaningless, in nuclear-free *peace* zones, the danger of even conventional conflict must be eliminated. Realistically speaking, it is pointless to ban nuclear and allow conventional weapons. A region truly wanting to be rid of nuclear weapons must develop a regional organization dedicated to the unconditional preservation of peace.

The 1967 Treaty of Tlatelolco stipulates that signatories establish an organization called Treaty Organization for the Prohibition of Nuclear Arms in Latin America to implement the provisions of the treaty. The organization is now carrying out inspection and other watchdog activities. Every nonnuclear region should have a similar supervisory organization that should be powerful enough to check and resolve immediately all trouble involving conventional weapons.

The peace-keeping function of the United Nations is a matter of maximum concern at the present time. Consequently, to strengthen that function, all peace-preserving organizations in nuclear-free zones should be formally made United Nations agencies.

I sincerely urge the present special session to create a United Nations committee to work on the establishment of peace-preserving organizations in nuclear-free zones. Such a committee could become a forum for discussion and a central board to examine ideas and plans for these zones. At the present time, peace-preserving organizations could help ease world tensions and encourage nuclear disarmament. If confronted with a sufficiently large number of nuclear-free zones, the United States and the Soviet Union would find themselves isolated in their arms race and faced with increasing risk of violating other nations' pacifist codes.

Merely exhorting the superpowers to disarm will lead nowhere. It will be far more effective to nip international troubles in the bud, ease tensions, and create environments compelling the United States and the Soviet Union to take action for disarmament. Achievement of what I have outlined is fully possible if all peoples truly want peace and unite in expressing their wishes for it. I appeal to the nonnuclear nations to unite in the creation of what might be called a global net of peace around the United States and the Soviet Union.

I am not optimistic enough to believe that a plan of this scale can take shape overnight. Total liquidation of nuclear arms is a long way away. But opposition to nuclear weapons exists everywhere, even among the peoples of the nuclear powers. The aim now is to mobilize that opposition.

Last year, George F. Kennan, former United States ambassador to the Soviet Union, proposed reduction by half of the total nuclear arsenals of both nations. And, according to a Gallup poll taken in December 1981, seventy-six percent of the people of the United States approved of his proposal (nineteen percent opposed and five percent made no reply). In other words, the people of the United States would support President Reagan by a strong margin of four to one if he were to propose to the Kremlin a mutual, fifty percent reduction of nuclear arms.

Belief in the efficacy of military strength, deep-rooted in both the Americans and the Russians, has long seemed an insurmountable obstacle to disarmament. Recently, however, a slight weakening of that belief has manifested itself with the deepening realization of the difficulty of elevating world living standards or satisfying pressing social and economic needs as long as the arms race continues.

Last year, at the request of the General Assembly, the United Nations published a document called *A Study on the Relationship between Disarmament and Development,* which was prepared by a group of government experts from twenty-seven countries, including the United States, the Soviet Union, and several Third World nations. According to this report, about five million people in the world are directly or indirectly engaged in military activities. Over twenty-five million are in the regular armed forces; over ten million are reservists; civilians employed by defense ministries total over four million; scientists and engineers working on military-related research and development are estimated at half a million; and at least five million are directly engaged in production of weapons or other military equipment.

The report said that between 1960 and 1980, worldwide military expenditures increased yearly by an average of about three percent and that total expenditures for 1980 alone reached 500 billion dollars. If expenditures continue at this rate, by 2000, the world total will be 903 billion dollars. As the report pointed out, this would mean that about forty-five percent of the resources needed for civilian life would be used for military purposes.

This is a criminal waste of resources, including human resources. The inability of military strength to ensure national security is beyond all question. Still, many—perhaps most—nations have at one time or another made the dangerous assumption that such strength is a guarantee of safety. And this assumption has led the world into the crisis it faces at the present time.

All nations everywhere must immediately abandon mistaken premises that security depends on ability to launch bigger counter threats or that military power determines a nation's prestige.

Peace will never come from the balance of terror generated in a situation in which horrifying nuclear weapons are pitted against each other. Confidence in the peace-preservation organizations of nonnuclear regions, implementation of disarmament, and easing of tensions promise a far more realistic peace.

If each country in the nonnuclear regions contributed part of its military budget, some of the world's staggering aggregate military expenditure could be channeled into a fund for use in creating peace-preservation zones. A special United Nations committee on peace-preservation organizations could set the level at which the fund should be maintained. And I hope that Japan would lead Asia in making contributions.

As I recommended to the first special session, converting a large portion of the total global outlay for military build-up—including nuclear development—to uses contributing not to human suffering but to human knowledge, welfare, and prosperity would have a significant impact on the world and could snowball into even bigger efforts. To implement the conversion, I propose the formation of a United Nations Committee on Economic Transformation for Disarmament to lay basic plans for the new international economic order that will become possible as disarmament progresses and military priorities disappear.

Problems already present in the world economy of the early 1980s indicate the urgency of starting disarmament now and of developing new, nonmilitary channels for the beneficial use of resources. Advancement of global disarmament and the surmounting of our military and economic crises will narrow the North-South disparity and strengthen the world's many national economies. Because of the exclusively positive gains it promises, all people will have enough stake in peace to work hard to preserve it. I urge the Second Special Session of the United Nations General Assembly on Disarmament to give the world the chance to make initial steps along a path toward global disarmament and a much brighter future for human society.

I further propose informing people everywhere about the horrors, the catastrophic power, and the current world deployment of nuclear arms, with the aim of inspiring a movement for the sake of international consensus on their total destruction. Unless people are deeply committed to the principles of peace and disarmament, the establishment of nuclear-free zones is impossible. More than any other factor, the activity and scope of the movement for the destruction of nuclear weapons will determine the successful establishment of nuclear-free zones.

At the time of the first special session, I suggested several of the many concrete ways of organizing grassroots campaigns against nuclear weapons. Now, as an initial step, I urge nongovernmental organizations to make special efforts to show, in as many countries as possible, the exhibition "Hiroshima and Nagasaki" that our group has prepared.

The Soka Gakkai Young Men's Division has shown an anti-war, anti-nuclear exhibit in all parts of Japan and, through it, has provided, for the sake of people who did not actually witness them in 1945, a graphic record of the horrors of nuclear attack. Another way of awakening people to the disaster nuclear weapons portend is to show films all over the world, with narrations in many languages, of the bombings of Hiroshima and Nagasaki. The mass media, especially television, are also an indispensable means of conveying the terror of nuclear arms.

In addition, I propose setting up in each nation what could be called an Anti-nuclear Peace Hall, which, functioning as a center, could strengthen determination to do away with nuclear weapons by holding exhibitions and providing all citizens with information. In Japan, the Toda Peace Memorial Hall and the Ikeda Peace Hall, established by Soka Gakkai, are well-attended and are helping to encourage peace and strengthen Japanese abhorrence of war.

Four years ago, I proposed the collection and exhibition, for all visitors to the United Nations headquarters, of documents, photographs, films, video tapes, paintings, and other materials conveying the tragedy and cruelty of war, the horrifying destructive power of nuclear weapons, the realities of the Hiroshima and Nagasaki bombings, and the extent and variety of current nuclear arsenals. The United Nations headquarters is an ideal location for a peace hall for exhibiting such materials and distributing them throughout the world. I envision a United Nations Peace Hall as a model for similar halls in other nations and as the inspirational core of a genuinely worldwide, mass movement against war and, above all, against nuclear weapons.

Although a civilian with no diplomatic expertise, I fully realize the enormous obstacles standing in the way of disarmament and peace. These obstacles are not, however, insurmountable. I make no suggestions about actual negotiations or the technical aspects of dismantling the world's lethal arsenals and military machines. But I am convinced that, if the people of all nations want peace, they can prevent their governments from preparing for war. In Japan, for instance, not only Soka Gakkai, but many other groups as well, have worked tirelessly to remind people of the tragedy our nation once went through. It is on the level of the ordinary people, who must be convinced of the futility of war, that I hope my suggestions may be helpful. I pray for the success of this session and hope that from it will arise a new determination to be transmitted to all nations.

Establishing Value in Your Life

Delivered at a Special Meeting of the Soka University Class of 1983, held at Hachioji, Tokyo, July 16, 1982.

It must have been more than twenty years ago, and I no longer remember either the title or the cast, but a scene in a motion picture I saw left a profound impression on me. It was the story of a young scholar who, during World War II, was drafted as a private second class and, at the hands of a devilish superior, subjected to inhuman suffering and to such humiliation as being forced to imitate chickens. In this abnormal world, the young intellectual always kept on his person, or by his side, a copy of Montaigne's *Essais* until, caught reading it, he was beaten. His precious book was kicked away from him and ripped.

As a young man, I too was extremely fond of Montaigne and kept a copy of *Essais,* along with the works of Emerson, at my side most of the time. Perhaps this is why the plight of the young man in the motion picture moved me deeply.

Recently, a student of foreign languages told me, to my surprise, that he had never heard of Michel Eyquem de Montaigne (1533–92). This is not good. A skeptic traditionalist, in his profound observations of human nature, Montaigne was guided by moderation, tolerance, and the belief in happiness. His influence on modern science, philosophy, and literature has been immense.

Like many other European philosophers, Montaigne stood on the side of the people, for whose sake he achieved much. And like them, for his thoughts and actions he suffered hardships, even imprisonment. Because I consider what he had to say of great significance, I should like to quote some passages from Montaigne: "Judging things great and lofty requires a great and lofty soul. Without it, we attribute to such things our own vice. In water, an oar must seem to bend. Not merely seeing things, but the way we see things is important." And again: "That all was marr'd within by vessels taint, What ever good was wrought by any art."

In other words, since the mind operates in wonderful ways and since a person's interpretation of his circumstances is important, we must strive to be spiritually and mentally as outstanding as possible. In Buddhist terms, it is said that no matter how logically the truth is expounded to him, a person with a disturbed mind distorts what he hears. As Montaigne says, the vessel is important. A cracked jug retains no water.

Here is another quotation: "In this breathie confusion of bruites, and frothy Chaos of reports and of vulgar opinions, which still push us on, no good course can be established. Let us not propose so fleeing and so wavering an end unto our selves. Let us constantly follow reason . . . ."

The way of the world constantly changes. A great undertaking makes no progress if the people responsible for it are concerned with popularity and the criticism of the world. In line with the thought of Montaigne on the same topic, George Washington, first president of the United States, said the best answer to slander and calumny is to keep quiet and do your duty.

Of course, the selfishness toward which human beings are prone hinders true progress. Society requires harmonious cooperation and a broad viewpoint. Nonetheless, each of us must have his goals and then must ceaselessly exert his best efforts for the sake of attaining them. Heedless of whatever the world may say, we Buddhist believers must remain unshakable in faith as we move toward the attainment of *kosen-rufu*.

Not all young people today demonstrate firm faith and well-established goals. I am deeply grieved by recently released statistics about juvenile crime. In the past year in Japan, 252,808 young people were arrested or taken into custody. Of these, 116,972 were middle-school students, 65,810 high-school students, and 20,222 elementary-school students. Furthermore, the nature of the acts for which they were arrested has grown worse. In many instances, incitement on the part of friends led these young people to go astray. Certainly the failure of the home to carry out its educational function and excessive emphasis on scoring well in tests exert a powerful influence. These statistics inspire great concern about the desolate state of education in our country and make me all the more aware of the tremendous importance of doing our utmost to solve this problem for the sake of the future.

In the midst of this darkness, however, I am greatly encouraged by the way in which education at Soka University and Soka elementary, middle, and high schools is proceeding along a correct path. I am confident that these institutions will hold up the torch of high ideals for the whole world of education. Although I leave the practical and academic affairs of Soka University entirely up to the faculty and staff, as founder, I consider it my responsibility to provide all possible moral support and to dedicate maximum effort to the creation of a fulfilled educational environment.

As the founder of the university, I have some requests to make of you members of the ninth graduating class. Most of you will be employed in the front ranks of society. Some will go on to graduate school, some will go abroad, and a few will remain on here.

My wishes for all of you are these. First take care of your health. Good health is the fountainhead of all other activity. Second, remember to think of your mothers. Fathers are stronger and can tolerate more. But under no circumstances cause your mothers worry. Watching you go forward, burning with hope, will enrich and brighten the lives of both parents.

Be very careful of human relations in society and on the job. Remember that, although they grow more difficult as the days pass, good personal relations are the first step to success. If you fail to keep this in mind, work and social life will become difficult.

Once you have a job, be prepared for an upward climb for the first ten years and set three years as the period in which you will lay the foundation for the rest of your career. It is seldom that all aspects of a job are pleasant. Remember that every success story has involved overcoming difficulties and making effort after effort.

At the bottom of all your actions and attitudes must rest a spirit of sincerity. On it as a basis, you must move forward, sometimes adamantly, sometimes in a spirit of unbending conviction, and sometimes with great forbearance, to establish your own value in your place of occupation and society at large.

You will have personal problems with seniors and contemporaries. People may overlook your hard work and achievements. You may have to face illness or accidents. And there may be times when you want to run away from everything. But making it through and triumphing are the meaning of human life. Time and time again, you will have to swim upstream, like the carp attempting to leap the waterfall. But do not give in to your trials. Instead, burning with the power of the universal force of life, rise to the challenge of difficulties, and be victorious. And in doing so blaze the trail for those that will come after you.

Daisaku Ikeda appeals for support of the United Nations at the Second Soka Gakkai International General Meeting in Honolulu, August 1981.

A discussion with French art critic and historian René Huyghe in Tokyo, April 1982.

Conferring with United Nations Secretary-General
Javier Pérez de Cuéllar in Tokyo, August 1982.

Reunion with Vice Premier Deng Xiaoping in Beijing, April 1975.

Talking with Dr. Henry Kissinger, former U.S.
secretary of state, Tokyo, September 1986.

Calling on Romanian President Nicolae Ceausescu in Bucharest, June 1983.

With the late Dr. Aurelio Peccei of the Club of Rome, in Paris, June 1983.

Mr. Ikeda receives an honorary doctorate from
Sofia University, Bulgaria, May 1981.

Talking with students at Fudan University, April 1975.

Javier Pérez de Cuéllar views the displays in the exhibition "Nuclear Arms: Threat to Our World" at the United Nations Headquarters in New York, June 1982.

A visit with students at Tokyo Soka Elementary School, October, 1981.

Conferring with Indian Prime Minister
Rajiv Gandhi in Tokyo, November 1985.

New Proposals for
Peace and Disarmament

A Proposal Made in Commemoration of the Eighth Soka Gakkai International Day, January 25, 1983.

Reverse the Course to Destruction

Today, all the nations of the world, including Japan, find themselves in an extremely complex and difficult predicament. In spite of a continuing global recession and the suffering it threatens to inflict, expansion of military establishments shows no signs of abating. As the economic situation deteriorates, both the industrialized and the developing nations take increasingly stubborn protectionist stands. A single misstep could set the world off on a careening course of destruction. It is no wonder, then, that people today frequently recall the 1930s, when Japan and most of the world were plunged into World War II.

With almost total pessimism, our time is described as "an unchartable age" or "an era whose future is unreadable." Undeniably we are entering a period of major chaos. And that is all the more reason why we, as Buddhists, must face the times with a clear, calm eye and attempt to plot our way into the twenty-first century.

According to a report released early this year by a well-known group of specialists in Washington D.C., the following two or three years will determine whether the nuclear arms race accelerates or we commit ourselves to the path leading to disarmament. The first half of the 1980s has already seen a build-up and strengthening of nuclear arms strategy as the great powers vie with other in the development of new strategic weapons. If, according to plan, American Pershing II missiles and Cruise missiles are deployed in Europe by December of this year, tension between East and West is certain to be aggravated. Outside of Europe, the Soviet Union has recently revealed plans to deploy a number of intermediate-range SS20 missiles in Siberia, apparently to counteract the build-up of American nuclear power in the Far East.

No doubt, the decision made by Japan and the United States at a recent summit conference to strengthen their military alliance will fuel tensions in Asia. Furthermore, steps of this kind force the Japanese people to suffer from uncertainty as to whether their nation is embarking on a pacifist or a militarist path.

All of these crises could rob man of his right to continued existence and might end in the destruction of the world. In short, this year, our planet is at a crucial crossroads between work for peace and the intensification of international tension.

Another critical issue is the deep entanglement of the arms race with economic, political, and social systems. It is well known that the military-industrial complex supports current destructive military power, but governmental bureaucracy and the academic establishment also provide support. Collaboration among military, bureaucratic, academic, and industrial organizations and institutions is becoming increasingly uninhibited. Forces with vested interests in the expansion of military power are determined to strengthen their positions. Because of the great strength of these sectors, attaining disarmament will evidently entail painful, sustained effort over a very long period.

The People Must Take the Lead

Though perhaps this is a sweeping statement to make, I believe that the increasing control machines and political organizations have steadily gained over humanity during the development of modern civilization is reaching its logical conclusion in the idea of nuclear power as an ultimate method of gaining desired ends. It seems possible that elite policy-makers who are apparently in control of the ruling structures supported by destructive military force might themselves actually be under the influence of an evil inherent in nuclear weapons and political power. In Buddhist philosophy, this kind of evil is called fundamental ignorance of the true nature of existence. In the darkness of such ignorance, humanity is certain to be relegated to a role of only secondary importance in all areas of society.

People who talk glibly of limited nuclear war display a lack of concern for humanity. The idea of such conflict goes beyond nuclear deterrence. Puppets of the nuclear devil, in their calculations of thousands and millions of dead—advocates of it fail to take into account the anguish of each individual who will inevitably be destroyed in such warfare. In the situation as they envisage it, nuclear weapons are the true protagonist; and humanity plays the wretched secondary role of defeated antagonist.

Not limited to nuclear arms, this kind fiendishness is apparent in all weaponry. Nuclear weapons merely represent its magnification to the utmost limits.

Clausewitz was able to call war a continuation of politics by other means because, in his time, humanity could be safely assumed to be in control of it. The advent of nuclear weaponry was the major, fateful catastrophe of modern times because it invalidated such reassuring assumptions. Concentration of control of the power structures on which nuclear might is based has spelled defeat for humanity and human dignity.

The fateful advent of nuclear arms demands that humankind once again take the lead in the drama of history. (And in this connection, I should like to reaffirm the immutable guiding principle that Soka Gakkai forever stands on the side of the ordinary people.)

The ordinary citizenry has been the main supporting force of the historically significant, worldwide anti-nuclear and disarmament movements that have experienced a great upsurge since 1981. And, as they have spread beyond national boundaries, these movements have inspired in me a sense of entering a new age in which ordinary people will recognize their responsibility to preserve peace in the face of nuclear arms, the enemy of all humankind. This self-awareness adds brilliance to a popular movement that, for the first time in history, has attained organizational power equal to that of governmental and international systems.

To broaden this popular movement, and in the hope of bringing the advent of the long-awaited age of peace even one day closer, I have done what I could by traveling as a private citizen to some forty countries, meeting with leaders, and promoting contacts and cooperation among different peoples. But the work has only begun.

One of the most pressing issues facing us today is to discover a way for the ordinary people to break through the great obstacles state and political power continue to present, and to open the way to permanent peace. I reject pessimism because I believe that despair and resignation cannot provide the answers we need. I agree with Karl Jaspers who, toward the end of his life, said that no situation is hopeless. We must persevere with hope and confidence that we can open the door to the twenty-first century.

In a similar vein, in conversations I recently held with the American sociologist, Professor Robert N. Bellah, of the University of California, who holds great expectations for our organization's many activities in the name of peace, he emphasized the importance of hope. He went on to say that simply terrifying people with the tragic consequences of nuclear war deprives them—especially young people—of hope and pushes them into self-centeredness. Instead of doing this, he added, we should sponsor peace movements to encourage people to hope for the reform of society and to assure them that humanity's most deeply rooted wish can indeed be satisfied.

Nongovernmental organizations (NGOs) are likely to play an increasingly important role in crystallizing the general wish for peace. Since they transcend the narrow confines of national interest, achievement of their goals inevitably requires the peace and welfare of all humanity. Soka Gakkai is one NGO actively cooperating with the United Nations Department of Public Information.

To provide a theoretical framework for the mass movements sponsored by NGOs and to study concrete methods and programs for realizing peace, it will be necessary to create a worldwide network of universities and research institutes and even to include local governments in that network. If a new order of peace is to be built, this will take a considerable amount of time because, in addition to nuclear arms, all of the other pressing issues threatening the survival of humanity must be dealt with.

A Forum for Peace

In *Proposals for Disarmament and Abolition of Nuclear Weapons* (June 1982), which I submitted to the Second Special Session of the United Nations General Assembly on Disarmament, I urged the nonnuclear nations to unite in the creation of a global network of peace around the United States and the Soviet Union. The achievement of this aim requires a multidimensional approach. As part of our efforts in this connection, this year, I am working with Soka University on projects that should set us on the right track. First, we are going to invite well-known scholars, peace activists, and personnel from the United Nations to participate in a Forum for Peace to be held in the fall of this year. This will be a gathering of intellectuals who will discuss ways of dealing with the global issues confronting humanity. In addition, in western Honshu, also during the autumn of this year, we intend to hold the Third World Peace Grand Culture Festival, a gathering of people from all over the world who are willing to pray and act for peace.

I hope to apply a similar global approach to the support we shall continue to provide the United Nations this year. One aspect of that support will be participation in a World Disarmament Campaign. The exhibition entitled "The Nuclear Threat to Our World," held last year at United Nations headquarters in New York, elicited a strong response and made significant contributions to boosting antinuclear and disarmament sentiment. In addition, it prompted Secretary-General Javier Pérez de Cuéllar to seek to establish permanent exhibits of materials on the atomic bomb in sixty-eight United Nations offices, including headquarters and the Geneva and Vienna offices. It can be said that the partial fulfillment of his wish has resulted because of the impact of the first exhibition on the nuclear menace.

In my proposal to the First Special Session of the United Nations General Assembly on Disarmament (*A Ten-point Proposal for Nuclear*

Disarmament, May 1978), I suggested that documents, photographs, and films dealing with the tragedy and cruelty of war, the horrifying destructive power of nuclear weapons, the realities of the Hiroshima and Nagasaki bombings, and the extent and variety of current nuclear arsenals be collected and displayed for all visitors to the United Nations. In addition, I urged that a Peace Archives be established within United Nations headquarters. I am overjoyed to see that the organization has taken definite steps to implement my suggestions.

Currently existing nuclear warheads have more than a million times the destructive power of the bombs dropped on Hiroshima and Nagasaki. But it is this extraordinary magnitude that makes the power itself difficult for ordinary human beings to comprehend. Consequently, it is essential to refer to the examples of Hiroshima and Nagasaki to bring the horror home on an understandable scale. For this reason and in the hope of encouraging greater public anti-nuclear and disarmament sentiment, we plan to hold another international exhibition on Hiroshima and Nagasaki this year.

At present, burgeoning support for the peace movement among young people seems especially promising. During the twenty-five years that have passed since my predecessor and mentor, Josei Toda, charged the youth of Soka Gakkai with the task of abolishing nuclear weapons, the peace movement of our Youth Division has taken deep root in society. To expand their efforts on a global scale, I suggest that they consider holding a Youth Culture Festival for World Peace in 1985, the twentieth anniversary of the adoption by the United Nations of the "Declaration on the Promotion among Youth of the Ideal of Peace, Mutual Respect, and Understanding among Peoples" and the year the United Nations has designated as International Youth Year.

For all nations, how the fervor and strength of youth are to be used in the twenty-first century is an issue of importance, and it will be significant for us to follow President Toda's injunction to concentrate youth power on the attainment of peace.

Courageous Decisions from World Leaders

In the closing words of her acceptance speech for the Nobel Peace

Prize last year, Alva Myrdal quoted from the will of Alfred Nobel in making a plea for a conference dedicated to peace. As is consistent with my belief that we must encourage a shift from emphasis on the elite to emphasis on the ordinary people, I heartily endorse her plea and renew my own appeal for a summit meeting in the name of peace.

Masao Maruyama, professor emeritus at Tokyo University, has pointed out that, unlike ambassadors and ministers, whose movements are necessarily restricted by national interests, top state leaders must focus on common human problems that go beyond the concerns of individual nations.

A summit meeting can naturally generate the bold ideas and actions and the courageous decisions that are essential. Prerequisite to such a meeting, of course, is the dissolution of the spell of nuclear power under which some world leaders currently labor. And, even though complete liberation from that spell may be impossible at once, by meeting and exchanging opinions, our leaders can at least make breakthroughs through which some fresh air may flow. The dramatic renewal of amity between the United States and China illustrates what human contact can accomplish.

Nuclear weapons are fateful because the negative force they exert threatens to annihilate humanity. To avert this doom, about which people all over the world are deeply concerned, the negative force must be converted into a positive one. I hope that people in positions of ultimate responsibility are considering how to accomplish this and I personally believe that a summit meeting can provide a catalyst for the resolution of this enormous problem.

It is especially important for the governmental heads of the United States and the Soviet Union to hold talks as quickly as possible. At this point in time, when Yuri Andropov has just assumed office as the chief of the Soviet communist party, it is impossible to overemphasize the importance of a meeting between him and his counterpart from the United States. At such a meeting, the two men could gain an insight into each other's general way of thinking and aspirations for their nations.

Buddhist philosophy and my own experiences in meeting many people all over the world have irrevocably committed me to faith in the value of daily human encounters throughout life. The accumulation of the intangible effects of honest talk and mutual stimulation, even between strangers, inevitably bears tangible fruit. This principle applies in all instances, including encounters between the top leaders of the United States and the Soviet Union.

In the ultimate analysis, to break through the impasse in which we now find ourselves, someone must have the courage to reduce armaments and effect true détente. The heads of the two most powerful nations in the world bear the weighty responsibility for doing this. Japan too has an important role to play in finding effective ways of encouraging lasting détente between Washington and Moscow.

In this connection, I have the following proposals to make and, as a world citizen, fervently, if perhaps idealistically, hope that action will be taken on the ideas in these proposals at a summit meeting between the two heads of state in question.

First, I propose giving top priority to a freeze in both nations on the production, testing, and deployment of nuclear weapons. The United States and the Soviet Union must first halt the arms race and then initiate talks oriented toward reduction of nuclear weapons.

Some American leaders insist that a freeze at the present time would be disadvantageous to their side. While remaining neutral, I suggest that both sides should rethink the issue of advantage, not in a narrow, nationalist perspective, but from the standpoint of long-term benefits for the entire world.

Continued mutual distrust has stimulated Washington and Moscow to continue the nuclear arms race, and therefore has impeded progress in arms reduction. Even their agreement on balanced reduction has gone round in circles leading nowhere because they have remained divided over the nature of the desired balance.

While the Second Special Session of the United Nations General Assembly on Disarmament was being held, I received a book written by United States senators Edward M. Kennedy and Mark O. Hatfield, both of whom have been working hard to put a nuclear-freeze bill through Congress. I am in total agreement with the sentiment expressed in the following passage from their book: "It betrays the lesson of the first nuclear war (Hiroshima, Nagasaki) to offer a freeze sometime in the future, or a freeze with preconditions, which would mean that both the United States and the Soviet Union could build more and more weapons, and negotiate at greater and greater length before entering into any agreement at all."

Mutual Trust—the Key to Larger Military Cuts

I propose a nuclear freeze first, because I believe it will stimulate between the United States and the Soviet Union the kind of mutual trust that can promote progress toward agreement on larger-scale arms reduction. In other words, it is of maximum importance to break from the vicious circle of mistrust that inspires escalating fear and the spiraling arms race.

My several visits to the United States and the Soviet Union have completely convinced me that the peoples of both nations long for peace. A reliable survey has shown that eighty percent of all Americans want to stop the production of new types of nuclear weapons and are now satisfied that the nuclear capabilities of the two nations are balanced. In addition, more than seventy percent of the population of the United States advocate prohibiting the storage and use, as well as the production, of nuclear weapons. I believe that Soviet citizens, twenty million of whom were victimized during World War II, feel the same way. The remark a Chinese leader made to me during one of my visits to his country illustrates why no people on earth actually want more nuclear arms: "We cannot feed or clothe ourselves with nuclear weapons."

Last year, the belief that it was the shortest route to preventing nuclear war and protecting the livelihood of the people supplied impetus for an upsurge in the nuclear-freeze campaign in the United States. I trust popular emotions of this kind and insist that the people's sensitive, realistic responses to the nuclear issue should be carefully heeded.

One of the reasons for my call for an end to the nuclear arms race is the desire to lighten the heavy burden of military expenditure oppressing the ordinary people and causing indirect economic dislocations in many countries. The effect on national economy of maintaining a military establishment is patent. For instance, the Vietnam War is widely recognized as a major factor in the decline in the once invincible American economy. In fiscal year 1983, the deficit of the United States federal government was estimated at a staggering two hundred billion dollars. Experts predict that the American economy will be unable to stand up much longer under the enormous military burden contributing markedly to this deficit. And the burden on the Soviet budget is considerable too.

According to specialists, the United States spends thirty-five billion dollars annually on nuclear arms. A nuclear freeze would save America half that amount; and progress in subsequent reduction talks would further reduce the expense required for the operation and maintenance of nuclear weapons.

A Center for the Prevention of Nuclear War

It is essential to stop as quickly as possible the colossal waste of manpower, machine power, materials, and money—estimated at six hundred and fifty billion dollars—spent globally on military establishments each year. In the industrialized nations, which account for the majority of this expenditure, more than twenty million people are jobless; and depression and inflation drain people of energy and the will to work for a better way of life. Instead of squandering money on military establishments, these nations should turn their attention to the widespread social instability caused by this situation, which is conducive to the emergence of fascism under a new guise and perhaps another global conflict.

Second, in the interests of stabilizing society, I propose that the United States and the Soviet Union agree to establish a center for the prevention of nuclear war. The alarming opinion entertained by some strategists that nuclear arms are actually usable aggravates the danger of the reality of nuclear conflict. As is often pointed out, false information from computers could accidentally trigger war. The so-called hot line between Washington and Moscow has been installed to prevent such a contingency but is far from an adequate safeguard. Even using the most sophisticated of modern high technology, it is impossible to go too far in reinforcing effective systems for the prevention of nuclear war. Only by means of a new center, set up in a neutral nation, and staffed by the best technological specialists from the United States and the Soviet Union, will it be possible to work out, from all conceivable angles, optimum measures to avert nuclear war.

To collect and analyze information and thus to spot and resolve crises immediately, a regular core staff of the best qualified experts in military, political, economic, and other relevant fields should have at their disposal the finest computer facilities and a network of satellite communications. Though initiated as an organization to deal exclusively with the aversion of nuclear war, later, the center could assume such additional functions as prevention of regional conflicts. When this occurs, the staff should be expanded to include specialists from all regions and many countries of the world.

International Conference to Freeze Military Expenditure

My third proposal is for an international conference to discuss ways to halt military expenditures. The moment they agree on a nuclear freeze, the United States and the Soviet Union should call the conference and guide all representatives in halting further increases in military spending.

Freezing nuclear weapons at present levels is insufficient to the purpose of lasting peace. In addition, an international consensus imposing ceilings on all military expenditures, including those on conventional arms, is essential. Indicative of the possibility of such a conference, last year, at the Second Special Session of the United Nations General Assembly on Disarmament, President Ronald Reagan of the United States proposed holding an international conference on military spending to establish a system for reporting and examining the arms budgets of all nations. Moreover, the recent Prague Declaration proposed opening negotiations between the nations of the Warsaw Pact and those of the North Atlantic Treaty Organization on measures for limiting military spending at present levels and ultimately for mutual reduction of military budgets.

Many of the industrialized nations now export large shipments of weapons to developing countries, a growing number of which, with total debts of six hundred billion dollars, find themselves on the verge of bankruptcy. As recent signs in the Mexican and Polish economies suggest, further accumulation of debt by such nations could create a worldwide financial crisis. Expenditures on weapons can only aggravate the dilemma facing such nations. This is why an international meeting to discuss compilation and implementation of immediately effective steps regulating such sales must be held at once.

Furthermore, the conference should produce an international agreement regarding a freeze on military expenditure and a carefully thought-out study on optimum uses for funds freed as disarmament goes into effect. These funds should be used in the promotion of peace and education throughout the world and in contributing to the improvement of human welfare and life styles, especially in the developing countries.

Easing International Tensions

As militarization increases in one nation after another all over the world, Japan's international role grows more pivotal and begins to have far-reaching implications. In our quest for lasting peace, our organization has consistently protected the Japanese constitution, which renounces belligerency, and strives to spread its spirit among all peoples of the world. Because it is based on trust in human nature and transcends the nation-state framework, I encourage our young people in their campaign to protect the constitution, article nine of which, in rejecting war, manifests some of the most far-sighted and wisest leadership of our time. On the basis of its pacifist constitution, Japan must take the lead in efforts to direct the current of the age and rebuild the human community along peaceful and humane lines. The only way we Japanese can fulfill this responsibility is gradually to encourage the entire international environment in the direction of true détente and arms reduction. This is the reason for my long efforts in attempting to establish friendly relations between Japan and all the other nations of the world. Friendship, not the notion of common destiny, is the only way to peace now. And such ideas as making the Japanese archipelago an "unsinkable aircraft carrier," as Prime Minister Nakasone said on a recent tour of the United States, is very dangerous.

Apparently, deeply moved by an English-language edition of *Peace Is Our Duty,* collected accounts of Japanese wartime experiences compiled by the Soka Gakkai Youth Division, Nobel prize winner Dr. George Wald recently wrote a letter to our organization saying that the need to prevent young people from ever being forced to undergo the horrors of war is of primary importance. This is certainly true. We must not allow war to destroy the bright futures of people whose period of greatest activity will be in the twenty-first century. If we wish our children to have any future at all, we the ordinary citizens of the world must make the wise choice of heeding the pacifist instinct in all peoples. In the coming year, as one of those ordinary citizens, I pledge myself to participating in the great wave of activity that will carry the people of the world to victory in peace.

Standing at a Crossroads
of Civilization

Delivered at the University of Bucharest,
Romania, June 7, 1983.

Cultural Traditions

Only the day before yesterday, when I visited the Village and Folk Art Museum, I was delighted to meet several young boys and girls who are being brought up with the beauty and strength of mind needed to ensure a bright future for Romania. The children performed folk dances in the museum plaza. And as I watched them, I fancied each of them, with bright-eyed youth and innocence, was calling for peace and bidding all of us to remember that without sunlight, freedom, and peace, the future of the whole world is dark indeed. Their call will remain with me all the rest of my life. In it I felt a powerful reverberation of life itself, indicating to us how much we must love peace and how hard we must study to ensure its preservation.

Examining the seventy-one village dwellings preserved intact at the museum reconfirmed in me the conviction that the soul of the Romanian people is pervaded by the desire for sunlight, freedom, and peace.

Before moving on to my main topic, I should like to offer my

148

profound thanks to Mr. Ion Iovit Popescu, rector of the university, and to the Socialist Democracy and Unity Front for inviting me to visit, for the first time, this beautiful country graced with abundant flowers and trees, and to speak at the historical University of Bucharest. In addition, I should like to express my gratitude to all the faculty members and students who have come today to hear me.

In the past, as founder of Soka University and as president of Soka Gakkai International, I have traveled extensively, exerting my best efforts for the sake of exchanges in relation to peace, culture, and education, and have been invited to speak at many universities in many parts of the world. For instance, at the University of California at Los Angeles, I spoke on "Toward the Twenty-first Century." At the Moscow M.V. Lomonosov State University, I discussed "A New Road to East-West Cultural Exchanges"; and, at Beijing University, "Personal Observations on China." At Guadalajara University in Mexico, I spoke on "Thoughts on the Mexican Poetic Spirit"; and, in May of the year before last, at Sophia University in your neighboring country, Bulgaria, I spoke on "In Pursuit of a Harmonious Fusion of Eastern and Western Cultures."

Today, as I speak on the topic "Standing at a Crossroads of Civilization," I shall keep in mind the immense possibilities your nation has for the new century—possibilities that are symbolized by your national emblem in which a brilliant sun rises in the distance behind oil derricks and mountains clad in venerable, ancient trees. At the same time I shall be hoping earnestly for the development of richer exchanges between Romania and Japan.

Your nation is well known in Japan, not only for the way you have used your abundant natural resources to achieve the most outstanding postwar economic growth in the socialist world, but also for your rich treasure trove of folklore. An important part of your traditional folk background is music. During the summer of the year before last, the people of many parts of Japan had an opportunity to hear and thrill to Romanian music, when three of your countrymen came to participate in a series of concerts called "A Musical Voyage along the Silk Road," sponsored by the Min-On Concert Association, which I founded. Japanese all over the country were especially pleased by the lighthearted sound of the folk instrument called the *nay,* in which we seemed to hear echoes of the soul of the Romanian people. But in those echoes, I cannot help hearing the sounds of a turbulent past history.

Beginning as a Dacian nation in prehistoric times, your land was conquered by the Roman empire, invaded by the Goths and Huns, amalgamated into the Byzantine cultural sphere at the time when the Slavs were moving southward, governed by the Ottoman Turks, and, after all these trials, began moving along the road to independence in the latter half of the nineteenth century. And throughout this vast historical drama, though it may have been temporarily locked beneath the frozen ground, the heart of the Romanian people never for an instant gave up its struggle for freedom and independence.

With admirable perspicacity, the great Greek historian Herodotus says of your ancestors the Dacians that they were the bravest and most just of all the people of Thrace. Later, when you came under the influence of Roman culture, it was not as an enslaved or subjected people. Your ancestors intermarried with the Romans, and the contacts with Roman civilization this association made possible contributed greatly to the development of your own distinctively Romanian culture. I always think of this historical background when I reflect on the determined policy of independent peace negotiations Romania pursues at the present time.

Throughout all those centuries, many different cultures have intermingled to enrich the spiritual soil of your nation. Certainly this has contributed greatly to your treasure trove of folklore. But I find it especially significant to note that Romania has been most deeply related to three of the great civilizations that have withstood the process of historical selection to survive to the present: European Christian civilization, Byzantine civilization, and the civilization of Islam. This aspect of your background makes me believe that historically as well as geographically, Romania is located at a crossroads of civilization.

As a consequence of the armed conflicts, invasions, and belligerence that have often characterized contacts among them, some civilizations have apparently vanished. Actually, however, they have occasionally persisted in the hearts of the people like an underground stream and, while undergoing various transformations, have burst forth into the light again when the time has been right. They are able to do this because of the power of cultural traditions. In the Orient, we have a saying to the effect that one comes to understand the new only by studying the old. This means that new vistas on the future will not open to people who do not respect and care for old historical cultures. The assumption that this is true is the standpoint from which I shall now attempt to take a look at the twenty-first century. In my opinion, establishing the correct balance between the significance of part and whole is the decisive key to the path we must follow in approaching the future.

Developments starting with the great age of navigation, in the fifteenth century, passing through the industrial revolution, and expanding to the modern civilization of scientific technology have drastically reduced the spaces that once separated peoples and civilizations. Today it is considered only natural for societies to bind themselves together to form one global whole. It is no longer possible to think of world economics solely from the standpoint of any one single nation. The oil shock and the subsequent counter-oil-shock have vividly illustrated how true this is. Modern technology works for instant, worldwide transmission of information and a resultant sense of greater international mutual acquaintance. For instance, satellite television transmissions brought into many Japanese living rooms the triumphs of your Nadia Comaneci during both the Montreal and Moscow Olympic Games.

But a much more vital and fateful example of the interdependence of all peoples everywhere today is the threat of nuclear war. If the Soviet Union and the United States should launch a nuclear war, there would be no victor and no defeated because all humanity would stand on the precipice of annihilation. In other words, nuclear weapons have galvanized the whole world into a single community sharing a single fate. When all of this is taken into consideration, it becomes patently clear that, unless we think of the entire world as, for better or worse, unified in one way or another, we will find ourselves incapable of acting. Nonetheless, the road toward a true unification of the world will not be an easy one.

The scale of the tragedy human folly has enacted throughout history is indicated by a few statistics related to recent time: at present there are forty armed conflicts taking place in the world with the participation, direct or indirect, of forty-five nations. This situation is all the more lamentable since, in war, human beings are often more brutal than any of the beasts.

But let us return to the main stream of the discussion. To unify the world in the true sense, the great obstacles posed by conflict among national states and peoples must be overcome. Doing this requires the persistent efforts of organizations like the United Nations.

New Humanism

National states and races constitute individual entities, but not necessarily what I mean when I use the word *part* in contrast to the word *whole*. States and races are divisions in which emphasis is placed on the political dimension.

Though they deserve respect in relation to what is called the "five principles of peace," they are no more than the product of the past few centuries of the growth of nationalism, in which the nations of Western Europe have played the leading part. Subsuming ideas like states and races, however, is the vast, fertile and infinitely varied human culture resting on thousands of years of history and tradition. This human culture has been passed on in distinctive local forms in the hearts of all peoples. As folklores reveal, the Romanians have their own distinctive culture, just as the Japanese have theirs.

The Swiss philosopher Verner Kaegi has said that a unified world will dominate our future and that, no matter what form it assumes, that world will survive only as long as within it the cell, like the village of old, where human beings oriental and occidental alike have been able to lead prospering spiritual lives, survives in good health.

Kaegi's village cell is synonymous with the distinctive cultures of each race and with what I mean by the word *part*. Unless these parts are respected, it will be impossible for us to advance toward the realization of the ideal of a unified world. The need to achieve the one without violating the other reveals the vital importance of proper balance between the two. And the difficulty of the task facing us in this connection is eloquently illustrated in the hardships many nations are experiencing as, attempting to modernize in scientific-technological terms, they often must sacrifice the traditional to attain the modern. Obviously, modernization is a different name for global unification.

Let us imagine a boat being rowed across a lake and let us equate the boat with traditional culture and the oars with the culture of modernization. No matter how stout the craft and no matter how vigorously the oars are pulled, no progress can be made if the waters of the lake are turbulent. In short, what is essential at this time is placid water, or peace. In my opinion, calming the waters requires a set of universal spiritual values that bind together all individual, local, and cultural traditions while allowing each to shine on its own. I am deeply afraid that, without the achievement of a worldwide spiritualization of this kind, mankind will be unable to cope with the relentless advance of modernization and developments of scientific technology.

Here I should like to recall the words of the religious philosopher Mircea Eliade, who, born in Romania, became world famous. Eliade expressed the wish that the encounter between the peoples of the modern West and those who either do not know the West or are unfamiliar with it would give birth to a new humanism. Only a man born and bred at a crossroads of civilization could have coined the simple expression *new humanism,* with its wealth of possibilities for the future. In spite of Eliade's wish, however, today new humanism still lacks a clearly defined outline. Moreover, the situation facing us today is beginning to drive some sensitive people to despair. For instance, Madame Alva Myrdal, the Swedish winner of last year's Nobel Peace Prize, has frankly said that people refuse to lend an ear to pleas for peace and that she herself is beginning to grow weary of the struggle.

I believe that we must keep our eyes, not on the appearing and disappearing froth constituting the superficial events of history, but on the deep currents that are the determining historical factors. I consider the masses of ordinary people to be like the great earth itself. If we put our ears close to that earth—if we rap at the doors of the hearts of the people—I believe we will hear the sounds of the truly determinant movements.

Pacifist Spirit

Stripped of all unnecessary external trappings, in the depths of their hearts, ordinary people everywhere are truly cosmopolitan in outlook and devoted pacifists. Perceptive writers of genius usually depict them in this way. One such writer is your own outstanding novelist Zaharia Stancu, whose famous novel *Barefoot* reveals warm traits of human understanding and friendship between the Romanians and the Bulgarians during a time of war between Bulgaria and Turkey.

As you all know, the scene of the book, the village where a certain Darie lives, is located just across the Danube from Bulgaria. Almost daily association with the Bulgarians, who come across the river to sell seeds in spring and vegetables in autumn, has given birth to a warm, earthy amity between the two peoples. Suddenly, however, when war with the Turks breaks out, the Bulgarians cease coming to the village. Before long, word gets back that such old familar Bulgarian friends as Ioan, Stoian, Berciu, and Anton have fallen in the field of battle. Then, to make matters worse, a militiaman comes to the village to take away Romanian men who are now going to be forced to go to war with the Bulgarians, people with whom they had formerly been on close, friendly terms. This scene stands out especially vividly in my mind.

Stancu describes how the villagers muttered among themselves when they heard this shocking news. "Fight against the Bulgarians!" "What have we got against them? They're our friends! It's a good thing Ioan and Stoian died in battle. If they were alive, we'd have to face them on the field. Can anything be as shameful as this? God, God! Why should we fight and shoot each other?"

As this beautiful, warm human outburst powerfully shows, the villagers may have been uneducated, but their very lack of learning kept them free of warped racial prejudices and animosities. They were firmly rooted in the earth of human life and vividly represent the profoundest aspects of human beauty and soul—aspects that far transcend consideration of nationality. In commenting a number of times on the lack of learning of the villagers, I do not intend to give the impression of praising ignorance. But it must always be remembered that learning and knowledge, no matter how great, must serve the vibrant interests of the life of the people.

As in all truly great literature, which must have the universality to appeal to everyone and to delineate the most minute elements of the heart and mind of a people, Stancu's work shows the pacifism and universal nature of the ordinary people that I commented on earlier.

The following historically factual episode, related by a noted Japanese author, reveals the same traits in the people of Japan. In 1904, at the beginning of the Russo-Japanese war, or at about the time depicted in Stancu's book, Japanese troops captured one Russian officer and one enlisted man and took them to a regimental headquarters. The first Russian prisoners to be taken, these men were something of a curiosity for the Japanese soldiers. When a regimental leader asked who wanted to go and take a look at the Russians, only about half the men present raised their hands. The leader then asked the others why they did not want to go, and one spoke out for all: "Back in my home village, I was a craftsman. When I put on a uniform, I became a Japanese soldier. These men are our enemy. I don't know what kind of people they are. But I think it is too bad that, now they've been unlucky enough to be captured, they have to be dragged around here and there and made a spectacle of. I feel very sorry for them and don't want to embarrass them by gawking at them." The leader was happy to hear this opinion. Gradually the other men came to see things the same way, and the trip to look at the prisoners was called off.

For me, the way that human sympathy expressed in the midst of war by one anonymous former craftsman swayed the thinking of a whole group of men has an uplifting and purifying effect. This man, who had no desire at all for war and who took pride in his own everyday work, which he considered worthy of the highest respect, refused to abandon his dignity as a human being even when forced to go to battle. I sense a certain regret in his remark that he does not know what kind of people the prisoners are. No doubt, in saying this, the Japanese soldier was reflecting that these people too had families and work somewhere in their own land. His feeling, and those of the villagers who hated the idea of going to battle with their Bulgarian neighbors from across the Danube, reflect the down-to-earth sympathy characteristic of ordinary people everywhere.

In both episodes, the idea of shame plays a prominent part. The Romanians considered it shameful to have to fight with their former Bulgarian friends. The Japanese soldier did not wish to shame the Russian prisoners by gaping at them. This common emphasis on one idea suggests to me that human minds can converge in harmonious understanding no matter what distances and differences seem to separate them.

An old saying has it that the answers to the most remote questions are to be found at one's own front door. This means we must appeal to elements common to all humanity if we are to generate the new humanism I referred to earlier. And, in my opinion, the most common element is the harmonious understanding that must be the soil in which the new humanism can grow and bloom. Ideologies and slogans will do no good; we must base our hopes on the soil of common sympathy found in the hearts of all ordinary people everywhere. When universal understanding and sympathy have calmed the waters of our lake, we can allow the boat of tradition and the oars of modernization—the whole and the parts—to advance in cooperation toward the twenty-first century.

The flow of history pauses for nothing, and the task of creating the new humanism rests on all our shoulders. As a believer in Nichiren Daishonin's Buddhism, which teaches the dignity of humanity, I am resolved to go on in the future, as I have done in the past, devoting my utmost efforts to the achievement of that task. And I hope that all of you will join me in working hand in hand for a new century when a unified world will be splendid and prosperous both materially and spiritually. In concluding my remarks, I should like to take this opportunity to express my deepest gratitude to President Ceauşescu, leader in the founding of your nation and ardent and tireless worker for world peace. *Mulţmescu* (thank you)!

A World Without War

A Proposal Commemorating the Ninth Soka Gakkai International Day, January 26, 1984.

A Crucial Year

Confusion and strife can be seen throughout the world, and conditions only grow worse as time goes by. Far from promising the creation of a new international order, the current situation is more unstable than ever before, and crisis is barely being held at bay. In this new age of nuclear instability, the dark cloud of the arms race hanging above grows blacker as fear and anxiety intensify. In such a world there can be neither stability nor order.

The fear of nuclear war has been intensified by the discontinuation of negotiations on the limitation of intermediate-range nuclear forces (INF) in Europe and the indefinite suspension of the United States-Soviet Arms Reduction Talks (START). If a consensus between the two superpowers is not reached within the year and the race in deploying intermediate-range nuclear missiles in the European theater is renewed, tensions involving nuclear weapons will reach a dangerous climax. The hand of the doomsday clock pictured in the American scientific journal, the *Bulletin of the Atomic Scientists* (January 1984) stands at three minutes before midnight, the moment

157

at which nuclear war will break out, ushering in the end of the world. At the end of 1953, that same clock showed two minutes before midnight. That was the year the Soviet Union conducted tests making it the second country, along with the United States, to possess a hydrogen bomb. The year 1984 is a crucial one, a year in which the world must turn toward disarmament, for the only alternative is ever-escalating arms expansion. The decision is up to the United States and the Soviet Union.

The television film *The Day After,* which depicted the horror of nuclear catastrophe, transfixed one hundred million viewers in the United States and aroused tremendous response in Japan as well. Part of it was broadcast on state-run television in the Soviet Union.

Earlier this year, a Soviet scientist announced the partial results of research, warning that a full-scale nuclear war between the United States and the Soviet Union would kill 1.1 billion people, that even survivors would be reduced to utter misery, and that the continued existence of the human species would be at stake. These predictions coincide with a description of nuclear war by the American science reporter Jonathan Schell in his book *The Fate of the Earth.* Though differences of ideologies and social systems are insignificant compared to the menace of nuclear war, the absurd race for superior arms— for more powerful means of mutual destruction—goes on because of the still strong belief in the validity of nuclear deterrence.

Bertrand Russell called nuclear weapons the absolute evil, and I fully concur. The evil lies not only in their overwhelming power to cause destruction and death, but also in the profound distrust emanating and growing out of their possession. It is this distrust that has created the so-called cult of deterrence, the belief that nuclear weapons are necessary for protection against nuclear weapons. Trust in nuclear arms is a negation of trust in humanity. The more people trust in arms, the less they trust each other. Ceasing to put their trust in arms is the only way to cultivate mutual trust among peoples.

Nuclear security and nuclear equilibrium are essentially impossible to achieve. Buddhism teaches the oneness of life and its environment *(esho funi),* which means that the subjective world is inseparably linked to the objective world. Because of this bond, as long as the objective environment includes the threat of nuclear weapons, humanity can know no peace.

The Danger of the Efficiency Principle

At the base of this erroneous policy of deterrence is the principle of efficiency, which has come to rule people's thinking in the modern world. Efficiency advocates stress the most effective, the most efficient, and the most convenient. Undeniably the pursuit of efficiency has stimulated scientific and materialistic advances. But its insidious tendency to reduce human beings to mere *things* is often overlooked.

At the height of the debate on nuclear deterrence, there was much talk of assured destruction, damage limitation, cost versus benefit ratio, and other similar terms. Such merciless and grotesque language derives from the cult of efficiency, which relegates human beings to the status of *things* and pursues expediency at the expense of countless human lives. Pernicious reasoning of this kind still rears its ugly head in different forms time and again. Recently, it has been governing the thinking of strategists who talk of nuclear preemptive strikes and nuclear arms control. As I have warned many times, it is the politicians and scientists—the elite of the nuclear civilization and establishment—who succumb most easily to the doctrine of efficiency.

Another manifestation of the efficiency-first syndrome is a kind of reductionism. Using this method of analyzing objects by reducing them to their simplest elements, modern science has made remarkable progress. While certain benefits have been derived from this approach, the emphasis on separate elements has meant sacrificing the comprehensive view of human life, including spiritual needs. This sacrifice to the god of efficiency has cast a dark shadow over all arms-reduction talks.

Deadlocked Disarmament Talks

The START and INF talks, especially the latter, seem hopelessly stalled and befuddled in a maze from which neither side can find an exit. One reason for the deadlock is overemphasis on parts at the expense of the whole. Perhaps advocates of nuclear stability and balance find it natural to categorize nuclear weapons into types and insist that separate talks be held for each category. But this apparently rational procedure has led them into total absorption with parts and ignorance of the whole issue before them. They cannot see the forest for the trees.

In spite of discussions about the capabilities of particular weapons and the number of agreements already reached, little progress has been made in connection with the whole issue. Current disarmament talks suffer from this critical blind spot.

But mere reduction or abolition of nuclear arms will not bring peace to the world. All the wars since the end of World War II have been fought with conventional weapons, the recent versions of which have tremendous destructive power. Moreover, nuclear and conventional weapons are inseparably connected. In short, reductions must be effected in both nuclear and conventional weapons.

The three hundred regional conflicts that have occurred since the end of World War II—many are still going on—are the result of various causes, particularly strife arising from racial or religious antipathy, which tends to be bitter and prolonged. With only a few exceptions, most modern wars have been initiated by sovereign states for motives of national gain and glory. At this very moment, thousands of people around the world are suffering because of the blind, stubborn wars among states.

In groping for workable answers that can lead to peace in the twenty-first century, we must examine the causes of strife in the period since World War II and hammer out effective methods for preventing war and preserving world peace. Concrete measures to institutionalize everlasting peace must be found. And it is toward this goal that all peoples must concentrate their intellectual powers. The most essential thing is a bold shift from parochial, nation-centered thinking to a global perspective. Increasing tension between the United States and the Soviet Union fans fires of continuing conflicts in various parts of the world.

As a Buddhist devoted to peace, I should like to offer some suggestions for a policy of peace for the twenty-first century.

The Peril of an Arms Race in Outer Space

Some time ago, astronaut Gerald P. Carr, who served as captain of Skylab III, shared his thoughts on religion with me.

He said, "As a young Christian man, I conceived of God as a rather fatherly figure, one who was paternal and watched over all of us down here on the Earth. Maybe he pulled a string or two to make things happen and kind of guided our lives. After having seen space, I was impressed by the great universal order of things. Today, I think that order of things in the universe is what we call God, or what other religions call something else. God is the understanding we have that there is order to all things in the universe. It is from this feeling of religion that I believe there is a common universality of all men. I think that is the basis for an understanding of the world community."

In reply, I said to Mr. Carr, "We call that order the Law, the Mystic Law that keeps harmony in the universe. It is the basic Law of all phenomena." No matter what name it is given, the idea expressed by Mr. Carr represents a dramatic shift from preoccupation with parts to an appreciation of the whole universe.

When I think of our great universe from the standpoint of peace and disarmament, I cannot suppress the gravest concern about the arms race that has recently begun in outer space. Reports mention the creation of antimissile defense networks in outer space and the development of weapons capable of destroying enemy military satellites. Nothing could be more dangerous for the future of the world than an arms race in outer space between the United States and the Soviet Union. How much more sensible it would be to cease spending billions of dollars on armament and to channel that money into the common endeavor of mankind to preserve and guard our precious Earth. To this end Washington and Moscow must immediately conclude an agreement prohibiting the deployment of weapons in outer space and the use of force in, or directed from, outer space toward Earth. The greatest possible number of people must become aware of the very real danger of the arms race in outer space and create so great a force of world opinion that the leaders of the United States and the Soviet Union are compelled to conclude such an agreement at once.

Spiritual Revolution

The year 1985 has been designated International Youth Year, and 1986 has been designated the International Year of Peace. Following that, the third special session of the United Nations General Assembly devoted to disarmament will be convened by 1988. In order to maintain the dynamism of the movement for peace represented by these events into the twenty-first century, not only efforts in disarmament, but also the determination to attain a world without war must spread more widely and more energetically than ever before.

I emphasized the importance of a world without war in my conversation with Gerald P. Carr, and he wholeheartedly supported my concern. Unless the world is free of war, abolition of weapons is no more than a meaningless dream. In the past, while talking about disarmament, both the United States and the Soviet Union have busily expanded their arsenals, as if they were kicking each other in the shins while shaking hands. Only distrust can grow out of such talks, from which no real achievements can be expected.

More than talks on the technicalities of disarmament, humanity requires an awakening of determination to create a world without war. The more widespread and deep this determination, the more obvious the absurdity of the arms race will become. Only under such circumstances can there be progress in nuclear disarmament.

No matter how unrealistic it may seem to some people, the attainment of a world without war is more vital in this nuclear age than it has ever been in human history. Efforts at the grass-roots level have helped to spread awareness of the threat of nuclear weapons throughout the world, and never before have so many human beings realized the absurdity of war as clearly as they do today.

Sentiments of the People

In 1948, at its third general assembly, the United Nations unanimously adopted the Universal Declaration of Human Rights, which, of special significance as a model of the guarantee of human rights for all nations in the period after World War II, defines in detail individual freedoms and fundamental rights in the areas of economy, society, and culture. In 1966, the United Nations converted the declaration into the International Covenants on Human Rights, which are legally binding on all signatories.

I propose that the United Nations adopt a Universal Declaration Renouncing War. Consensus among nations on such a declaration would be an important breakthrough in actualizing eternal peace. Lest I be criticized for overoptimistically believing the goal can be attained at once, I further propose that, as a first step, non-governmental organizations (NGOs) begin the process by building up a foundation for the ultimate adoption of a Universal Declaration Renouncing War in the United Nations. Discussions between states tend to give priority to strategy and considerations of gain and loss, and this precludes consideration of the basic revulsion against war shared by people at the grass-roots level everywhere. Because of their nonpolitical nature, NGOs more accurately reflect the concerns of the ordinary people.

Now, more urgently than ever, we must call on all peoples to contribute actively to generating a united movement in support of a world without war.

Like the tributaries flowing into a mighty, invincible stream, the movement will gain new impetus from the International Year of Peace in 1986 and will provide the fundamental spirit for the Third Special session of the United Nations General Assembly on Disarmament. From this will emerge a global network of people who, abhorring war, encircle and restrain war-mongering superpowers.

The Ultimate Tragedy

I place great hope in the ability of young people to lead a dynamic movement in pursuit of a world without war. During International Youth Year, young people in NGOs across the world must link their efforts with the movement for peace, disarmament, and an ideal world without war.

I most earnestly call upon the youth of Soka Gakkai International to renew their determination to rid the world of war and to take the initiative in that endeavor.

As Professor John D. Montgomery, Chairman of the Department of Government of Harvard University, remarked when we met recently, both the winners and the losers in war suffer tragic losses. After its defeat in World War II, Japan promulgated what has come to be called the Peace Constitution, which renounces war, and the nation has enjoyed miraculous economic prosperity. Although a winner in the same war, the United States has been involved in a succession of military conflicts including the Korean War and the Vietnam War, in which an immense number of human lives were lost. We must always remember that, in the words of Josei Toda, "War is barbarous and inhuman. Nothing is more cruel, nothing more tragic."

Renouncing all war is absolutely necessary for the survival of the human race in the nuclear age. Since even conventional war can escalate into nuclear war, complete freedom from fighting is indispensable to the survival of mankind.

The twenty-first century is fast approaching. Our organization will continue to strive for the cause of realizing a world without war and, at the same time, trust the sensible young people of the world to launch a new age, an age of no war. Now is the time when a bold first step must be made toward eternal peace, the goal long cherished by the peoples of the world.

A Spiritual Silk Road

Delivered at the Meeting Commemorating the Ninth Soka Gakkai International Day, Held at the Tokyo Community Center, Tokyo, January 29, 1984.

Like science, religion must know no national boundaries. Nichiren Daishonin appeared in this world and taught the Buddhism of the Sun—*Nam-myoho-renge-kyo*—for the peoples of the entire world. For this reason, his Buddhism recognizes no boundaries, nor does Soka Gakkai in its efforts to take that Buddhism to all peoples.

Albert Einstein said, "And certainly we should take care not to make the intellect our god; it has, of course, powerful muscles, but no personality. It cannot lead, it can only serve; and it is not fastidious in its choice of a leader. This characteristic is reflected in the qualities of its priests, the intellectuals. The intellect has a sharp eye for methods and tools, but is blind to ends and values. So it is no wonder that this fatal blindness is handed on from old to young and today involves a whole generation.

"Science without religion is lame, religion without science is blind.

"I am firmly convinced that the passionate will for justice and truth has done more to improve man's condition than calculating political shrewdness which in the long run only breeds general distrust" (*Out of My Later Years*).

165

In short, the intellect is a double-edged sword and must not be regarded as absolute in matters of goals and values.

The famous story of Galileo (1564–1642), the mathematician, astronomer, and physicist, illustrates the incompleteness of religion without science and the harm political maneuvering, even in the church, can do.

In 1609, observing the heavens with an improved telescope that he made himself, Galileo discovered the satellites of the planet Jupiter, the valleys and mountains of the moon, and sunspots. In addition, as revealed in "Dialogue Concerning the Two Chief World Systems" (1632), he proved the Copernican theory that the Earth rotates and, in doing so, fell afoul of the official teachings of the Church of Rome and was condemned for heresy by the Inquisition.

Because of his fame, the Inquisition could not sentence him to death but resorted to trickery. Along the corridor leading to the courtroom where his trial was to be held, they displayed various grisly instruments of torture in the hope that the sight of them would make the already aging Galileo recant. Instead, however, he demonstrated his fierce devotion to his mission by saying that he would not die yet because he had much work left to do for humanity and the world.

Convinced that history would be an impartial judge, while enduring eight years of incarceration, he continued his research and writing with renewed vigor. Ultimately, however, the Inquisition triumphed. The famous words to the effect that, no matter what he was forced to say, the Earth *does* move are probably an attribution by posterity.

When he heard of the Inquisition's triumph in the case of Galileo, Descartes immediately hid the manuscript of his study on the nature of light, on which he was working at the time. And when an emaciated Galileo was finally dragged back to his own house, he found that all of his former followers had vanished.

His story reveals how the name of religion, without the intellect and science, can be used to oppress. But history has proved Galileo correct. And last year, three and a half centuries after the event, the Pope renounced this trial as an error. As Josei Toda said, though people may not recognize it now, in two centuries, history will prove the absolute correctness and justice of Nichiren Daishonin's Buddhism and the undertakings of Soka Gakkai in the name of the attainment of *kosen-rufu*. Regrettably, calculated political brilliance is stimulating increasing psychological pollution and distrust in society today. And, for this reason, our movement for a Buddhist human revolution and for peace, education, and civilization based on Buddhism reflects the most forward-looking approach possible for mankind.

This year, many of our Japanese members, in keeping with Nichiren Daishonin's desire to take the teachings to all mankind, are overcoming differences of language and culture to carry out a mission that glows with virtue and merit. I am convinced that Nichiren Daishonin himself, the True Buddha of the Latter Day of the Law, Nikko Shonin, the great leader in the propagation of the Buddhism of Nichiren Daishonin, and Nichimoku Shonin, guide in carrying the teachings to the whole world, all praise our efforts, as does Nittatsu Shonin, the sixty-sixth high priest, who attended the first World Conference on Peace, held on Guam nine years ago.

To carry on our praiseworthy work, I want all of our members to devote themselves to blazing what I call a spiritual Silk Road, a path along which all kinds of spiritual contacts and exchanges can be made, among all the peoples of the world, just as all kinds of goods and information were carried from place to place over the ancient Silk Road that linked Orient and Occident. Such a road will lead us all to expressions of gratitude from Nichiren Daishonin. In addition, it will lead all of our members to eternal and limitless happiness and all mankind to lasting peace.

Peace and the Mission of Youth

*Delivered at the First United States-Japan Joint Youth Division
General Meeting, held at the San Diego Sports Arena,
March 11, 1984.*

~~~

The coming together here today, in this bright and smiling weather, of twenty thousand representatives of Japanese and American youth has historical significance as a signal bell of hope for the other generations of young people who will come after you. Young people are always the driving force in the building of the future, and theirs must be a ceaseless search for values of peace, culture, and life.

Politics, economics, and science are, of course, important; but we must never forget that they all essentially arise from, and must return to, human beings, and should therefore always serve the best interests of all humanity. Since this is true, attempting to uncover the meaning of humanity and of life itself is a topic of maximum importance. The Buddhism of Nichiren Daishonin clarifies the essential nature of life more thoroughly than has ever been done by any other philosophy or religion in such of its doctrines as *ichinen sanzen* ("a single life-moment possesses three thousand realms"), the Ten Worlds, the Three Truths (nonsubstantiality, temporary existence, and the Middle Way); the Three Bodies, and "Time without Beginning."

This is why all of you must study and practice true Buddhism in order to receive verification of its merits so that you can bring the universal new human revolution to all humankind and create a new era for a society that has already reached an impasse. Without an understanding of the importance of such study and practice, all measures intended to deal with the political and economic problems of the world are doomed to failure since they are like a house built, foundationless, on sand. In short, revitalization and a flowering of happiness for individual human beings and for whole societies and nations require a firm philosophical and religious foundation.

An Age Without a Philosophy

The impasse I have said faces humanity today ultimately results from the lack of a truly valid philosophy for individuals, peoples, and nations. Though they held sway in the minds of many people for various lengths of time, the teachings and thoughts of past religious leaders and of such philosophers as Socrates, Aristotle, Descartes, Kant, Marx, and Hegel have now lost their power. This indicates that our time and our society are unfortunate, because the absence of a leading philosophy renders human beings incapable of discovering deep values and makes them the rootless prey of idleness and depravity. They therefore lose all hope and submerge themselves in indolence and frivolous pleasure. The only cure for a situation of this kind is a religion or philosophy that convinces, that can be put into actual practice, and that offers clear answers to the questions of life. I say without hesitation that the religion perfectly fulfilling these requirements is the heretofore unprecedented Buddhism of Nichiren Daishonin.

To my young friends of the United States, a land of freedom, I express my sincere hope that in the future you will expand your knowledge of this great Buddhism, intensify your practice of its teachings, and deepen your knowledge of it as much as possible for the sake of the twenty-first century and all the centuries to come in the infinite future.

You must not think that, in urging you to study the Buddhism of Nichiren Daishonin, I am attempting to export Japanese culture to the United States. Indeed there is no need to do such a thing. Nonetheless, mutual exchanges of culture stimulate development every-where. As you know, in the past few decades, American culture has had a startling influence on the people of Japan. As is said in economic circles, "If the United States sneezes, Japan catches a cold."

Humanity's Need for Buddhism

When the sun rises, all humanity basks equally in its light. Similarly, all human beings everywhere can bask in the radiance of the new, eternally universal great Law of Buddhism. Furthermore, that great Buddhism is bound to spread all over the world because, deep in their hearts, all people crave it.

But attention must be drawn even to the great Buddhism. And carrying out that mission is the significance of our efforts to prop-agate the teachings of Nichiren Daishonin; that is, the meaning of the *kosen-rufu* movement.

Nor should it be considered strange that we Japanese carry this message to non-Japanese peoples. Cross-cultural contacts are im-portant in many fields, including not only philosophy and religion, but also scholarship, science, and art. Though many Americans today are Christian, Christ himself was a Jew. Shakyamuni Buddha was born two thousand five hundred years ago in India, but his message has crossed boundaries to move into many countries. The spreading of the teachings of Nichiren Daishonin, who was born in Japan, to all parts of the world in the Mappo Era (the Latter Day of the Law) may in some sense be compared to the spread of the Buddhism of Shakyamuni.

Values

Earlier I mentioned the importance of the search for values. Indeed, it can be said that the ability to create value (the word *soka* in the name of the Soka Gakkai means "value creation") is one of the salient traits setting human beings apart from the other animals. A close examination of human activities reveals three categories of values: profit (which is largely economic and provides the founda-tion supporting life), good, and beauty. Good is opposed to evil. The greatest possible evil is killing, at its most horrible in the form of the mass killing that is war. The taking of life is folly and brings only unhappiness. The great Mystic Law permeating each individual, all society, and the entire universe is the supreme good that can banish this evil and bring paramount happiness to all peoples.

In the value called beauty must be included all of the cultural aspects that have a psychologically cultivating and enriching effect on human life. We followers of the teachings of Nichiren Daishonin know that the Mystic Law is the source of all value creation and, through our efforts for peace, culture, and education, we are striving to take to all society creative efforts in the name of profit, good, and beauty.

Our work in the name of peace is nonpolitical and free of ideological connection. As the sole nation in the world ever to have undergone an atomic bombing, we Japanese are profoundly aware of the respect due to life itself. Obviously, this respect is part of the teachings of Nichiren Shoshu, and we strive to take this message everywhere as part of our efforts for peace. Though, as a Japanese, I consider my own country important, I realize that Japan's population of one hundred and twenty million is small in comparison with the over four and a half billion people on earth. Because I realize how important it is to them, I have devoted myself to carrying the Mystic Law to the population of the whole world and, at the same time, to promoting peace, culture, and education everywhere I go. In spite of our efforts, however, and in light of the unrest plaguing much of the globe and of the hundreds of millions of people facing starvation in underprivileged areas, I insist that the United Nations still has a vitally important role to play in human affairs.

Unity of the Youth of the World

Certainly, political measures are important in abolishing nuclear weapons and in arms reduction; but lasting peace will be unrealizable unless the youth of the whole world band together in an ever-forward march in its name. The twenty thousand young defenders of the Mystic Law who have assembled here today must take the leadership in that march.

Already young people in many lands are joining in our drive: warmly enthusiastic people from Brazil, others from sun-drenched Peru, and still others from such nations as West Germany, Italy, Spain, Switzerland, Hong Kong, Malaysia, Singapore, Panama, the Dominican Republic, Belize, Mexico, Canada, some socialist nations, Ghana, Kenya, and Nigeria (in Africa, the continent of the twenty-first century). All these comrades are blending their voices with ours in a cry for peace.

My beloved young friends, the youth of the world has made a vow and is starting its march toward the new century. This is truly the opening curtain of a splendid period filled with new faith, wisdom, and fervor. As the *Gosho* exhorts us, "Do not waste this lifetime and regret it for many existences to come" (*Gosho Zenshu,* 970).

As Buddhism teaches, each of you has received the gift of life and has a mission to perform. Though your individual part in the work may be inconspicuous, each of you participates in the movement for peace that will bring courage and hope to all the suffering people of the world. The knowledge that this is true plus great faith will enable all of you to find fulfillment and satisfaction in life. In conclusion, let me offer my prayer that, as good citizens of the United States, this home of the free, you will study diligently and be as active as possible in society.

The Royal Road to Peace—
A Personal Observation

Delivered at Beijing University, China, June 5, 1984.

Wen and Wu

This marks my sixth visit to Beijing University. Today, as was the case four years ago, I have kindly been given an opportunity to address the members of the university. I would like to begin by saying how deeply grateful I am for this honor and by expressing my sincere thanks to President Ding Shisun, the distinguished members of the faculty, the members of the student body, and others in the audience today.

The day passes all too quickly, and I have determined to spend this particular, very memorable day by attempting to deepen, if only in a small way, the bonds of friendship between China and Japan.

In the remarks I made here four years ago, entitled "Personal Observations on China," I tried to present my view of the true nature of the Chinese people as I see them.

I have entitled my address for today "The Royal Road to Peace—A Personal Observation," and in it I should like to describe, from the standpoint of a single individual, prospects for the establishment of lasting peace, a goal I firmly believe in and have been working to attain over the past years.

In recent years, in addition to addressing the members of Beijing University, I have visited the University of California in Los Angeles, Moscow State University, the University of Guadalajara in Mexico, Sofia University in Bulgaria, and the University of Bucharest and have delivered addresses at each of these campuses. I have done so because I firmly believe that without sincere understanding and mutual exchange among the peoples of the world there can be no hope for peace, and that such understanding cannot be achieved without concerted effort. If my modest remarks today can to some degree help to strengthen the ties of peace and understanding between China and Japan, I will be deeply gratified.

Whether it is a petty quarrel between individuals or a full-scale war between nations, contention breaks out when self-restraint ceases to function. When warfare has broken out on a national scale, then, as Plato or the English philosopher Hobbes pointed out, the state becomes a kind of superhuman monster whose self-restraint is all but impossible to bring into effective operation. When Goethe remarked with a sigh that, regrettable as it is, there has never been a state that armed itself heavily and maintained a complete system of national defense and, to the end, was willing to use its military might for self-defense only, he had precisely that difficulty in mind.

The ideal situation, of course, would be to maintain no national armaments at all but it would be unrealistic to hope to reach that goal all at once. There has probably never been an age when peace was so persistently called for as it is today, and yet the efforts at disarmament we see around us appear to show no sign of progress. Thus, though the journey may be long, we have no choice but to work for peace step by step, advancing from one stage to the next along the road to our objective.

The pressing need now is to call into play the forces of *wen*—the arts of peace and civil accomplishments without which culture and civilization cannot flourish, and to employ them to control and restrain the forces of *wu*—the arts of war and militaristic ways of thinking. It is these civil arts and concerns, as opposed to military ones, that I should like to refer to as the self-restraining powers of a nation.

In regard to this point, the three-thousand-year history of China seems to me to be fraught with suggestion. The overall view we cannot fail to be strongly impressed by is the way that China, on the whole, has honored *wen,* or civil virtues, over *wu,* or military ones. This of course is a relative matter, since no nations devote themselves solely to military concerns or concern themselves with civil pursuits alone.

The question is which of these factors has on the whole been the main focus of concern. And, with the exception of certain atypical periods, I cannot help feeling that attention to civil virtues and ideals has been the principal motivating force in China's history.

To be sure, in the early days of the Han empire, in the second and first centuries B.C., or in the thirteenth and fourteenth centuries A.D., when China was under the rule of the Mongols, military force and expansionism came to the fore. Of course, over the centuries China has always had to pay attention to border defenses, as the virtually endless miles of the Great Wall dramatically illustrate. And, in the matter of internal strife as well, China has experienced upheavals and outbreaks of fighting on a scale far surpassing anything known in the relatively narrow and isolated island nation of Japan.

Moreover, as I am well aware, the spirit that seeks to honor civil and peaceful pursuits has led at times to a kind of effeteness in Chinese culture. This has been especially true in the closing years of a dynasty's reign, when a prevailing air of decadence has all but invited men of ambition to rise in rebellion and seek to topple the current rulers.

And yet, in spite of these various reservations, in comparison with many other great empires that have appeared on the stage of history, only to flourish for a time and then fade away, over the ages, China has shown relatively little inclination to rely solely upon military might to accomplish its aims. And, even though military concerns may for a certain period have occupied the nation, in the end they have been absorbed into the larger sea of peaceful and cultural pursuits that surrounded them.

China has been called the world's most historical nation because of the voluminous records of its past that have been compiled and preserved. And each of those volumes of historical records is dominated by an intense concern for ethics and morality. That is because the nation places overwhelming emphasis upon civil and humanitarian concerns, and from this attitude is born the strength to restrain impulses toward military aggression or adventurism.

The belief that foreign aggression runs counter to the Way and is a violation of virtue is said to have first made its appearance in China at the time of the Sui and Tang dynasties, or around the close of the seventh century and in the centuries immediately following. This was a period when China enjoyed heights of culture and civilization all but unparalleled anywhere in the world at that time. And the appearance of such a moral concept at that time seems highly suggestive of the power inherent in the culture and civilization.

As evidence of such a belief, when Emperor Yang (604–18) of the Sui dynasty launched against the Korean state of Koguryo a campaign that inflicted terrible hardships upon the Chinese populace, his action was bitterly attacked in an antiwar song that circulated among the people.

Later, in the closing years of the reign of Emperor Xuanzong (r. 713–55) of the Tang, when vast sums of money and countless human lives were being needlessly expended on border campaigns, Du Fu wrote his famous poem entitled "Song of the War Chariots," in which he not only expressed antiwar sentiments, but also condemned as immoral all types of foreign aggression.

In the poem, Du Fu describes conscripts being sent off to military duty and in the following passage depicts the grieving parents, wives, and relatives who are seeing them off.

> They drag on clothing,
> stamp their feet,
> block the road weeping;
> the sound of their weeping
> rises straight up
> to strike the clouds.

By the roadside
   a passerby questions
      the marching men;
the marchers merely answer,
   "They keep calling
      up more troops!"

Some from the age of fifteen
   have been north
      guarding the Yellow River,
and now at forty
   they're off west
      to farm the garrison fields.

When they set out,
   the village headman bound
      their heads with turbans;
they've come home now,
   heads gray, and it's off
      to man the border again.

In border regions,
   blood flows like
      water in the sea,
but the Martial Sovereign
   must expand his borders,
      not yet content.

Have you not heard
   how in two hundred
      districts of the Han
         east of the mountains
a thousand villages,
   ten thousand hamlets,
      are now overgrown
         in weeds and vines?

Thus, speaking for the marching men, the poet decries the senseless waste of war and aggression. Out of sentiments such as these were born the conviction that all kinds of foreign military action are unjust and contrary to the dictates of morality. It is interesting to note that this conviction, this consensus of feeling, seems to have taken shape just around the time when China and Japan were first entering into formal diplomatic relations through the Japanese embassies dispatched to the Sui and Tang courts. The form these relations took was in a sense an expression of the conviction condemning the use of force in foreign relations.

The Moral and Spiritual Leader

Traditionally, China looked upon itself as the moral and spiritual leader of the East Asian area and expected the countries surrounding it to acknowledge that leadership. But, with a very few exceptions, it made no attempt to conquer neighboring nations outright. Instead, it asked only that they submit tribute as indication that they recognized the sovereignty of the Chinese ruler. When foreign embassies like the ones from Japan journeyed to the Chinese court and presented their tribute, they were in effect acknowledging China's sovereignty and their own role as ministers of a subject nation. The Chinese ruler would then present the members of the embassy with various articles of Chinese manufacture by way of return gifts, and in this manner exchange of diplomatic relations was combined with a kind of foreign trade.

Underlying this trade and diplomatic encounter was the conviction that, through the influence of its culture and civilization, China could win the admiration and allegiance of the countries surrounding it, a further indication of the degree to which it prided itself upon civil and peaceful accomplishments rather than military might.

Such an arrangement did not necessarily work to the material advantage of China. As host to the foreign embassies, it was naturally obliged to bear the expense of housing and supplying the envoys and their numerous retinue during their stay. Moreover, it was customary for the Chinese sovereign to present to foreign envoys gifts that exceeded in value the items of tribute presented by the embassies. In actual fact, the tributary nations customarily received goods valuing five or six times the amount of the goods they themselves presented. It is said that one reason for the restrictions on shipping and the seclusionist policy adopted by Emperor Taizu (r. 1368–98), the founder of the Ming dynasty, was his feeling that China could no longer afford the expense involved in the old system of tribute missions from abroad.

One of course may dismiss the bounties distributed by the Chinese ruler to his tributaries as no more than the largesse expected of a rich and powerful nation. Yet the whole system displays a sense of hierarchy and noblesse oblige that is not necessarily to be encountered in other parts of the world. I frequently have occasion to travel to the countries of eastern Europe, where even today one observes the scars inflicted by the rapacity and greed of the Ottoman empire when it dominated the region. In comparison to the Turks' policy of merciless exploitation of the countries within their sphere of dominance, the Chinese system of tribute and trade is outstanding for its mildness and generosity and its reliance upon peaceful persuasion instead of force.

This sense of hierarchical order and moral obligation that accompany it stand in sharp contrast to the type of nationalism that developed in Europe in recent centuries, and the concepts of dominating and dominated nations that underlay it. At the time of the May Fourth Movement in China, the British philosopher Bertrand Russell, who was visiting Peking (Beijing) University at the time, remarked, "If any nation in the world could ever be 'too proud to fight,' that nation would be China. The natural Chinese attitude is one of tolerance and friendliness, showing courtesy and expecting it in return."

The Problem of China, 1922

As you probably know, the Chinese writer Lu Xun and others took violent exception to Russell's judgment, asserting that he had failed to take note of the negative aspects of the feudal mentality that it reflected and that still prevailed in China. I cannot help feeling, however, that Russell, with the eyes of an outsider, fixed upon one of the truly admirable characteristics of Chinese culture.

Be that as it may, I should like here to try to discover what force or strength it is that allows individuals or nations to control brute impulses, to master and restrain disruptive instincts. Unless we learn to identify that force and to cultivate it to the fullest, there is no hope that we will be able to advance along the road to peace by controlling and eventually ending the arms race.

Some sixteen years ago, when many people in my country were still talking about the menace of Chinese power, I proposed that steps be taken to restore normal diplomatic relations between China and Japan. At that time I said it was inconceivable that China should ever resort to direct military force to carry out a war of aggression, and I based that judgment solely on the history and tradition of the country. Diplomatic relations have now been restored between China and Japan; China has once more become a member of the United Nations and since then has on frequent occasions proclaimed that it will never go the way of the superpower nations. And, because I feel I have at least some insight into Chinese history, I am convinced that this pronouncement is prompted by more than considerations of temporary strategy.

Focus on Humanity

If we inquire a little more deeply into the background from which comes the power of self-mastery and self-restraint, we will find that it derives from an outlook and a manner of thinking consistently focused upon the human being.

As an outstanding scholar of my country who is especially well informed on the subject of Chinese thought has put it, "Chinese philosophy has sought first of all to define the goal of human life. The speculations of Chinese philosophers have never strayed in their area of concern from the human being. Even when the philosophers speculated upon the natural world, they approached the problem as one aspect of speculation on human life and developed a theory of naturalism on that basis. In other words, for them, philosophy was above all the study of humankind."

To say that the philosophers "never strayed in their area of concern from the human being" is to say that they made the human being the starting point of their inquiries. And I believe this may be said not only of philosophy, but of such other fields as religion, science, and politics as well. In all the areas of human endeavor in China, concern for the human being has constituted the underlying foundation. The result is philosophy, religion, science, and politics all for the sake of the human being. In the great river of Chinese history, with its interweaving streams of weal and woe, fundamental concern for the human being has remained an unwavering constant.

Nor is such a condition common in human history. In areas where such monotheistic religions as Christianity or Islam prevail or have prevailed, particularly in Europe in the Middle Ages, God, not man, has been the constant by which all goals and values were measured. Man was no more than the servant of God and philosophy was looked on as the handmaiden of theology. All fields of human endeavor—philosophy, religion, science, or statecraft—existed for the glory of God, not for the sake of humankind.

Even in modern times, when the old reliance upon God has become a thing of the past, this attitude has not changed easily. In place of God, the concept of progress has become the constant by which everything is measured, and science and technology have been elevated to the status of a new religion. But, as has often been pointed out, modern science has not always confined itself solely to the area of human concerns but has shown an unmistakable tendency to become an exercise in pure intellect, intellect in search of self-expression and self-fulfillment, regardless of how those ends affect humanity.

Of course, I have not the slightest intention of disparaging the accomplishments of science and technology or of denying the benefits they bestow. But we must not forget that great pitfalls lie in wait for a science that has ceased to be governed by concern for humankind.

With regard to the question of peace, the concept of colonialism, which has been a chief cause of war and contention among nations in modern times, is based upon habits and patterns of thought that wholly disregard the rights and dignity of human beings. Such patterns of thought, which led the countries of Western Europe into arrogantly believing they could divide all human societies into the categories of "civilized" and "uncivilized," fostered in them the view of themselves as a chosen people and lent covert support to the tenets of colonialism. In this sense, although European civilization in modern times has contributed much in the way of both material and spiritual attainments, its overall tendency has been not to restrain or control but merely to camouflage the more barbarous passions of human beings.

Movement and Action

In Chinese culture the idea or complex of ideas designated by the word *tian,* or Heaven, to some degree corresponds to the Christian concept of God. The word is used in a wide variety of contexts pertaining to religion, philosophy, ethics, and even the natural sciences. But, with the exception of usages in the very early period of Chinese intellectual history, it has never been perceived as a supernatural being like the Christian God. Heaven is conceived by the Chinese not as an a priori or transcendental being which looks down upon and speaks to man, but as something that is perceived a posteriori by man and sought for within himself.

Just what connotations the word *tian* may have in modern Chinese I am not in a position to say. Probably the concept is regarded at least in part as a relic of feudal morality and its attendant ills and abuses. What concerns me here, however, is not so much the nature of the concept of *tian* itself, but the manner in which it has been perceived and sought after; that is, *tian* has tended always to be defined in human terms and regarded as something immanent in and to be sought within the individual, rather than in the external world.

In my address given here four years ago, I spoke of the Chinese tendency to "view the universal in the light of the particular," and this seems to me to be another example of the same kind of thinking. The emphasis is upon the sustained effort and activity by which man examines reality, seeks to discover and define the concept of Heaven therein, and then reconstitutes his perception of reality on that basis. It is, in other words, a process that focuses on movement and action instead of on stasis.

In contrast, the process of value judgment constantly refers to a set of fixed concepts as its basis and, by adhering too rigidly to them, loses sight of the fact that such concepts are nothing more than products of the constantly shifting and evolving progress of human endeavors. As a result of such thinking, people come to make a virtual religion out of their faith in theory, a particular system, or efficiency, and allow themselves to become slaves to their beliefs. Belief in the power of nuclear deterrents is one of the most mistaken faiths of our time, because it fails to approach the problem from the human angle. It is a faith built on foundations of mutual distrust and hatred and fear among human beings, and these are precisely the elements that must be eliminated if we are ever to hope for the abolition of nuclear weapons.

Active Striving for Peace

In connection with the active search for a solution to the problems mentioned above, I should like to turn now to a work by the modern Chinese writer Lu Xun entitled *Feigong,* or "Against Offensive Warfare." This piece deals with the famous ancient philosopher Mozi (470–391 B.C.?), who lived in the turbulent period know as the Era of the Warring States and is remembered for his condemnations of warfare and his vigorous efforts to achieve peace. The title of Lu Xun's work has been rendered by one Japanese translator in Japanese terms meaning "The Story of How to Stop a War."

According to Lu Xun's story, which is based upon the actual writings of Mozi and his followers, Mozi, a native of the state of Lu, received word that Chu, a powerful state in southern China, was planning to attack and destroy a small state to the north of it known as Song. Moreover, it was said that the immediate impetus for the attack was a device known as "cloud ladders," for scaling walls of enemy cities, the invention by Gongshu Ban, a native of Mozi's own region, who had presented it to the king of Chu. Greatly pleased when the device was presented to him, the king of Chu decided to put it into action.

When Mozi received word of the impending attack, he immediately took to the road and hurried to the state of Chu to try to put a stop to the plan. As he hastened through the state of Song along the way, he noticed how poor it was. Later, when he reached the territory of Chu, he marveled at its riches and could not help wondering why so wealthy a state should wish to attack poor Song.

Arriving in Chu, he first of all met with Gongshu Ban and lectured him on the stupidity of going to war. Gongshu Ban replied that he had already talked to the king of Chu about his scaling ladders and it was therefore too late to do anything. Mozi then persuaded Gongshu Ban to arrange an interview for him with the king of Chu. The king agreed with Mozi's arguments against the initiation of hostilities but replied that, since Gongshu Ban had gone to all the trouble of inventing the "cloud ladders" for him, he had no choice but to employ them in an attack.

Mozi then arranged for himself and Gongshu Ban to carry out a tabletop simulation of the attack in the presence of the king. Representing the party under attack, Mozi proceeded to win a resounding victory. Gongshu Ban began to hint that it would be well to have Mozi put to death, but Mozi once more outwitted him by telling the king that he had in fact already given advice to the ruler of Song on how to make his cities absolutely impervious to attack, and warned that though he himself might be put to death, his three hundred disciples were standing by, ready to carry on in his place. Thereupon the king of Chu abandoned his plans for attack.

Lu Xun has declared that Mozi is his favorite among all the philosophers of ancient China, and certainly his treatment of the story is deeply moving and shot through with subtle touches of satire. In particular, the argument of the king of Chu that, because the "cloud ladders" have been expressly created for him, he cannot do otherwise than put them into use reminds us very much of arguments employed today by exponents of arms expansion.

I have brought up this story by Lu Xun because it seems to me that, even in our present world, the kind of active striving for peace that Mozi exemplifies offers the surest way of unlocking the barriers to peace. To act and speak out on behalf of peace—to take positive measures of this kind, no matter how indirect their immediate effect may seem—constitutes in my belief the Royal Road to Peace, the only means of transforming mistrust, hatred, and fear into trust, love, and friendship. And such measures will in the future, I am convinced, open up channels of communication linking the hearts and minds of all men and women everywhere.

The eminent Chinese writer, Ba Jin, whom I have had the pleasure of meeting on other occasions, attended the forty-seventh International PEN Congress, held in Tokyo last month, as president of the China PEN Center. In the address he made, he spoke of the opportunity such a congress offers for the participants to "make friends through literature," surely a most appropriate observation for the delegate from a country that, as I have stressed, has always honored the arts of peace.

Later in his address, in describing the power of literature, Ba Jin said, "Like water wearing away a rock, the dissemination of literature over the course of several generations has a profound effect on people. With literature as our weapon, we can reveal the truth and expose evil, strike out at the forces of darkness, and rally around just causes; if all the people in the world who long for peace and stand for justice could unite in a single body, taking their destiny into their own hands, all world wars and nuclear conflicts could be avoided."

I am of the same opinion. Though the efforts put forth by each individual may seem to have no more force than a trickle of water, they will in time wear a channel through the rock, and indeed will come to constitute a mighty river capable of sweeping away huge boulders. Only the gradual accumulation of resolute actions and dialogues based upon courage and vision can advance us toward our goal.

With what limited ability I myself possess, I intend to push ahead in that manner. And I should like to close my remarks today by asking all of you, upon whose shoulders rests the future of China, to join me in walking the highway to peace.

History Is Made
by Human Beings

Delivered at Fudan University, China, June 9, 1984.

Chinese Concern for History

A few days ago I had the pleasure of giving an address at Beijing University which I entitled "The Royal Road to Peace—A Personal Observation." Today, to my further honor and gratification, I have been given this opportunity to address Fudan University, an institution with a history of close to eighty years. I understand that Honorary President Su Buqing and President Xie Xide are at the moment visiting America, but I should like to extend my sincere thanks to the members of the faculty and student body who are present here for making this occasion possible.

In my remarks delivered at Beijing University, I spoke of the pronounced tendency in Chinese civilization and culture to honor civil or peaceful accomplishments over those associated with military ideals, and of how this tendency has acted to restrain the nation from engaging in warfare and military activities. And, to the extent made possible by my limited knowledge, I tried to trace the origins of that tendency in China's traditional ways of thought. Today I should like

186

to limit my attention to the Chinese view of history, a theme that I barely touched on in my earlier remarks, offering a few observations on how history relates to the question of human life and its meaning.

Few countries in the world can rival China in the depth of its concern for history. India, for example, though situated in the same general area of eastern Asia, provides a marked contrast because of its relative lack of interest in the subject of history. In the past, the Chinese have been almost fanatical in their efforts to observe the events of history and to get them all down in written form. The voluminous literature that has resulted has been aptly described in the colorful Chinese phrase *hanniu chongdong,* meaning books so numerous that they "make the oxen (transporting them) sweat, and fill (the house they are stored in) to the rafters."

Over the centuries, the Chinese people have paid honor to two other proverbs: "to study the old (in order to) understand the new," and "to borrow antiquity to explain the present." These phrases amply testify to the traditional belief that history is a mirror reflecting the present, a source of light serving as a guide to the present age.

Just what view of history prevails in China at present I am not in a position to say. Certainly since the revolution in China there has been a tendency in all fields of study to concentrate upon the role of the common people.

The late Chairman Mao has stated that "the people, the people alone, are the motive power that creates history." And this would certainly seem to suggest a view of history that places the masses and their interests in the center of the stage. This marks a clear and decided break with the traditional Confucian-inspired view of history that focused upon the role of the ruler and held up as its highest ideals the mythic sage-rulers of antiquity, such as Yao and Shun.

At the same time, the intense concentration upon history that has marked the Chinese tradition in the past and has continued over a period of several thousand years, whether looked upon as a good thing or a bad, cannot be easily changed. That is no doubt why the modern writer Lu Xun, who was aware of this acute consciousness of history and regarded it as a kind of cannibalism, thought it was important for men and women to undergo a kind of revolution in their thinking, difficult though that may be to achieve, and to free themselves from the old ways of thought.

Mirror and Source of Light

My own view is that the traditional view, which held history in high esteem and looked on historical experience as a mirror and a source of light to illumine the present and give direction to the future, has not only dominated the long centuries of China's past, but also continues even today to be a vital force. I am constantly struck with admiration by the apt manner in which the Chinese employ quotations from their classical literature in speeches and writings. And this tells me that, in their eyes, history is fraught with didactic import and is a living reality in the present.

We may note that the Chinese view is very different in nature from the interpretation of history and the historical consciousness that have prevailed in Europe since the eighteenth century, particularly as they were shaped by the currents of nineteenth-century historicism. To be sure, historicism has won a measure of recognition because of its emphasis upon the objective approach and the need to support contentions with factual proof. But more important has been its tendency to objectify history, to treat it as the same kind of subject for objective observation and study as the phenomena of the natural world. As a result, history has come to be thought of as subject to laws of its own; its vital connections with the human being have been cut off, and it has come to walk an independent path.

The German philosopher Nietzsche, who so clearly foresaw the crises of modern European civilization, said: "We employ history for the sake of life and action; we do not employ it for the sake of any easy succession from life and action, and we certainly do not employ it to dress up or disguise a life that is egotistical or actions that are cowardly or base."

I think it is possible to substitute the words "human being" for the word "life" in Nietzsche's pronouncement. Nietzsche never ceased attacking the subversion of values that envisions history as walking a path of its own and that relegates life or the human being, who in fact plays the leading role in the creation of history, to a subsidiary position.

The traditional Chinese view of history as something that assists in the creation of a better today and tomorrow, as food for life and the human being, represents a wholly different dimension from the type of outlook that Nietzsche was chastizing. The Chinese concern for history, which is perhaps best symbolized in the work of the early Chinese historian Sima Qian (145?–c. 90 B.C.), far from viewing history as a cold, impersonal entity subject to laws of its own, constantly approached it in a mood of passionate subjectivity and moral concern, demanding to learn from it how human beings ought best to live.

Questioning of Human Destiny

I would like here to quote a famous passage from Chapter 130 of the *Shi Ji* (Records of the Historian), Sima Qian's voluminous history of China's past in which the historian comments upon the relationship between literature and human suffering. It is a passage that never fails to move me with its courage and conviction:

"Of old when the Chief of the West, King Wen, was imprisoned at Youli, he spent his time expanding the *Book of Changes;* Confucius was in distress between Chen and Cai and he made the *Spring and Autumn Annals;* when Qu Yuan was exiled, he composed his poem 'Encountering Sorrow'; after Zuo Qui lost his sight, he composed the *Narratives from the States;* when Sunzi had his feet amputated, he set forth *The Art of War;* Lü Buwei was banished to Shu but his *Lü-lan* has been handed down through the ages; while Han Feizi was held prisoner in Qin, he wrote 'The Difficulties of Disputation' and 'The Sorrow of Standing Alone'; most of the three hundred poems of the *Book of Odes* were written when the sages and worthies poured forth their anger and dissatisfaction."

By citing these various works of early Chinese history and literature and the harried authors who produced them, Sima Qian was saying that it was suffering and persecution that brought about the creation of these great writings. And because such is their origin, historical writings constitute a questioning of men's fortunes and misfortunes, joys and sorrows, good and evil acts, a questioning of human destiny as a whole that strikes at the very heart of the matter. This same questioning, we may note, is a motif running throughout Sima Qian's *Records of the Historian.*

Viewing history as a questioning of human destiny means that the record of historical events is thought of not as something existing outside human beings, but always as something internal. One might go so far as to say that history is none other than the personal history of the individual. And in that thought one envisions the individual, standing alone, unflinching, bravely taking upon himself all the possible destinies of humankind.

There is a saying in Buddhism to the effect that "all the eighty-four thousand teachings are the daily record of the individual." In this context, eighty-four thousand is not intended as a definite quantity but merely indicates a very large number; the word "teachings" refers to all the various doctrines that Shakyamuni Buddha preached in the course of his life. All these countless doctrines are contained in the daily record of the individual—that is, in the workings of the life force of a single human being. Though on a somewhat different level, this doctrine too gives a sense of the human being as standing on his own, not swayed by praise or blame, but bravely facing whatever fate may await him.

Solidarity of World Citizenry

The flow of history never ceases for a moment. In the words of Li Bai (also known as Li Po), one of China's greatest poets, "Heaven and earth are an inn for the ten thousand things of creation; time is the traveler of a hundred ages." And the time has now come for human beings, and the common people in particular, to cease being content to play only a subsidiary part in history. We must firmly establish the role of the free and independent individual in the making of history and, at the same time, link individual to individual in cooperative movements that, spreading in successive waves, bind together the entire citizenry of the world.

With the swift passing of time and the changes that accompany it, the world is rapidly becoming, in every sense of the word, a single entity. Whatever may have been the past histories of China or of Japan, under present circumstances all of us who are passengers on the Spaceship Earth are inevitably faced with a common destiny. From now on, our history is that of the world as a whole. And to ensure that, whatever sudden shifts and vicissitudes the flow of history may bring, we are able to face the coming century with hope and confidence, we must once and for all learn to look upon history as something in which human beings play the decisive role. At the same time, we must all become aware that, as fellow passengers on the Spaceship Earth, we need to develop a sense of solidarity appropriate to the citizens of a single globe.

May I close my remarks by congratulating Fudan University on the part it has played in the past eighty years in training men and women of talent, and express my sincere hopes that, for the sake of China and the world at large, it will continue its educational activities with even greater vigor and success in the future.

Resolution
Determines the Outcome

*Delivered at the Leaders' Commemorative Meeting,
held at the Nagano Culture Center, Nagano Prefecture,
on July 30, 1984.*

＿＿～～～～

One year at the summer training course at Taiseki-ji, the head temple of Nichiren Shoshu, the second president of Soka Gakkai Josei Toda addressed a group of young people, the builders of the future, with advice to venerate the *Gosho,* the written works of Nichiren Daishonin, from an early age. He then continued with an exhortation to avoid a shallow education and to read eagerly the classic works of literature of both East and West. Behind his advice was the knowledge that depth and self-refinement determine the worth of a human life. In addition, he was well aware that veneration of the *Gosho* makes other good literature more meaningful and that a knowledge of literary classics helps an understanding of the *Gosho.*

Certainly the *Gosho* is the basis and ultimate of all things. And the writings of none of the other religious leaders of the past approach it in terms of a perfect development of the nature of life, accurate observations of humanity, and immense compassion.

On this occasion, I should like to spend some time on the famous novel *War and Peace,* the composition to which Leo Tolstoy gave all his strength between his thirty-sixth and forty-second years. As is well known, the book deals with the Napoleonic Wars of the early nineteenth century and especially with the French attacks on Austria and Russia, and the celebrated battles of Austerlitz and Borodino. Its vast canvas continues to depict the French occupation of Moscow and finally their retreat in defeat. It involves more than five hundred characters, ranging from the tsar to peasants, and, in attempting to deal with such fundamental issues as the meaning of war, peace, human life, death, marriage, happiness, and society, it reveals the author's views on these issues and on life and history as well.

I cannot help wondering what Tolstoy, and such other great Russian writers of about the same period as Dostoevski, Turgenev, and Gorki would have been like if they had been given the chance to come into contact with the Buddhism of Nichiren Daishonin. (Similarly, I cannot help feeling that history would have been different if Napoleon had had contact with that same Buddhism.) In spite of the splendid spiritual radiance he emitted, Tolstoy died unhappy. While the progress of kosen-rufu is due to the Buddha's will, it is our honor and pride to strive to carry the Buddhism of Nichiren Daishonin to peoples everywhere. Perhaps if we had been active in his day, we might have lightened his final years. Though our *kosen-rufu* movement may seem small now, it will certainly someday bring limitless peace and happiness to humanity in the future.

Awakening the People

A profound and permeating theme of *War and Peace* is the idea that it is not single heroes, but the people, who make history. This finds reflection in our own work since we, as faithful believers in the Mystic Law, are working for the sake of a new future for the ordinary people. Without being controlled by authorities or power, we have gathered together under the Mystic Law in what is certainly the most wonderful forward drive by the people ever witnessed throughout history. On level after level, we must build a unity of the common people that spreads throughout the whole world. We are the main creators of future history. The time when we could leave the work up to someone else has passed. The task is ours. Position, fame, wealth, and reputation are bubbles that are bound to burst. But our work is of such enduring significance that stopping it would mean the worst possible misery for the future of humanity.

The flow of time is mighty. No doubt none of the ordinary rank-and-file cavalry and artillery soldiers in the Napoleonic Wars wanted to fight. But because the times were moving in the direction of war tens of thousands of people lost their lives. The same thing occurred in World Wars I and II. And, if there is a World War III, no one will survive. The wise power of the ordinary people is necessary to put a halt to this threat. As long as they remain unawakened and under the sway of political power, the ordinary people will never attain their own happiness, peace, and victory.

Many of the leading figures in *War and Peace* are young: Prince André, Pierre, Natasha, Maria, Nikolai, Platon Karataev, and others. I feel that, in his desire for the happiness of these young people, the far-seeing Tolstoy, even if only emotionally and conceptually, manifests something corresponding to the Buddhist desire to make people happy in actual life. No matter what the situation is in novels, however, in reality, though they may grasp fleeting, relative joys, people can find absolute, indestructible happiness only through the Buddhism of Nichiren Daishonin. In the profound misery surrounding his own death, which has been variously explained as suicide or the frailty of old age, Tolstoy vividly demonstrated how difficult it is to find absolute happiness.

A Realm as Lucid as the Sky

In a celebrated scene in the novel, Prince André, who has been wounded by rifle shot, is lying on the battlefield looking up at the sky. "There was no longer anything above him but the sky—the lofty sky, not clear, but somehow immeasurably high, with gray clouds creeping slowly across it. 'How quiet, peaceful, and splendid! Not at all as it was while I was dashing about' thought Prince André. 'Not the way it was when we ran, screamed and fought. Not the way it was when, with enraged and frightened faces, our artillery and the French tugged at their cannon-cleaning rods, not at all the way the clouds move across that high sky. How is it I have never seen that lofty sky before? I am happy that I have recognized it at last. Yes, everything is empty, everything is deception except that lofty sky. There is nothing, nothing but it. And even the sky doesn't exist. There is nothing except quiet and calm.' "

This passage recalls for me the significance of worshipping the Gohonzon, the manifestation of the universe, and the maximum and irreplaceable happiness a human being attains from quietly contemplating the Great Law, which is loftier than the sky itself. André's comment that everything is empty and deception, except the lofty sky, is clear indication of the futility of worldly fame and glory.

In a slightly later scene, Napoleon passes the place where Prince André lies wounded. Though formerly one of André's heroes, Napoleon seemed ". . . a small, insignificant person in comparison with what was taking place at the time between his soul and the high, endless sky with the clouds scudding across it."

Perhaps André's admiration had been only a manifestation of his own ambition, which had been completely annihilated in the confrontation he is experiencing between life and death.

Many people are unable to triumph over their ambitions. Indeed, in my thirty-seven years of experience with religious faith, most of the people I have known who have gone back on or betrayed their beliefs have done so at the mercy of their own thirst for fame and glory. It is my hope that none of you will be swayed by base, worldly concerns but will, instead, live in keeping with your faith, chant Daimoku, work for the sake of *kosen-rufu,* and follow the Way leading to personal happiness and peace for society and the world.

Inner Resolution

In another scene, in talking with one of his subordinates, Prince André says that never in history has success in military operations been determined by position, weapons, or numbers of combatants but always depends on the passion in the hearts of individual soldiers. From our standpoint, this passion is resoluteness of faith. We must always remember that the Law-battle for *kosen-rufu* will be determined by the deeply-ingrained, adamant, and indestructible resoluteness of the faith of each of us. In the struggle between correct and false, good and evil, happiness and unhappiness, the Buddha and the devils, the Buddha, the True Law, and the powers of good must triumph if we remain resolute.

Prince André continues in a similar vein to say that the person who has decided in his heart that victory will be his will actually win. Considerations of position or whether the left flank is weak or the right flank overextended are insignificant. Awaiting the soldiers in the following day's battle are hundreds of millions of chance occurrences. Escape from misfortune, and who comes out alive, and who dead, determine the outcome of the battle. On that day, ten thousand Russians will confront ten thousand Frenchman, and the outcome will depend on who fights the more furiously and unselfsparingly. One of the main points of *War and Peace* is the determination in the hearts of the masses of the Russian people, a determination that ultimately drives the army of Napoleon from their country. In spite of the importance of planning, strategy, and calculation, it is the power of inner resolution that counts. This is especially true of the resolution of faith that is essential in the minds of all of us in the unprecedented undertaking of *kosen-rufu*.

Building an Ideal World

Delivered at the Representative Leaders' Training Session,
held at the Nagano Training Center, Nagano Prefecture,
August 8, 1984.

Faust's Message for the Young

Today I take this opportunity to discuss with you Goethe's *Faust,* which ranks with Dante's *Divine Comedy* as one of the great pinnacles of world philosophical literature and, through this discussion, to share with you some of my own recent ideas.

The Buddhist law is tantamount to all laws. This means that Buddhism embodies all knowledge. Our own view is that all things are given life from the dimension of the Mystic Law, which is a summation of all other laws. Consequently, for the sake of mastering a maximum amount of knowledge, I want the officers of our organization to come into as intimate contact as possible with the outstanding literature of the world and thus become more cultivated and discerning. The age in which we live requires this of us.

The drama *Faust* is the product of amazing perseverance. Goethe spent sixty years completing it, although the weight of other tasks prevented his working on it for twenty of those sixty years. I am only fifty-six and all the rest of you are still young, so the amount of time

Goethe spent on this one work should encourage us to remain youthful and realize how much we have before us.

Faust, the protagonist of the play, which is divided into a prologue and two parts, is traditionally thought to have been a scholar who, though doubt exists, is believed to have been a master of medicine, art, mathematics, and philosophy. Before Goethe, such other writers as the English dramatist Christopher Marlowe used Faust (or Faustus) as a subject, but the content of their work is unsatisfying. And it was left to Goethe to take up the topic in earnest, to plumb its full depths, and to give it a splendid artistic and philosophical setting. I believe that the spiritual history of Doctor Faust embodies all of Goethe's own philosophy.

Having passed the age of fifty-five and mastered all learning, Faust comes to the conclusion that "there is nothing we can know."

His attitude can be compared to the humility of the learned man, what Socrates called knowledge of ignorance. In my travels throughout the world, I have met and talked with many great scholars: Arnold J. Toynbee, René Huyghe, and Réne Dubos, and the thing they all share in common is humility. It is very regrettable that many scholars in Japan are deficient in this quality and are therefore incapable of training good people to succeed them.

I have decided to speak on the topic of *Faust* because, as I mentioned a few days ago when we discussed Tolstoy's *War and Peace,* I cannot help wondering what Goethe would have written and done if he had been acquainted with the Buddhism of Nichiren Daishonin. If a man of his genius—a man who was capable of examining, through the story of Faust's pact with Mephistopheles and the ensuing struggle, the heights and depths of which humanity is capable—had known the true Buddhism, I believe European thought might have been different from what it is.

Though it is impossible to summarize its content in brief form, I think the play attempts to answer two questions of maximum significance. First, what are the meanings of beauty, religion, love, and politics for human beings and human life? Second, what is the correct way for a man to live?

As a drama, *Faust* depends on dialogue, a form of communication employed in many ways. Dialogue plays an important part in Nichiren Daishonin's *Rissho Ankoku Ron* (On Securing the Peace of the Land Through the Propagation of True Buddhism). The philosophy of Socrates is set forth in the Socratic dialogues, and we of Soka Gakkai employ dialogue in our discussion meetings. Though it seems simple, this is a very important point. As Goethe well knew, dialogue—exchanges between two or among more than two individuals—is what makes human beings human.

The following is one of my favorite passages in *Faust*:

> No escarpment, no immuring,
> Trust oneself is all one can;
> Fortress firm for sure enduring
> Is the iron breast of man.

Though the dimensions in which they operate are different, it is possible to equate this passage from the drama with a kind of prologue to Buddhism. From our viewpoint, the "oneself" in which the character Euphorion in the play says he finds his sole point of reliance becomes indestructible faith. In a relation of reaction and exchange with the Dai-Gohonzon, this indestructible faith generates in our minds limitless merit and life force. This is why we must always be diligent in faith.

Another extremely acute observation is to be found in this passage:

> Yet not in torpor would I comfort find;
> Awe is the finest portion of mankind;
> However scarce the world may make this sense—
> In awe one feels profoundly the immense.

The awe of which Faust speaks as the "finest portion of mankind" may be compared to the thrilling tension and unshakable resolution we feel when confronted with difficulty in the form of the Three Obstacles and the Four Devils or the Three Powerful Enemies. Experiencing this kind of awe is indeed to acquire a supreme jewel and is in keeping with the spirit of Nichiren Daishonin's *Kaimoku Sho* (The Opening of the Eyes).

Still another important passage is this: "Were I but Man with

Nature for my frame, / The name of human would be worth the claim." Standing resolute—like man in this passage—in the face of fate and, as a manifestation of the precious Mystic Law, carrying out the struggle for one's self and for *kosen-rufu* is the heart's blood of the way all human beings should live.

What Goethe says in this passage relates to the need imposed on all of us—and especially on the young—to proceed along the way of faith without being retarded by excessive concern for prosperity, decline, disgrace, honor, praise, censure, suffering, and pleasure (the so-called Eight Hindering Winds). During my last meeting with the late Arnold J. Toynbee, I asked him to offer me a word of advice. He declined, saying that he was a man of scholarly pursuits whereas I am a man of practical action to whom he would not presume to give advice. Nonetheless, he urged me to go ahead with my work courageously. This is what Goethe means when he speaks of the worth of being human when one is Man within the framework of nature. His message is far removed from the ivory tower of learning for its own sake.

Faust wishes to build a castle that will be a realization of the human dream. He says, ". . . To bring to fruit the most exalted plans, / One mind is ample for a thousand hands."

This has bearing on a remark made by a certain intellectual to the effect that one should sway an organization without being swayed by it. From our viewpoint, the ultimate spirit that is "ample for a thousand hands" is the spirit of prayer and the doctrine of *ichinen sanzen,* which clarifies the oneness of ultimate truth and the world of phenomena.

Faust is a practical, not a conceptualizing, man. With executive ability, he wishes to be responsible for what today would be an amalgamation of ministries and agencies to create a strong society: "I'd open room to live for millions / Not safely, but in free re-silience."

With your offerings, we are erecting temples, culture centers, and training centers all over the country and are thus opening room where people can train themselves and live freely. These places are a firm foundation for a great future of *kosen-rufu.*

Like Faust, the Buddhism of Nichiren Daishonin is practical and of this world. Other religions in the Daishonin's time concentrated on escapist longings for the Paradise in the West or other divine realms removed from the world of actuality. In contrast, the Buddhism of Nichiren Daishonin teaches that the secret of success of a religion or philosophy is the way it deals with changing and improving the actual world. Such change and improvement are the outcomes of practical actions arising from a philosophy.

The world situation today certainly demands improvement in the realm of practical actions. Not long ago, I watched a television program depicting the misery that would be caused by a nuclear conflict. At present, in their arsenals, the United States and the Soviet Union possess weapons 1.5 million times more destructive than the atom bomb dropped on Hiroshima. The use of these weapons would turn the world into the kind of House Afire that Shakyamuni describes in the famous parable in the third chapter of the Lotus Sutra. Shakyamuni says the ordinary world of humanity—the *saha* world—is like a house engulfed in flame. But for the sake of the true happiness of humanity, instead of running away, we must find practical ways to put out the blaze.

Action—the deed—is the important thing. In attempting to translate the New Testament, Faust, displeased with, "In the beginning was the Word," first renders the text "In the beginning was the Sense." But this too fails to satisfy, and he tries "In the beginning was the Force." But finally he rejects this too for "In the beginning was the Deed." I cannot help seeing in this transition from Word to Deed something like the oriental method of deduction or something akin to poetic intuition. Like Faust, we are practical people who cannot afford to ignore the acute observation of a poet whose vitality and activity at the age of eighty is a model for us all.

Happiness Must be Won

In another part of the drama, Faust says:

> This I hold to with devout insistence,
> Wisdom's last verdict goes to say:
> He only earns both freedom and existence
> Who must reconquer them each day.

Winning existence and freedom through daily struggle is comparable to gradual accumulation of merit through faith, or, in other words, through the steady practice of both Gongyo and the chanting of Daimoku. Faith, like true happiness, is not remote but must be won through daily struggle. Though in stages, Goethe's meaning gradually approaches the realm of Buddhism, the ultimate realm of true human nature. And in this, I think his work is more profound that Dante's. After making a deep examination of humanity, he concentrates on actuality and in this way enters the realm of religion in his pursuit of beauty.

When asked by Mephistopheles whether he may try seductions on Faust, God says, "The worthy soul through the dark urge within it / Is well aware of the appointed course."

In the vicissitudes of life, strong faith is essential. Even though driven by "the dark urge," the person whose faith is true will follow the correct path in life. The most important thing is for the individual to walk steadfastly and in a way suited to his own best nature down the road that leads to universal, eternal happiness.

In human relations, guiding and convincing other people are of major importance. (It is of special significance to people like you who are leaders in the drive for *kosen-rufu*.) At one point in the drama, a character called Wagner questions Faust about eloquence; and Faust tells him,

> Seek you but honest recompense!
> Be not a fool with jangling bells!
> For solid reason and good sense
> With little art commend themselves.
> If you're in earnest to be heard,
> Should there be need to chase the word?

In other words, there is no need to use low-level stratagems to sell one's self. The desired effect is the natural one, in Buddhist terms.

Unadorned truth is the thing that moves the human mind. In the recently concluded Los Angeles Olympic Games, the Japanese gold-medalist gymnast Koji Gushiken said, "I had no idea how many points I was making. I only wanted to perform as well as I could."

His attitude indicates what Goethe meant by saying that speaking honestly has no need of decoration and is of the utmost importance in our difficult task of presenting a clear, accurate picture of true Buddhism to others.

Commonly held images are often far from the truth. A certain journalist has reported that many Japanese people think the word *jobutsu,* which means to attain Buddhahood, connotes the same thing as dying. Obviously, we have a great deal of convincing to do if we are to rectify such incorrect interpretations. To achieve our goal, we must speak honestly, with no ornamental flourishes, and avoid the kind of flowery speech employed by politicans in their search for power.

These words of Faust reveal Goethe's view of mankind:

> Should ever I take ease upon a bed of leisure,
> May that same moment mark my end!
> When first by flattery you lull me
> Into smug complacency,
> When with indulgence you can gull me,
> Let that day be the last for me.

Determination of this kind is a trait common to all people who have achieved important things. Anyone who would complete a great work in this life must adopt this stand. In keeping with the sacred teaching to strive to grow stronger day by day and week by week, such determination never to give in to sloth or pleasure is part of the spirit of Soka Gakkai.

Frustrations in life are almost always a product of compromise with the devil in one's own mind. In many years of observing people who have failed in diligence, I have discovered that the cause is always to be found within the people themselves and is usually vainglory, jealousy, resentment, or conceit. Such people dwell in the state of Anger *(Asura)* and seek only to justify themselves with fine words. Today, as in the time of Nichiren Daishonin, out of desolation or envy, people of this kind attempt to destroy the purity and happiness of the Soka Gakkai world.

Faust continues by saying that stagnation means slavery and that a man must remain active always, without rest: "Once come to rest, I am enslaved." This reminds me of the words of the sixty-fifth high priest of Taiseki-ji, Nichijun Shonin: "The cemetery is the place to rest." Josei Toda, like me, was deeply impressed by this comment. The drive for *kosen-rufu* requires just this kind of perseverance and endurance.

> *Faust*: And what to all of mankind is apportioned
> I mean to savor in my own self's core,
> Grasp with my mind both highest and most low,
>   Weigh down my spirit with their weal and woe,
> And thus my selfhood to their own distend . . .

Though it is susceptible to various interpretations, I think this passage relates to the great compassion that strives to expand the individual life to the Buddha world.

Through worshipping the Gohonzon our individual selves meld with the universal source and expand to universal proportions. Our enlarged selves are our true selves, and manifesting them is our reason for living.

Once again to return to the topic of eloquence, when Wagner asks how he can move the minds of others, Faust tells him:

> What you don't feel, you won't hunt down by art,
> Unless it wells from your own inward source,
> And with contentment's elemental force
> Takes sway of every hearer's heart.

In other words, a speaker may have a good text but will fail to convince his audience unless he makes the message his own.

The strength of Soka Gakkai is in the profound interest, based on faith, with which we can stimulate the minds of the people. We must remember that absolute eloquence deriving from the experience of Buddhism is the reason for our having advanced as far as we have. Faust continues speaking to Wagner:

Of parchment then is made the sacred spring,
A draught of which forever slakes the thirst?
From naught can you refreshment wring
Unless from your own inmost soul it burst.

Memorizing books and speaking beautifully are not everything. This
vividly calls to mind the Daishonin's comment that action and study
must spring from faith. Without the heart of faith, which gushes forth
like a fount from the spirit, mere intellectual worshipping of the
Gosho is fruitless. The Daishonin's teaching is reasonable. It is the
teaching of *ichinen sanzen*. We must remember that to make it our
own we must make it our own ultimate reality.

Faust's spiritual journey leads him upward toward the Buddhist
doctrine that one's actions must be for the instruction of others. In
the first part of the drama, he makes a pact with Mephistopheles and
then carries out the ensuing struggle. In the second part, he tries to
discover the optimum way for human beings to live and act and
finally comes to the conclusion that true human happiness is found
only in working for others.

Finally, in search of himself and believing that he is creating an
ideal realm, the blind Faust dies. Actually, however, the thing that
Faust had been building, under the delusion that it was an ideal realm
was, as a consequence of the work of Mephistopheles, no more than
his own tomb. Mephistopheles attempts to steal Faust's soul from the
tomb but is, if I remember correctly, prevented by a band of angels
descending from heaven.

On a certain level this story of the battle between Faust and the
devil resembles the struggle between the Buddha and evil. We must
not let evil win. *Faust* is called a tragedy; we must not allow our
battle to end tragically. Our ideal realm of *kosen-rufu* must not go the
way of the ideal world Faust thought he was building.

To ensure that this does not happen, we must keep our eyes firmly
fixed on reality. Each of must have strength to augment wisdom with
faith as, united and enlightened, we compose our song of victory.

Thoughts on Aims of Education

*A Proposal Commemorating the All-Japan Educators'
Meeting of Soka Gakkai, August 25, 1984.*

Restoring Humanity to Education

Not a day goes by without a serious discussion of the sad state of our educational system. The problem has reached nationwide proportions. Such phenomena as juvenile delinquency, violence at school, truancy, and prevailing lethargy among the young constitute no more than the tip of the iceberg. In spite of the fervent attempts being made both at home and in the schools to deal with it, because of the breadth and depth of the issue, so far no general remedy has been prescribed.

As one person earnestly desiring the wholesome growth and development of youth, I cannot help being anxious. Since I am not a specialist in the field, I have no intention of discussing individual educational methods or the various aspects of the educational system that require reform. All of these things must be handled with wisdom and in the light of world trends and the situation in Japan. Avoiding hastiness, qualified people must approach these problems remaining fully aware that cultivating today's youth will determine the fate of tomorrow's Japan.

I should like to say, however, that politics must not be allowed to take the lead in educational reforms. In all ages, political power has tended to subjugate education and everything else to its own purposes, as was vividly illustrated by modern Japanese education after the establishment, in 1872, of a system dominated by political aims and giving first priority to the achievement of nationalistic goals. Slogans such as "increase production and promote industry" and "enrich the country and strengthen the military" were hoisted aloft like imperial banners to which education was obliged to give service. Though this policy may have been partly justified on the basis of the desire to catch up with the Western powers, we must not avert our eyes from the loss it entailed.

Nor can it be said that the constitution and the Fundamental Law on Education adopted after World War II succeeded in avoiding the same pitfalls since, generally speaking, it was politics again that took the lead in the postwar democratic education system. Education was once again called on to serve nationalistic aims with the difference that postwar striving to become a great economic power replaced prewar and wartime striving to become a great military power. Under such circumstances, when the national aim collapses, educational aims are left dangling in the air. It is therefore by no means coincidental that the dark cloud of educational devastation covering our country from the 1970s into the 1980s coincides with the Japanese course of high-rate economic growth and its frustrations.

The true goal of education should be the cultivation of the individual personality on the basis of respect for humanity. We must admit, however, that in modern Japan education has been used as a means for cultivating people who will be of value to the nation and big business, that is, people who will function effectively within the national and commercial structure.

For some time I have advocated the establishment of a fourth branch of government, that of education, independent of the present three branches—legislative, executive, and judiciary—as a method of combatting the ills and distortions created by education dominated by politics. The thing that has been lost in the modern Japanese system of education, led as it has been since the late nineteenth century by political considerations, is humanity.

On the basis of his many years of practice and study in teaching, the late Tsunesaburo Makiguchi, first president of Soka Gakkai, defined education concisely and clearly in the following way. The goals of education must not be set by scholars and must not be taken advantage of by other parties. The goal of education must be one with the goal of life. And this means that it must enable children to attain a life of happiness.

Putting to good use his more than thirty years' experience in practical education and adding to that his astute sociological observations, Makiguchi evolved a definition of happiness in the form of his original theory of value. He was able to achieve this because throughout his life he always kept an enlightened eye turned on humanity.

In this connection, I am always deeply moved by a passage from the writings of Victor-Marie Hugo, the great romanticist who devoted himself to the establishment of the autonomy of education, the relief of poverty, and the ensurance of freedom for all:

> Light that makes whole. Light that enlightens. All fruitful social impulses spring from knowledge, letters, the arts, teaching. We must make whole men, whole men . . . (*Les Misérables*)

I do not think we need Hugo's words to realize that the main significance of education is to make "whole men." I insist that all future educational reforms must be made for the sake of humanity, not politics. I further insist that the nostalgia—sometimes expressed today—for the nationalistic Japanese education of the past is stimulated by doubt concerning the situation of the present and represents refusal to learn from history.

Three Principles

The question has been argued, and studies and proposals have been made on it from many different angles, but in my opinion, educational reform dominated by considerations of humanity must not be made within the framework of the established system but must be guided by these three principles: totality, creativity, and internationalism.

Totality of Wisdom   In speaking of totality I imply interrelation. No thing or event exists in isolation; everything is interrelated in some way with everything else to produce one great total image. To take an immediately apparent example, I might cite the human body itself, in which head, hands, torso, legs, internal organs, and all individual cells are intimately intermeshed to form the whole. We cannot overlook the connection between the physical and spiritual being. Modern depth psychology and ecology show that interrelations expand infinitely to connect human beings with each other, with the world of nature, and with the entire universe. Inseparably bound together, the microcosm and the macrocosm work together in wondrous rhythm. In the words of Goethe's Faust: "Lo, single things inwoven, made to blend. To work in oneness with the whole, and live . . . "

From ancient times, perceiving the invisible threads interweaving all things has been considered a kind of wisdom. But modern civilization has turned its back on this wisdom and has pursued instead a ceaseless course of fragmentation. Though perhaps an inevitable part of the development of human knowledge, this tendency, while producing great results in the physical realm, has created a condition in which the cords that once bound man and man, to say nothing of man and nature, have been severed, and the individual man himself groans in the small, enclosed, and lonely space into which he has been driven.

In terms of learning and education, this state of affairs can be compared to the way in which mankind has ignored the totality of wisdom and instead has allowed departmentalization of learning to exist for its own sake. Unrelated to the values of human happiness and a better way of life, learning goes its own way, expanding to ever vaster proportions.

The immensely important educator Yukichi Fukuzawa (1835–1901), who lived at a time when modernization was the major trend in Japan, saw this from a very early date.

"Such an informed person is informed about things but not about the connections among them and is ignorant of the principle mutually connecting this and that. Learning consists solely in understanding mutual relations among things. Learning that does not take such relations into consideration serves no useful purpose."

Further, he observed: "The informed person who does not know connections among things differs from a dictionary only in that he eats and the dictionary does not."

In other words, the person who, like a dictionary, is a compendium of unrelated information, knows much but ignores interrelations and is therefore idle and fruitless.

Of course, Fukuzawa, who was the author of *An Encouragement of Learning,* and who studied much himself and stimulated others to do the same, is attacking not learning as such, but learning and knowledge for their own sake only. Nor do I think his words reflect pragmatism and practicality alone.

Fukuzawa speaks of connections among things (the Japanese word *en* which he uses in this meaning is found in such famous Buddhist terms as *engi,* the pivotal doctrine of dependent origination). Determining what connection study and learning have with oneself, that is, what meaning they have, represents an inclination toward the kind of totality I have been speaking of, the same kind of inclination that can be seen in the philosophy of Henri Bergson, who made the famous statement, "Living comes first of all."

Undeniably, the pursuit of learning for learning's sake has been a great driving force in the development of modern science. But results of this development, such as nuclear weapons and environmental pollution, force us to examine the scientist's social responsibility. In other words, the scientist must ask himself what connection his learning has with his own fate and with that of all mankind.

On the more practical plane of actual education, I often hear of students who no longer read great classics and literary masterpieces but content themselves with digests giving all the information they need to pass examinations. They know and have no desire to learn more than the digests tell them. Even in our audiovisual and mass-media-oriented age, this is cause for concern.

Information learned from a digest for nothing but the purpose of an examination is no more than knowledge for knowledge's sake. Reading great literature is an opportunity to make connections with the spirits of outstanding writers and in this way to improve and broaden one's self for the sake of further development. Such spiritual improvement comes only from direct contact and cannot be obtained through digests. Although it may be possible to obtain much superficial information without actually reading great books, people who choose this path become spiritually shallow and biased.

Not only in literature, but in all other branches of learning as well, educators and students alike must make unceasing and diligent efforts to establish connections between compartmentalized learning and the totality of wisdom. Obviously, abuses in the educational system—such as excess emphasis on examinations—must be corrected. But, even if the system remains imperfect, as long as such efforts are made, students will grow into people of sufficient scale to transcend its faults. Such people will go beyond petty egoistic thinking to become total human beings who, while considering the whole of wisdom, relate their own lives to the fate of all mankind. I am firmly convinced that cultivating excellent human beings of this caliber is the true meaning of education.

Creativity: The Badge of Humanity   Creativity could be called the badge, or proof, of our humanity. Human beings are the only creatures capable of striving positively and dynamically, day after day, to create newer, higher values.

Creativity is the womb from which individuality is born. All humans are different. Each has a unique personality. But often the personality withers in the bud before it has a chance to come to full flower. In different terms, before coming into individual radiance personalities frequently freeze at the stage where they are characterized by mere idiosyncrasies. Creativity is a stimulus operating from within to thaw this imbalance and allow the personality to grow and bloom fully.

Creativity is a brilliant force rising from within. This is what Alfred North Whitehead (1861–1947) had in mind when, addressing a group of English students about to leave school in the devastation following World War I, he said they had all the essential sources of growth within themselves. Knowledge can be obtained from without, but creativity and imagination must be stimulated from within. Schools and other institutions of learning today seem to me to fail most sadly in stimulating and cultivating creativity.

Young people may be oriented toward good or evil. It is of primary importance for people concerned with education to believe in the creativity of each young person with whom they come in contact and to cultivate it warmly and persistently endeavor to bring it to vigorous bloom.

I do not deny that, in this case too, abuses in the system—such as being absorbed in acquiring the technique to pass examinations—constitute a great barrier to improvement. But it would be irresponsible to lay all the blame at the system's door, because exchange between human beings is the soil in which creativity grows. The creative life gushes forth fountainlike as a consequence of stimulation brought on by spiritual exchanges, sometimes severe, sometimes warm, between human beings who share complete trust, given with no thought of reward.

In this connection, I am reminded of a passage in the famous *Epistles,* in which Plato says of people who claim to understand the quintessence of his philosophy—which is projected against the background of what he himself learned from Socrates—as a result of hearing him or other teachers or through their own discoveries, "It is impossible, in my judgment at least, that these men should understand anything about this subject . . . . For it does not at all admit of verbal expression like other studies, but, as a result of continued application to the subject itself and communion therewith, it is brought to birth in the soul of a sudden, as a light that is kindled by a leaping spark, and thereafter it nourishes itself."

Plato's saying that this lofty spiritual subject is born in the soul suddenly, as light kindled by a leaping spark, and that it thereafter nourishes itself is highly pertinent to modern education. Recognizing each student as a unique personality and transmitting something, sparklike, through contacts with the instructor are more than a way of implanting knowledge: they are the root essence of education.

In certain parts of Japan, child education is called *koyarai,* a term that means allowing the child to stand on his own, out in front, while the parent or educator, pushes him from behind. According to the famous folklorist Kunio Yanagida (1875–1962), this is exactly the opposite of the modern educational tendency to stand in front of the child and attempt to pull him forward. The *koyarai* philosophy has something important to say to contemporary educational thought, which considers a child less than a complete, or mature, human being until he has completed a prescribed curriculum. Recognition in the field of anthropology of the three elements that modern civilization has overlooked—the primitive, the subconscious, and the childlike—is called one of the great discoveries of the twentieth century. Undeniably, education today stands at a turning point in relation to discovering children, in the sense of attempting to learn ways to recognize and appreciate the individual personalities of young people.

Educators must make the effort to call forth the creative powers latent in their students. In this undertaking, they require endurance, courage, and affection. To cultivate others, an educator must have a glowing, appealing personality. Socrates' powers to move others were once compared to the shock of a stinging ray. When told this, Socrates said that the ray stings others because he is stung himself. Similarly, the teacher himself must be constantly creative if he is to evoke creativity from his students. If he is not, all his talk of creativity will remain fruitless words.

There is nothing wrong with keeping in step with advances in the computer age by introducing all kinds of new equipment to make education more convenient and efficient. But no amount of equipment compensates for the absence of those old, but forever new, merits of effort, endurance, courage, and affection. When these things have become exhausted, the situation is very grave; and relying on the latest equipment to alleviate it is putting the cart before the horse.

International Outlook   In this age, when internationalization is accelerating throughout the world, the future of Japan can well be said to depend on the ability to cultivate capable people with truly international viewpoints.

For better or worse, Japan has become one of the economic leaders of the world, and, as recent trade friction demonstrates, what Japan does has an immense influence on what the world at large does. Henry Kissinger, whom I have met on several occasions, says history offers no reason why an economic superpower will not develop into a military superpower. From my own standpoint, however, no matter what past history may have been like, to continue to enjoy peace and prosperity, Japan must follow a course other than militarization. And, if that path has never before been trodden, Japan must be courageous and take pride in blazing it.

The path I speak of is that of a nation devoted to culture. As an outcome of my many private attempts and undertakings, I have come to see clearly that, although it may seem inconspicuous, mutual understanding achieved through cultural exchanges is very powerful.

An episode during the Russo-Japanese War of 1904–5 which I read about recently is pertinent to this topic. As the war was drawing to a close, Japan was looking about for a nation to serve as mediator between the two countries. In strict secret, the Japanese government dispatched two envoys: Kentaro Kaneko to the United States and Kencho Suematsu to England.

Perhaps to some extent because the two men had been classmates at Harvard, Kaneko was able to convince President Theodore Roosevelt to assist him. The president, however, asked Kaneko to give him information that would help him explain the Japanese viewpoint to the American people. Kaneko gave Roosevelt a copy of a book, written in English by Inazo Nitobe, called *Bushido, the Spirit of Japan,* in which the code of the warrior is explained as the basis of Japanese moral education. The president read the book in an evening, found it convincing, and agreed to serve as mediator between Japan and Russia.

Suematsu, on the other hand, attended English salons, where he spoke boastfully of Japan, a land as much on the way up as the rising sun—in other words, he used an approach similar to the contemporary insistence on such things as the gross national product—and was laughed at for his pains.

This episode illustrates the way in which culture, like that explained in Nitobe's book, can prove more influential than economic bragging. Unfortunately, after the Russo-Japanese War, Japan pursued a course of headlong militarization. And, today, we will find ourselves in a very dangerous predicament unless we strive to make culture the underpinning of our economic power.

To achieve this, the most important thing is educating people who are broadly cultivated and who have mastery of languages. Because this is now being realized, Japanese linguistic education, which has in the past been criticized as useless, is now, I am happy to say, being reappraised. I want to make it clear, however, that though an essential element, linguistic proficiency alone does not make a truly international person. As I have said, this requires broad cultivation, not only practical expertise in politics and economics, but also understanding of one's own culture and tradition and those of other peoples as well. Unlike the knowledge of what Yukichi Fukuzawa calls the "informed," the kind of cultivation I have in mind must be so deeply ingrained that it manifests itself in behavior and deportment. As T.S. Eliot says, culture is living. It is not a mere surface accretion but is acquired only when it has been bred into a person since childhood, like training in manners. Consequently, a nation devoted to culture must be a nation devoted to education.

In commenting on the need for what he called two-legged scholars, the great writer Ogai Mori (1862–1922) said, "I divide modern Japanese scholars into those with one and those with two legs. The new Japan is a whirlpool in which the cultures of the East and the West combine. Some scholars stand in the Eastern one and others in the Western one, but both kinds are one-legged. . . . The age needs scholars with two legs, one planted in each culture. Truly moderate debate is possible only with such people, who are the elements of harmony necessary at the present time."

The problem indicated here by Mori, who was himself a man of great cultivation in Japanese, Chinese, and Western cultures, remains unsolved to this day. I think we can expand his meaning of two-legged to represent not merely knowledge of the cultures of East and West, but also wide and well-balanced cultivation in general. Today, as internationalization continues to advance, we are in greater need of such necessary "elements of harmony" than the people of Mori's time.

In relation to the need for balance and harmony, I should like to mention something that has been on my mind recently. The attitude of the Japanese people toward their own traditions and the traditions of the rest of the world seems to me to have swung, pendulum-like, too wide and too fast in the last fifty years or so. Before World War II, when we were taught that Japan was a divine nation, total rejection of everything un-Japanese was taken for granted. Since World War II, on the other hand, Japanese tradition—even the best parts of it— has been despised and ignored. Recently, the pendulum seems to be swinging back in the opposite direction. If this change of attitude is part of an arrogance born of economic success, I am deeply afraid that it could lead Japan in a wrong direction. Rejection and adoration of the foreign are two sides of the same coin, and both indicate lack of self-confidence and independence. Vacillations and imbalance are the outcome of lack of self-confidence. People who persist in such a state can never be called truly international, no matter how much they may pretend to direct their view outward.

United Nations of Education

Economic and military power can breed arrogance but not self-confidence, which can be cultivated only through cultural development. This is why, in Japanese schools, I think it would be a good idea to place more stress on the proper use of the Japanese language and on the study of such aspects of our irreplaceable heritage as great literature and the traditional arts. Without mature knowledge of one's own language, foreign-language studies cannot produce the best results. From all that I have seen or heard, people who excel in international contacts are bright and appealing as Japanese personalities. Cultivation in one's own culture as well as in other cultures is what it takes to make a true cosmopolitan, and I think our institutions of learning ought to set the development of such international people as one of their goals.

Although, as I have said, I am no specialist, I have enumerated these three points—totality, creativity, and internationalization—because I think a profound understanding of them is essential to the reforms that must be made in our current educational system.

In addition, on the basis of a new interpretation of youth and its growth and development, I should like for all of us to join in the evolution of a new theory of education suited to the needs and circumstances of today.

Our own Soka Gakkai Education Division has a splendid tradition based on the work of our first and second presidents. First president Tsunesaburo Makiguchi, who had unrivaled enthusiasm for teaching, arranged his philosophy on its practice in a coolly scientific manner in his book *Jinsei Chirigaku* (The Geography of Human Life), and subsequently in his most significant work *Soka Kyoikugaku Taikei* (The System of Value-creating Pedagogy), compiled from random notes and jottings accumulated during the course of two decades of teaching at elementary schools. Second president Josei Toda was also an outstanding educator with abundant experience in public teaching and in the Jishu Gakkan, a private tutoring school he founded himself. He compiled his educational theories in a work entitled *Suirishiki Shido Sanjutsu* (Deductive Guide to Arithmetic).

Through meetings to report on actual experiences in teaching and educational research projects and the records of teaching activities, I expect our members to go on making further progress in this field and am certain that, as one ripple stimulates others, our educational activities will swell into a great tide sweeping into the twenty-first century.

I hope that next year, which, as you know, is designated as the United Nations "International Youth Year," young people with great vitality and creativity will engage in truly global contacts with others and will realize their mission as pioneers in the next century. The responsibility of educators in awakening youth to its mission is very heavy. In that connection, I should like to make the following concrete proposals.

World Council of Educators

First, I propose that next year, in Hawaii (or possibly Hiroshima), we sponsor the first world council of educators, during which educators and their representatives from all nations would come together to hold significant discussions of present educational conditions and attempt to work out the optimum educational system for the future.

For some time now I have enthusiastically advocated the establishment of a United Nations of Education. This is why I tentatively suggest that the first world council of educators be entitled a Conference of Educators for Deliberation on the Formation of a United Nations of Education. An organization of this kind, which would represent a pooling of the wisdom of the ordinary people of the world, is urgently needed now, especially in the light of the many problems facing the United Nations Educational, Scientific, and Cultural Organization (UNESCO).

Because of the complications and difficulties involved in organizing such a conference, it will no doubt be necessary to set up preparatory organizations in Europe and Asia to study regional and local conditions. The project will take time, but we must address ourselves to its perhaps slow but sure accomplishment.

I further propose that the world council of educators adopt a declaration concerning education in the twenty-first century. The document should be the outcome of the most thorough discussions possible of what future education should be like in terms of both the individual human being and all humanity. Gradually obtaining a widening circle of endorsement of its principle as a consequence of the efforts of educators in all regions will stimulate global educational unity and further enhance the vitality of young people everywhere.

International Exchange Program

As the founder of Soka University, I have traveled all over the world meeting educators and discussing problems with them. I intend to go on doing the same kind of work, and, to amplify my efforts and make them effective on many levels, I request even greater effort and cooperation on the part of teachers and educators. A group teaching social sciences at Soka Gakuen schools recently visited China, where they traveled to the Dunhuang caves and many other parts of the country, enjoying meaningful exchanges with Chinese educators. Some members of the Education Division have done similar work in China and the Soviet Union, and many of them have traveled to America, Europe, and Southeast Asia on related missions. In the future, I hope exchanges of this kind will be made on the widest possible scale and with the greatest possible depth.

In the future, I should like to hold discussions with teachers on the possibility of sending peace delegations of boys and girls to various parts of the world. Young people have many years ahead of them. And stimulating them to make friends with other peoples all over the world will augur well for a brighter future for mankind.

In addition, I am entertaining the possibility of instituting the Soka Education Prize to recognize great achievements for the improvement of human education.

Youth must bear the burden of the future. But it is the teachers who must open the doors of the life force of the young. Whether young people will prove vigorous enough to revolutionize our age depends on the attitudes of the men and women who educate them. Teachers' ways of thinking influence the actions of parents and society. I hope teachers will ensure that their efforts have the very best influence by always carrying out their work with courage, enthusiasm, and compassion.

~~~

New Waves of Peace Toward
the Twenty-first Century

*A Proposal Commemorating the Tenth Soka Gakkai
International Day, January 26, 1985.*

~~~

Pooling the People's Power to Eliminate Nuclear Arms

January 26, 1975, a day that deserves lasting commemoration in the history of our work to carry the teachings of True Buddhism to the whole world, was the occasion on which, in the presence of Nichiren Shoshu Sixty-sixth High Priest Nittatsu Shonin, at the World Peace Conference held on Guam, Soka Gakkai International (SGI) was founded. The hard work and unflagging activity of more than one hundred fifty modest representatives from fifty-one countries present that day have made it possible to achieve the flourishing growth we see today in our international organization.

The historic Fourth World Peace Culture Festival, held at the Hanshin Koshien Baseball Stadium in the Kansai area in September of last year, drew participants from fifty-five countries and two territories of the world. This brilliant event was a milestone marking the advent of a new era for SGI and a fitting tribute to round out its tenth year.

With the support and good wishes of fellow believers all over the world during the decade since the founding of SGI, I have traveled extensively, holding conferences with many people in positions of leadership and, to my great happiness, as the founder of Soka University, calling on educators in many of the most important educational institutions of the world: Columbia University, the University of Chicago, and the University of Hawaii in the United States; Moscow State University in the Soviet Union; Beijing University, Wuhan University, and Fudan University in China; the Chinese University of Hong Kong; the University of Paris IV (Paris-Sorbonne) in France; the University of Sofia in Bulgaria; the University of Bucharest in Rumania; Complutense University in Madrid in Spain; Delhi University, Jawaharlal Nehru University, and Rabindra Bharati University in India; the University of Brasilia in Brazil; the National Autonomous University of Mexico and the University of Guadalajara in Mexico; the National University of San Marcos in Peru; and the University of Panama. I took delight in the exchanges these visits made possible, since I am confident that mutual relations among human beings with profound interest in education and culture are the true foundation of lasting peace. The numerous honorary doctorates and professorships conferred on me by these institutions are less honors for me personally than recognition for the educational, cultural, and peace activities of SGI.

I should like to express my sincere respect for the immense devotion our members in all parts of the world have shown to their mission in the past ten years. At the same time, I hope that the next ten years will see further strengthening of the roots of our resolute movement in the name of peace and that, with January 26, 2001 as a goal, we will persevere in vigorous activity that will be engraved in the history of *kosen-rufu*.

SGI and the Peace-making Role of Nongovernmental Organizations

On the occasion of this tenth anniversary, I should like to reiterate some of the basic policies of SGI.

1.   As good citizens, the members of Soka Gakkai International

resolve to contribute to the prosperity of our respective societies and countries, while respecting their individual cultures, customs, and laws.

2.   The members of Soka Gakkai International resolve to aim for the realization of eternal peace and the prosperity of humanistic culture and education, based on the Buddhism of Nichiren Daishonin, which clearly defines the dignity of human life.

3.   The members of Soka Gakkai International resolve to contribute to the happiness of humankind and the prosperity of the world, while strongly denying war and violence of any kind; to support the spirit of the Charter of the United Nations; and to make positive steps toward cooperating with its endeavor to keep world peace, with the abolition of nuclear weapons and the realization of a warless world as the supreme purpose.

The realization of the goal of a warless world demands uniting the masses of the whole globe. To contribute to its achievement, with the cooperation of the United Nations and the cities of Hiroshima and Nagasaki, since 1982 the Soka Gakkai Youth Division has been sponsoring an exhibition entitled "Nuclear Arms: Threat to Our World," in the hope of consolidating the will of all people to oppose nuclear war and work for the abolition of nuclear weapons.

Realizing that easing of tensions in Europe is an urgent part of peace for the world, the year before last we sponsored this exhibition in such cities as Geneva, Vienna, and Paris. Last year it was shown in Stockholm, Helsinki, Oslo, and Bergen. This year it is being held in West Berlin. Wherever it has gone, it has aroused tremendous response. Fully aware of its significance, I intend to give the exhibition the greatest possible support.

The exhibition started with a showing at United Nations Headquarters in New York on the occasion of the Second Special Session of the General Assembly on Disarmament, in June 1982. At that time, UN Secretary-General Javier Pérez de Cuéllar said he wished every ambassador, minister, and diplomat attending the conference would see it. I hope that it can be shown at the Third Special Session of the United Nations General Assembly on Disarmament and serve further to stimulate public opinion against nuclear arms.

Since its first showing, the exhibit has been in wide demand and has toured many parts of the world. It has been highly regarded by people connected with the United Nations, intellectuals, and workers for peace everywhere. In the future, as part of the World Disarmament Campaign, it is scheduled to be shown in such socialist countries as China and the nations of the Soviet bloc and in such Third World countries as Kenya.

The exhibit does more than merely stimulate world opinion: it clearly points up the importance of the role of private groups and nongovernmental organizations (NGOs) in all future work for peace. As a valuable example of successful cooperation between NGOs and the United Nations, the exhibition is especially significant for the way it accords completely with the ideals of the United Nations Charter, which stresses the will for peace shared by ordinary people everywhere. I hope that, as an NGO of the United Nations, in the future SGI will be active not only in exhibitions of this kind but also in many other activities connected with global issues.

The proposals I made to the First and Second Special Sessions of the United Nations General Assembly on Disarmament and the abolition of nuclear weapons represent my desires as a man of religion and express my hope, as leader of SGI, to protect and support the United Nations.

Still another phase of our work for peace is the holding of disarmament seminars representing a coming together of the wisdom of many people as groups of our members engage in exchanges with leaders concerned with peace and disarmament. For example, last year, such an exchange was made between our representatives and Prime Minister Olof Palme of Sweden, chairman of the Palme Commission (Independent Commission on Disarmament and Security Issues).

Another field in which I hope SGI will play a prominent, helpful role is refugee relief. I am deeply moved by the shocking recent reports of dire famine in Africa. The year before last, in September, when I met Mr. Poul Hartling, United Nations High Commissioner for Refugees (UNHCR), I told him that, in Buddhist terminology, UNHCR's efforts in protecting human life are part of the work of the bodhisattvas and as such deserve the highest respect. It is impossible to overlook the importance of aiding refugees as a positive way of working for peace by protecting human rights.

Last year, the Soka Gakkai Youth Peace Conference conducted a fund-raising campaign to aid famine-stricken African refugees and was able to present to the UNHCR about 150 million yen (about 577,000 U.S. dollars). Starting in 1973, Soka Gakkai has conducted seven refugee-relief fund drives, raising a total of 431 million yen (about 1,658,000 U.S. dollars); has sent representatives to refugee camps in Indochina, Afghanistan, and Africa four times; and has participated in the International Conference on Assistance to Refugees in Africa (ICARA). Hereafter, we shall go on taking part in work of this kind, which is a fundamental expression of a desire to protect the dignity of humanity.

Proposals for Peace

This year marks the tenth anniversary of the founding of SGI, the twenty-fifth year since I began my journeys for world peace, and the fifty-fifth year since the founding of Soka Gakkai. I should like to take advantage of the opportunity the occasion presents to make a few proposals.

Like many others, I have the greatest interest in the resumption of disarmament talks between the United States and the Soviet Union that has taken place in this important fortieth year after the conclusion of World War II. Last year, on the ninth annual SGI Day, I made a proposal for a wide-reaching movement to rid the world of war, expressed deep concern over the continuing tension between the Soviet Union and the United States, and advocated the conclusion of an agreement prohibiting the deployment of weapons or the use of force either on, or directed toward, Earth from outer space. Feeling this way, I openly welcome recent conferences between the foreign ministers of the two nations and the resumption of arms talks. Though we cannot predict their outcome, we must be glad that discussions with the elimination of nuclear arms as their ultimate goal have resumed.

Two years ago, on the eighth annual SGI Day, I urged an immediate summit meeting between the top leaders of the United States and the Soviet Union because I believed that, from such an encounter, made possible by surmounting the difficulties between the two parties, bold thoughts and actions could break through the impasse then prevailing between them, and could lead to further courageous decisions. This year, too, as a citizen ardently longing for peace, I urge such a summit meeting, at the earliest possible date, because it would be an opportunity both to put a stop to the overall arms race between the great powers and to take a big step toward nonmilitarization of outer space. Past disarmament conferences have repeatedly ended in failure; and it is my great fear that, if the present ones drag on to a great length, militarization of outer space will become an established fact. A summit meeting is essential if this is to be prevented.

Exchange of opinions between their top leaders is the best way to eliminate the deep-rooted distrust that exists between the two nations. And, in the long view, removing this distrust can become an indirect cause leading to disarmament and serving as an important key to the achievement of global peace.

Certainly the road to disarmament is long and rocky. Nor does the far-from-successful course of past arms negotiations inspire unmitigated optimism. Nonetheless, the road must be followed. And, in this connection, I suggest that we all keep in mind the following lines by the famous Indian poet Sir Rabindranath Tagore:

> Asks the Possible to the Impossible,
> "Where is your dwelling-place?"
> "In the dreams of the impotent,"
> Comes the answer.
>   *(Stray Birds)*

Human hands produced nuclear weapons and weaponry systems, and human hands should be able to reduce and eliminate them. If we stand idle and fail in this, we will rob future generations of their dreams and earn from future generations the dishonorable epithet of "the impotent." But even more horrendous, given the total-destruction capabilities of contemporary weapons, we could rob future generations not only of their dreams, but also of their very existence.

In his *Giving Up the Gun; Japan's Reversion to the Sword, 1543–1879*, Dartmouth College professor Noel Perrin has several thought-provoking points to make.

During the half century from the late sixteenth to the early seventeenth century after the famous warlord Oda Nobunaga's victory at the battle of Nagashino in 1575, the use of firearms was at its height in Japan. Both in technological quality and in absolute numbers, guns were almost certainly more common in Japan at that time than in any other country in the world. For centuries thereafter, however, throughout the Tokugawa period (1603–1867), the warrior class "chose to give up an advanced weapon and to return to a more primitive one," in spite of the greater killing power of the former. That is to say, they rejected the rifle and returned to the sword. And from that time onward, the quantity and quality of guns used in Japan dropped sharply.

Professor Perrin gives a number of reasons for this reversal. One of the most arresting is the nature of the sword as a symbol of the human spirit and of morality. In other words, the Japanese based their choices of weapons on what could be called purely internal aesthetic awareness. As a consequence, Edo (modern Tokyo), which had the largest population of any city in the world at the time, gradually and peacefully developed a high level of technology in waterworks, sanitation, and transportation systems, while the manufacture of firearms moved from controlled production to such a state of reduction that, by the middle of the nineteenth century, most people had entirely forgotten how to use guns.

Saying "The Japanese did practice selective control," Perrin evolves two precepts that the Japanese experience proves. First, a no-growth economy is perfectly compatible with prosperous and civilized life. Second, human beings are less the passive victims of their own knowledge and skills than most men in the West suppose.

The second point offers especially encouraging hope in promoting contemporary disarmament negotiations. Of course, there is no exact analogy between the world's present dilemma about nuclear weapons and the geopolitical conditions that enabled the Tokugawa shogunate to adopt a seclusion policy and to maintain largely peaceful control over the country from the seventeenth to the nineteenth century.

Nonetheless, making their choice on the basis of internal, spontaneous motives of moral and aesthetic considerations instead of on efficiency of weapon performance alone, the Japanese people of that time were virtually able to abolish firearms. Their success in this strikes a bitter blow against passive and pessimistic modern views that what is done is done and is irreparable. In particular, it is my desire that, confiding in the voluntary strength of the people to change existing circumstances, the leaders of the United States and the Soviet Union will sit at the same table and have a frank exchange of opinions as soon as possible.

Peace Culture Festivals

During this year, which the United Nations has designated International Youth Year (IYY), the role that young people can play in fostering the cause of world peace will be spotlighted. In Honolulu and Hiroshima, Soka Gakkai plans to hold World Youth Peace Culture Festivals. Both already have the support of the United Nations as an undertaking planned to contribute to the success of IYY. In the past, the members of SGI have held an international festival once a year in the name of world peace. This year, in connection with the tenth anniversary of the founding of our organization and with the twenty-fifth anniversary of our early attempts to carry the Buddhist message to the whole world, they will participate in two festivals. Hiroshima was chosen as a venue partly to commemorate the fortieth anniversary of the atomic bombing and partly to stimulate in that city a concentration of power for the global elimination of nuclear arms.

Parallel with the peace festival, the first World Council of Educators is scheduled to take place in Hiroshima. Through events of this kind, together with independently sponsored local culture festivals, we intend to concentrate the energy of all peoples who are eager for lasting peace. The only way to achieve this end is to start at home. Dots must be connected to form lines, and lines expanded to cover whole surfaces until peace reaches every corner of the globe.

French sociologist Roger Caillois concludes his famous book *Bellone ou la pente de la guerre* (The Descent to War) with the following comment: "Humanity has produced a great mechanism to serve the needs of mankind. While serving, however, that mechanism demands obedience from humanity. All thinking people must become aware of the evil in such a situation. When we try to see things in their fundamental meanings and attempt to do something about it, we find that the problem is extremely subtle and virtually limitless. But, in essence, it is a human problem, a solution to which must be found first in human education. No matter how long it takes, this is, in my view, the only way to restore to its proper functioning a world in which education has become perilously faulty. Still, I become terrified when I think that, proceeding at our current lagging pace, we must somehow overtake the rapidly advancing danger of absolute war."

Although his view is somewhat pessimistic, I consider his comments about seeing things in their fundamental meaning and about finding a solution first in human education very important. And, though it may sound a little like blowing our own horn, I am confident that, through our various peace and culture festivals, we are helping to create a new style of education. I cannot suppress my excitement and hope for the peace of the twenty-first century when I see our young people growing and developing as they pool their energy and strength in the difficult work of preparing and presenting those festivals. Nothing can be a stronger force for peace than the confidence these young people, and all human beings for that matter, cultivate by facing and overcoming difficulties.

On a slightly different level, I place great hope in the Third Special Session of the United Nations General Assembly on Disarmament. Of course, the groundwork for the meeting must be carefully laid, and preparations must embody sincere, earnest reflection on the experiences of the preceding two UN special sessions. The primary importance of the meeting is as a challenge from the ordinary people to reverse the current worldwide trend toward increasing militarization and to ease dangerous international tensions. Next year, which has been designated the International Year of Peace by the United Nations, will be especially significant as the time when preparations for that third special session must be made.

In connection with this special session, I place great stress on the need to declare a comprehensive nuclear test ban because the halt this would cause in weapons research would be a revolutionary step in the direction of the elimination of nuclear armaments.

An Age of Asia and the Pacific

Since, at present, Asia and the Pacific zone are being closely observed everywhere, I believe that, as we stand looking toward the twenty-first century from the vantage point of the fortieth anniversary of the conclusion of World War II, how peace is to be achieved in this part of the world is of special importance.

Obviously, the conflict between the Soviet Union and the United States is a matter of the greatest concern to the peace of the Asian region. Both of these superpowers have recently shifted strategic emphasis to this part of the world and, lamentably, with nuclear weapons positioned in the Pacific, glare at each other. This is an immense threat. And, if the current situation continues, Asia could well become a bigger stage of Soviet-American confrontation than Europe has been. It would be especially dangerous and foolish should Japan be drawn into this conflict.

Currently, a mood of dialogue among the Asian nations is gaining impetus. I am especially glad to see the movement in this direction represented by recent attempts to improve contacts between North and South Korea, regions considered especially perilous tinderboxes. Efforts to ease tensions between the two Koreas is highly encouraging for all people who wish for peace. But I fear that strategic emphasis placed on the Asian region by the United States and the Soviet Union could have negative effects on this and other similar movements.

In June of last year, during my sixth visit to China, when I met Chinese Communist Party Secretary General Hu Yaobang, because I was especially concerned about the matter, I inquired about the possibilities of peace between North and South Korea. Hu Yaobang shared the Chinese view on the subject with me. As I said, in mentioning the possibilities of resolving tensions between the United States and the Soviet Union, in this instance too, it is essential for the top-ranking leaders of the two Koreas to come together in a summit conference. I am certain that this is what their peoples want and that such a meeting would have immeasurable significance for reducing the tension between them.

Though the Olympics have been made unstable because of excessive political influence, the 1988 Olympics in Seoul—the second Asian city after Tokyo ever to host the games—will be of no small importance. From ancient times, the Olympics have been regarded as a festival of peace, an opportunity for young people from all parts of the world to try their skills and abilities, and a gathering place for mutual exchanges among peoples. All of Asia will welcome the easing of tensions that can be generated by the Seoul Olympic Games, which I confidently trust will be important to peace throughout this part of the world.

Recognition of the vigor and vitality of the Asian nations and of their latent power has made current the idea of a coming Age of Asia and the Pacific and the concept of pan-Pacific cooperation. Twenty years ago, the gross national product (GNP) of Asia, including Japan, amounted to no more than one-tenth that of the world. Today, valued at two trillion dollars, it is twenty percent of the world total and is likely to grow more and more as we approach the end of the century. At present, interest in Asia is mainly economic, and in the future too the amount of trade conducted in this part of the world is likely to increase dynamically.

Deepening ties of economic cooperation and mutual interreliance throughout the area is in itself excellent. But, as history proves, when economic factors alone are taken into consideration, conflicts of interest produce friction among nations. When this happens, the idea of a Pacific Age will remain no more than pie in the sky. We Japanese must remember that, because of the horror of World War II, many nations of Asia are deeply worried by the idea that Japan might once again become a great military power. Even though we have become an economic power, if we fail to take their fears on this issue into consideration, we will be unable to evaluate our role accurately.

Human relations and mutual respect among different cultures must be the basis on which the Pacific Age is built. This indeed will be its historical significance. In 1970, during our more than ten hours of dialogue and exchange, Richard E. Coudenhove-Kalergi, founder of the European Community, told me that Japan must first exert maximum effort for world peace and then work for the creation of the Pacific civilization of tomorrow. He added that he felt the world is now in a transitional phase and that Japan must take the leadership in the shift of emphasis from the Western civilization of Europe and the United States to a new civilization centered in the Pacific region. He further insisted that Japan has been given the important mission of leader and principal player in this transition.

On the basis of his own distinctive interpretation of history, the late Arnold J. Toynbee, with whom I spoke on close terms on several occasions, foresaw the coming of a Pacific Age and expressed opinions similar to those of Coudenhove-Kalergi. In my frank opinion, both of these men were groping for a way to explain the open and peaceful civilization that they envisioned as characteristic of the Pacific Age.

In December 1984, during discussions I was privileged to participate in, the Norwegian authority on peace research and the rector of the New Transnational University in Paris, John Galtung mentioned his particular interest in the role religion can play in bringing peace to the world today. As we talked of Christianity, Islam, Buddhism, and Marxism, I suggested that, in connection with the human longing for peace, Buddhism, with its spiritual basis of compassion and tolerance and denial of war and violence, is especially valuable.

All three of these Western intellectuals—Coudenhove-Kalergi, Toynbee, and Galtung—demonstrated the greatest interest in the interior world of the oriental spiritual heritage. When, with the argument of force, the Europeans invaded and colonized in the nineteenth century, the nations of Asia were living in relative peace and respected each other's cultures. Asia gave wealth, art, and culture to Europe, whereas, from the age of the great navigators, Europe used force to victimize Asia. Today, when the limitations of the world's natural resources are evident and when peaceful coexistence is indispensable, Western intellectuals are becoming profoundly aware that peaceful coexistence should replace force and domination in order to save the world from the threatening crisis. The time has come to understand thoroughly that the approach to the creation of a Pacific, or an Asian, Age must not lean too far in the direction of politics, arms, or economics, but must instead include ample consideration of the oriental spiritual world, which constitutes the wisdom of the Orient.

Sino-Japanese Amity Is Essential

My mentor and the second president of Soka Gakkai, Josei Toda, often expressed his belief that China would play an important role in future world history. He was deeply concerned about the welfare and happiness of the peoples of all Asian nations, most of which now have, or at one time had, connections with Buddhism, and publicly stated his interpretations of the Korean War, which was taking place at the time.

During my visit to China last year—when I had an opportunity to meet Deng Yinchao, widow of the late Premier Zhou Enlai—Wong Zhen, honorary president of the China-Japan Friendship Association, presented me with a copy of the Sutra of the Lotus of the Mystic Law. In expressing my personal thanks, I attempted to include some of Josei Toda's profound interest in China by saying, "Your country is our benefactor because it was through China that Buddhism reached Japan."

In many of my own writings I have dealt with Asia and with ways of making peace grow and thrive in our part of the world.

In September 1968, I proposed the restoration of diplomatic ties with China. At that time, both Japan and the United States regarded China with animosity. And, in this prevailing mood, China remained isolated from many countries. Nonetheless, I advocated the resumption of relations and on three occasions thereafter delivered addresses and greetings at Beijing and Fudan universities and spoke on, among other things, the contributions Chinese civilization can make to world peace.

In urging the restoration of diplomatic ties, I had in mind the peace and stability of all Asia, in the achievement of which the roles of both China and Japan are extremely great. My approach to the issue was this: first, China and Japan must establish enduring ties of amity, then, sharing the work with other Asian nations, the two of them must take the initiative in creating peace in Asia. Because this is my fundamental philosophy on the issue, though it may sound audacious, I was the early flag-bearer in restoring diplomatic ties between China and Japan. This was why I traveled to China on six occasions, exerting utmost efforts to promote friendly relations with leaders and ordinary people alike. Moreover, in connection with my desire for peace in Asia, I made several goodwill trips to the Soviet Union to establish amicable exchanges.

But peace must be absolutely unrelated to force, neither economic nor, much less, military. Peace hiding behind force is no peace at all. We must never forget that the other nations of Asia look with considerable mistrust on a very powerful China or a very powerful Japan, even though they both may strive to be peacemakers.

Last year, on a trip to China, I made a speech entitled "The Royal Road to Peace—A Personal Observation" at Beijing University. In it, I said, "If we take the overall view, we cannot fail to be strongly impressed by the way China has, on the whole, honored *wen,* or civil virtues, over *wu,* or military ones." And I observed that in the case of China, with the exception of certain atypical periods, attention to civil virtues and ideals has been the principal motivating force in the nation's history. Further, I tried to discover the force or strength that allows individuals or nations to control brute impulses and master and restrain disruptive instincts.

Of course, choices of leaders and people will determine the path China travels in the future. But, on the basis of my own encounters and experiences there, I can say that China is now engaged in changes and progress all undertaken with the twenty-first century in mind. It is my frank impression that, in order to feed its billion people, China must stimulate economic growth, and therefore, abandoning the great-nation posture, will pursue peace. Moreover, the Chinese realize that their modernization for the next century requires a peaceful international environment. It is because I prize their eagerness for peace and want to make it known to people everywhere that I have requested the leaders in Beijing to allow the showing of our exhibition entitled "Nuclear Arms: Threat to Our World" in their city. They have agreed.

The most historically significant aspect of the Asia-Pacific Age will be the way it abandons control by the power of authority and arms in favor of control by culture and humanity. Long ago, I defined culture as something that leads the masses to happiness without the use of authority or arms. Whether it is possible to make all concepts converge in agreement on this one point is the key to the creation of a new Asia-Pacific Age. The civilization of that age must be "of the people, by the people, and for the people."

It is impossible in this limited space to explain Japan fully in relation to the rest of Asia. Nevertheless, I should like to mention one point that my meetings with people in various Asian nations and my other experiences convinced me the Japanese must keep in mind. It may sound trite, but the point is this: understand the heart of Asia. Unless we Japanese understand how other Asian peoples feel and think, we cannot play the role we must in making the twenty-first a better century. And this must begin with a recognition that all cultures—languages, life styles, customs, histories, traditions, and so on—are on a footing of perfect equality. A feeling of oneness and trust is born from mutual respect for each other's cultures and from sincere, open exchanges among hearts and minds.

Exchanges in Education and Culture

All cultures have different histories and have developed in distinctive ways. Our understanding of another culture is in most cases superficial. To understand the complexities behind what we know of other cultures requires a kind of compound eye making possible a wide, inclusive view of many factors and the willingness always to put oneself in the other party's position.

My own travels throughout the world have convinced me that, as long as this attitude is assumed, it is possible to find things in common with all peoples everywhere. This is why, recognizing the great importance of exchanges in learning, culture, and education, I have engaged in open discussions transcending national boundaries with many different peoples of many different historical backgrounds and various manners and mores. Unfortunately, however, although Japan is an economic power, the Japanese themselves are little respected in this part of the world because too many of them fail to understand the mind and hearts of other Asian peoples.

Though I speak in terms of Asia, the region is actually composed of extremely diverse and varied component nations and peoples with many different problems that cannot all be resolved in one way. Each nation has its own difficult decisions to make. Each has its own coordinates of internal development and growth, and it is perilous to try to set one model for all.

In an earlier work, I said that I felt peace and prosperity in Asia depended on the interrelations between tradition and modernization. In April of last year, Natth Bamarapravati, rector of Mahidol University in Thailand, visited Taiseki-ji, the head temple of Nichiren Shoshu, and expressed the opinion that Soka Gakkai has succeeded and grown because of the way in which it has been able to harmonize Buddhism and modernism. In our subsequent discussion of modernization and tradition in general, I said I felt tradition should be a light shining within the process of modernization and that, to enable it to serve this purpose, international exchanges are extremely imporant.

I am fully aware of the danger of trying to impose a model of modernization on development in all Asian nations. Resting largely on heavy and chemical industries, the modernization of Western nations does not necessarily fit the diversity and variety of the Asian scene. All Asian nations now face the problem of reconciling tradition with modernization. Japan's trial-and-error struggle with this same issue since the middle of the nineteenth century has produced both good and bad results. But the Japanese experience can be of considerable instructive value to other nations.

Of course, other Asian nations place great expectations on Japanese economic power. But, in the future, instead of limiting ourselves to cooperation in the field of economy or to exchanges and transferrals of technology alone, we must institute a free, open, multilevel system of cooperation extending to cultural and educational fields and centering on the training of the best possible personnel. This will make economic cooperation all the more effective.

In the past, I have traveled throughout the region making private-level exchanges on education and culture with leaders and with ordinary citizens. In the future, I intend to expand these efforts still further in the hope of acquiring an even deeper understanding of the way the minds and hearts of other Asian peoples work.

I am happy to say that yearly the numbers of students from other parts of Asia who attend Soka University—an institution founded on the spirit of the slogan "Be a fortress protecting the peace of humanity"—increase. I have expressed to the university authorities my desire that as many as possible of the members of the generations who must bear the responsibility of the future come to our country, learn something about Japan, and return to become leaders in their own nations.

Nothing inspires as much hope for the future peace and prosperity of Asia as exchanges among the young people of today. Perhaps my generation cannot achieve the goal, but we hope to pass on the will to attain it to those who come after us. We are now preparing to open the Soka University campus in San Diego, California, and have already opened the Soka University European Linguistic Center near Paris. For the sake of the future, I propose building a similar Soka University branch somewhere in Asia where young people from other Asian lands may study the Japanese language and culture and where Japanese students may do research on other regions. I believe such an institution would truly be a cultural fortress protecting the peace of Asia.

Beginning in the summer of last year, the music-promotion organization known as the Min-On Concert Association (Min-On) initiated a series called "A Musical Voyage Along the Marine Road," which is highly interesting in that it promotes cultural exchange, introduces the music and dance of Southeast Asia, and attempts to trace the influences on Japanese culture of civilizations along the marine route that was once as important a sea route linking the nations of Southern Asia as the Silk Road was a land route. The first in the series was "Brilliant Dances from Thailand and Okinawa."

This year has witnessed the fourth in Min-On's series "A Musical Voyage Along the Silk Road," which featured a joint performance by representatives of China, the Soviet Union, Turkey, and Japan. The gathering and performing together in Japan of musicians and dancers from these countries was an event of great significance. To date, ten nations have cooperated by allowing research teams to investigate their music and by sending performers to Japan for the

Silk Road series: China, Mongolia, India, Pakistan, Nepal, Iraq, Afghanistan, Rumania, the Soviet Union, and Turkey.

In 1975, in a commemorative address entitled "A New Road to East-West Cultural Exchanges," which I delivered at Moscow State University, I said, "At no time in history has there been so great a need as there is now for a spiritual Silk Road, extending through all the cultural spheres of the globe, transcending national and ideological barriers, and binding together all peoples at the basic level." In that address, I further expressed a wish for a new spiritual Silk Road binding together not only East and West, but also North and South. I am delighted that, though on a small scale, Min-On is doing something to make that wish come true.

The Cultural Richness and Diversity of the World

At present, in economic terms, the world is roughly divided into the industrialized North and the developing South. But this division does not necessarily accurately reflect cultural superiority and inferiority. Among the developing nations are those whose cultural achievements rank among the most important aspects of the heritage of all humanity. In terms, not of economy alone, but of such things as art and literature, the world is astonishingly diverse and much too complex and rich to be divided simply into North and South.

True cultural exchanges stimulate mutual respect among peoples of different races and cultural backgrounds and create ties of peace among the hearts of human beings. As its founder, I hope Min-On will further advance its work in cultural and artistic exchanges and in this way set up a milestone on the road to the creation of a world without war.

There can be no lasting peace in Asia unless the people of each Asian nation independently assure their own individual peace and prosperity. But Asian problems cannot be solved outside a frame of reference including Europe and all other regions of the globe. Furthermore, for the sake of finding solutions to the problems facing humanity, the ordinary peoples of all nations must unite in a spontaneous, dynamic movement that will ultimately result in a green and flowering path of peace extending from Asia to the whole world.

Only fifteen years remain until the year 2000. Twice in the first half of this century, the nations of the world have experienced the tragedy of global war and still have not shaken off the curse of conflict and distrust. The time has come for all peoples to pool their strength and change the current from one of fear and conflict to one of mutual understanding, trust, and peace.

Always Young and
Always Eager To Learn

Founder's Message, Delivered at the Eleventh Graduation Ceremony of Soka University, held at Hachioji, March 20, 1985.

Let me begin by extending my sincerest congratulations to all of you on your graduation and my deepest thanks to the faculty and staff of the university, all of your family members, and our distinguished guests, who have braved the cold to be with us today.

In his speech, delivered earlier, Professor Yamaguchi mentioned the way people who have just finished university education begin their new jobs with simple but essential tasks. For instance, the new employee at the National Railways may be assigned the duties of a ticket taker, and the novice in a bank may be required to count bills. These comments are both important and pertinent to the two points I should like to bring to the attention of you young people about to face the severity of modern society.

The first point is the significance of living fully in each passing moment. No one who takes the weak attitude of shirking the problems he encounters in his current course or of passing responsibilities on to others can expect to triumph in the harsh realities of a highly competitive world.

The American philosopher Ralph Waldo Emerson has something to say that has a bearing on my meaning. He remarks that the roses blooming under his window do not refer to their predecessors or superiors but are content to manifest their own characteristics. Roses are active, not only when in full bloom, but also before buds and leaves appear and, in their roots, after all foliage has fallen. It is the nature of the rose to find its own satisfaction and to bring satisfaction to nature in each instant of its life.

Unlike the rose, human beings reminisce, long for the past, and refuse to live in the present. Or, failing to realize the treasures surrounding them, they attempt to dwell in the future. But, Emerson goes on, unless, together with nature, human beings live in the present they cannot become happy and strong.

Undeniably, there is a tendency among many people today to attempt to escape from the issues facing them because of the stifling, imperfect nature of our oversupervised society. But ultimately, such escapism leads to defeat and the abandoning of the idea of living itself. We Japanese are said to be especially self-indulgent in this respect. It is my hope that all of you will rid yourselves of such attitudes if you have them, and starting today, resolve always to be willing to face the problems of the present. Whether you can spend your lives realizing that everything surrounding you is, as Emerson says, treasure, depends on your own attitude.

My second point is an exhortation to be strict with yourselves and lenient towards others. The general human tendency to go easy on oneself and hard on others hinders the formation of bright, open human relations. During your college careers, to an extent at any rate, you have been able to choose compatible and pleasant associates. In society, however, you will be forced to come together daily with seniors and colleagues who may be less attractive. Under such circumstances, for the sake of good human relations, being hard on yourself and indulgent of others becomes all the more important.

Mahatma Gandhi went through the great drama of his life wearing what might be called glasses that diminished the faults of others and magnified those of the self. I am convinced that this desire to forgive and minimize others' failings while strictly judging one's own is one of the major elements accounting for Gandhi's still persisting fame.

You are now setting out on a life extending far into the future. It is my hope that you will be as sharp with yourselves as the autumn frost, while, as warm as the spring breezes with others, you smilingly create growing circles of rich and meaningful human relations and expand your worlds to the maximum.

The Austrian-born British philosopher Ludwig Wittgenstein (1889–1951), became famous with the publication, in 1922, of his book *Tractatus Logico-Philosophicus,* which was actually an expansion of notes on reflections made while the author dashed about in the front lines of the battlefields of World War I. In other words, as he physically wandered between life and death on the battlefield, his inner being was constantly engaged in research in the meaning of human existence. To his truly important pursuits, it made no difference whether he was surrounded by the scenes of war or the calm of the university classroom.

In Wittgenstein's achievement I sense the kind of youthful life force associated with people who remain in their prime into old age, who are always creative, and who are prepared to make everything they do part of an extended course of education. It is my fondest wish that, no matter what field of endeavor you select, all of you will be victorious in your use of the precious gift of life, be forever young and willing to learn, and always bear Soka University in your hearts and minds wherever you go.

Cool-headed and Warm-hearted

Founder's Message, Delivered at the Fifteenth Matriculation Ceremonies of Soka University, held at Hachioji, April 7, 1985.

First I should like to express my gratitude to all of you for having chosen our university as your place of study. Next I should like to request University President Takamatsu and the entire faculty to do their utmost in the training of these young people, who may well be towering leaders of the future.

To all of you students, I should like to stress the importance of study and to tell you never to forget that learning is the great purpose of your university life. The earlier comments of Professor Takano, head of the Department of Education, on the proper attitude toward learning, which I heard with the greatest interest, are related to what I have to say.

Unfortunately, among the many university graduates in my acquaintance not a small number make me doubt that they have actually completed a course in an institution of higher learning. I do not want any of you to stop at the kind of shallow learning such people demonstrate. Their associates look down on persons who, though university graduates, lack the power of knowledge. Winning and losing determine much in society and the world, where people without the power of knowledge are unqualified to be winners.

The English philosopher Alfred North Whitehead has said that learning demands the patience to master details minute by minute, hour by hour, and day by day. He adds that, in learning, there is no elegant, royal road leading to eye-opening generalizations. Learning is the accumulation of wisdom built up by humankind from the distant past, and there is no easy way to acquire it. I hope that, without looking for what Whitehead calls a royal road, all of you will be runners in a race leading you through a thorough investigation of human wisdom.

At the present time, learning tends to be too specialized and compartmentalized. On this topic, Norman Cousins, an outstanding American journalist and participant in the movement for global peace, has warned that no matter how much our harvest of knowledge contributes to the creation of a richer world and no matter how skillfully we can relate technology to theory, unless our powers of thought and our technology are useful in the work of creating a safer, better world, our education is incomplete and somehow mistaken.

I am completely convinced that what he says is correct. Learning is not for the sake of fame and glory but must be used for the sake of the happiness of all humanity.

Everyone knows of the solar-centric theory of the great Polish astronomer Copernicus (1473–1543). Fewer people, however, realize the versatility of this outstanding scholar. In addition to taking part in literary activities and cartography, he carried out reforms in both currency and the calendar. As a qualified physician he battled with persisting plague and distributed medicines, free of charge, to the poor of his region. I am deeply moved by the way in which this scientist put his learning to use in working for the good of society as a whole. Moreover, this man, who possessed true wisdom, always looked down on himself for leading a life devoted to research. The following anecdote reveals his attitude.

When local leaders fled in fear from a band of Teutonic Knights invading Poland, Copernicus became a leader of the resistance and fought against the invaders to the last. And it was during this time, while constantly facing imminent death, that he completed the first volume of his historical work *De Revolutiones*. As is well known, in considering his pressing activities and the environment of the time, people in later centuries have regarded his achievements as nothing short of miraculous.

Fully aware of the objections society would raise against it, at first Copernicus considered withholding his theory that the earth revolves around the sun. But, with courage and decisiveness, he later avowed that he would ignore people who criticized and reviled his theory on the basis of no more than a few passages of scripture twisted and distorted to suit their own aims.

Knowing the ugly complications, calculations, and jealousy besmirching many human relations, Copernicus nonetheless understood the beauty of the world and of the heavens surrounding it, and in his search for the fundamental truth of the universe, had nothing but love for all humanity. In this he was like the fragrant lotus blooming in immaculate beauty, though rising from muddy waters.

In conclusion, let me express my prayers that all of you will develop into people who are attentive and strong and who, in the words of a famous scholar, always have a cool head and a warm heart.

Cultivation as
Refined Common Sense

Delivered at the First Matriculation Ceremonies of Soka Women's Junior College, held at Hachioji, Tokyo, April 8, 1985.

Together with my congratulations to you on the occasion of this first matriculation into Soka Women's Junior College, I want to express my hope that you, the members of the first class, will nobly and steadfastly plot a path that students who come after you will be able to follow.

Though brief, the two years you will spend in junior college are of profound importance as a major demarcation point in your lives. And it is my hope that, working in unity with your faculty, you will achieve as much as, or even more than, students in a four-year university course. In my congratulatory remarks today, I should like to touch on three points.

The first is the importance of planting, in your youth, ideals deep in your mind. In a favorite passage of mine from the work of a certain great writer there occurs the idea that a person with ideals knows the path he must follow. The soul of a person with great ideals compels him to walk a great road.

I believe that a person with ideals is strong and, in all kinds of labyrinths, is able to guide others surely, like a lamp shining in the darkness of night. An interesting episode connected with Inazo Nitobe, agricultural specialist, pacifist, and formerly under-secretary-general of the United Nations, illustrates the significance of having ideals. (Nitobe's face is now familiar to all of you because it appears on the five-thousand-yen bank note.) Once, while he was still a student at the then Tokyo Imperial University (Tokyo University), a professor asked what good studying English literature could do. Nitobe replied that he hoped it would enable him to serve as a bridge over the Pacific Ocean. And it was because he had this ideal as a young man that later he was able to become a bridge of peaceful exchange by introducing Japanese thought abroad and importing the ways of thinking of other nations into Japan. I urge all of you to seek and embrace the ideals best suited to you and to cultivate them steadily through your course of daily study.

My second point has to do with self-training, a special privilege of the young. A house built on weak ground will soon collapse. Similarly, it is impossible to hope for true happiness and satisfaction in life unless, during your young years, you train and strengthen yourselves physically, mentally, and spiritually.

In my own youth, in this connection, I was deeply moved by the thought of the great French essayist Michel Eyquem de Montaigne, who said that fate gives us neither happiness nor unhappiness, but only the material and seeds. More than fate, it is strength of mind that alters these materials at will. Our minds are the controllers; they are the sole causes of happiness and unhappiness.

Each of you young people must bear a unique burden of fate. In the course of time, you will no doubt stumble and become frustrated or even desperate. But fate is only the seeds and the raw material. As Montaigne says, more than fate, it is strength of mind that interprets these things, either in a defeatist way, as unhappiness, or in the reverse, as springboards to happiness.

And this is where training is vitally important. I hope that the training to which you subject yourselves during your two years here will enable you to proceed with certitude toward a richly blooming life in your forties and fifties.

The third point I wish to discuss is cultivation. For young ladies in Japan, this term is often interpreted to mean study in such things as the tea ceremony, the koto, and calligraphy. But when I use it, I mean more than such intellectual and technical accomplishments.

The thing lacked by some socially prominent people who are criticized and disliked for lacking cultivation is the kind of distinctive, bright personality that is the womb of discernment and that serves as a lubricant in the formation of good human relations.

Among all the animals, only civilized human beings are capable of this kind of cultivation, which manifests itself in appearance and action that are sublimations of a pure mind. Though people speak in terms of sophisticated and general cultivation, I think that, ultimately, all cultivation can be described as refined common sense. The first prerequisite to its attainment is a pure and spacious mind that sees correct things correctly and recognizes beauty for what it is. Important ways to attain this state are to have a true faith that purifies the mind and the life force, to come into contact with and read as many outstanding books as possible, and to enjoy associations with good senior and contemporary friends and acquaintances.

But you are all adults and college students who do not need me to tell you what cultivation is. It is sufficient for me to express my wish that all of you will discover the truest meaning of the word and manifest it in your lives.

In conclusion, permit me to express my prayer that all of you will grow into the kind of people visualized in the mottoes of this institution, which sets out to educate women rich in mind and fortune, firm in faith, determined to work for the harmony of humankind, and endowed with broad social and international views.

Dialogue for Lasting Peace

A Proposal Commemorating the Eleventh Soka Gakkai International Day, January 26, 1986.

On this eleventh Soka Gakkai International (SGI) Day, I should like to share with you some of my recent thoughts, which I hope will supply impetus for the further growth and development of our organization.

Last year was especially significant as the fifty-fifth anniversary of the founding of Soka Gakkai and the tenth year since the founding of SGI. In connection with this, during the year, in the presence of Nikken Shonin, the sixty-seventh high priest of Nichiren Shoshu, who came from the head temple Taiseki-ji to join us, we held World Peace Youth Culture festivals in Hawaii and Hiroshima.

In 1957, my teacher and mentor Josei Toda, second president of Soka Gakkai, entrusted to the youth of our membership the task of working for the abolition of nuclear weapons. The holding of a successful World Youth Peace and Culture Festival in Hiroshima eighteen years later is a fitting conclusion to the SGI's tenth year of existence. In addition, it provides stimulus for the uniting of our worldwide membership in the drive to fulfill Mr. Toda's behest of abolishing nuclear weapons entirely.

Our goal now is to create, on the basis of the Mystic Law, a firm foundation for the work of the forces of global peace. In connection with the achievement of this goal, I should like to redirect your attention to the fundamental meaning of Nichiren Daishonin's *Rissho Ankoku Ron* (On Securing the Peace of the Land Through the Propagation of True Buddhism), that is, the realization of permanent world peace and a tranquil human society. My most heartfelt wish is that, in the coming decade, all of you will join me in moving forward courageously toward the attainment of this aim.

For the past several years, on every occasion that presented itself, I have insisted that a summit meeting between the leaders of the United States and the Soviet Union is indispensable to the achievement of world peace. For example, In May 1981, on one of my three visits to the Soviet Union that year, I met with Nikolai A. Tikhonov, then premier, and told him how reassuring it would be for all humanity if the leaders of his nation and of the United States would come together for thorough, far-ranging discussions in some suitable place outside Moscow. In the proposal I made in 1983, on the occasion of the eighth SGI Day, and again, last year, on the occasion of the tenth anniversary of the founding of SGI, I emphasized the importance of holding such a summit meeting at the earliest possible opportunity and of the mutual understanding of each other's thoughts and aspirations that frank, sincere exchanges of opinion at such a meeting would make possible. I was convinced then, as I remain now, that, by overcoming difficulties and holding meetings, the leaders of these two nations, which are largely responsible for the peace of the world, could generate the kind of bold thoughts and actions and the courageous decisions required to relax tensions and break from the present impasse.

Fresh Dialogue between the United States and the Soviet Union

For this reason, I warmly welcome the summit meeting that did materialize last year. Though the true results of those meetings will depend on the ways the United States and the Soviet Union conduct themselves from now on, I greatly appreciate the relaxation of tensions the meetings created throughout the world. The climate of bright hope and peace that the meetings themselves generated must not be underrated.

The confrontation that has been continuing for some time between the two nations has been severe enough to result in what has been described as a new Cold War. Stalemate in the nuclear-arms race has led to such great reduction in their scales that some people now believe in the actual usability of such weapons and often resort to the pernicious notion of the so-called nuclear preemptive-strike syndrome.

At the second SGI general conference, held in Hawaii in August 1981, I pointed out, with as much severity as I could, the inhumanity and peril of current nuclear strategy. In light of this peril, in complete agreement with the opinion expressed at last year's summit meeting that there can be no victor in nuclear conflict, I consider it highly meaningful that, in the joint communiqué made after the meeting, both parties agreed to the advisability of striving to avoid all conflict—both nuclear and conventional—and of ceasing competition for military supremacy.

I have continually underscored the importance of a summit meeting between the Soviet Union and the United States for two main reasons. First, I believe that in the name of humankind, before the whole world, both parties should make a clear statement of their rejection of all belligerence. Second, I believe that such a statement can be forthcoming from a summit meeting precisely because the participants are in positions of paramount responsibility in their nations. Indeed, the summit meeting did send out a beam of the hope-giving light of peace.

On the fifteenth of this month, Secretary-General Gorbachev made a new arms-reduction proposal calling for a three-stage elimination of nuclear arms by the end of the century. This and President Reagan's display of interest in the proposal represent a welcome movement in the direction of nuclear-arms reduction.

The noted American pacifist Harold Willens has said, "The myth of expertise is exactly that—a myth. It takes scientific skills to make a hydrogen bomb. It takes only common sense to know when there are too many hydrogen bombs. And common sense is precisely what is needed now."

Mr. Willens's "common sense" can be replaced with words like *good sense* or *conscience,* both of which are more readily exercised by top leaders than by administrative specialists or scientists. Common sense establishes circuits with ordinary citizens. And, when an infinite number of such circuits is established in all directions, the resulting network of peace will enable national interests to extend to the whole globe.

For a number of years, relations between Japan and the Soviet Union have been chilly. But the recent visit to our country by Foreign Minister Shevardnadze, on behalf of Secretary-General Gorbachev, has epoch-making significance in that it opens the way to the conclusion of a peace treaty between the two nations and can mark a great turning point in an undesirable situation that has prevailed between them since the end of World War II.

In the proposals I made at the time of the eighth SGI Day in 1983, I urged the establishment by the United States and the Soviet Union, on the specialist level, of what I call a Nuclear War Prevention Center. I therefore welcome the agreement expressed in the summit meeting joint communiqué to set up a Danger-reduction Center, on the specialist level, for research to reduce the peril of nuclear war. Arrangements to forestall the possibility of a fortuitously instigated nuclear conflict are extraordinarily important to the actualization of a vow to eliminate nuclear conflict entirely.

Far from taking an optimistic view of the future, I continue to believe in the necessity of keeping a stern eye on the conduct of the United States and the Soviet Union in the years to come. The thing that disturbs me most is the possibility that, during extended negotiations, bit by bit militarization will make real advances into outer space. The past history of new arms-limitations talks between the two nations suggests that such a thing is very possible. The matter must be resolved during this and the coming year, when another summit is supposed to take place.

First of all, as a prerequisite to their abolition, what the new summit should deal with is a freeze on nuclear arms at their present levels. After this first step, the leaders of the world should make sweeping reductions in nuclear arsenals. This is imperative because, in the past, instead of leading to positive steps for the reduction of nuclear arms, such negotiations as the Strategic Arms Limitation Talks (SALT) have largely confined themselves to arms control. It is no longer permissible to concentrate on balance of nuclear might and preservation of the status quo.

Consequently, I sincerely hope that a summit dialogue between leaders of the two powers will extend as far as prohibition of all nuclear experiments. Such prohibition would be good news indeed for nonnuclear signatories to the Nuclear Nonproliferation Treaty.

The leaders of the Soviet Union and the United States must remember that all peace-loving peoples are keeping a stern watch on their actions in this matter. In addition, it is highly desirable for these two nations to conclude a new treaty relative to limitations on the militarization of outer space.

In spite of the great weight they exercise in such affairs, however, the United States and the Soviet Union are not the sole parties responsible for the construction of an enduring peace. The task belongs to the rest of us as well. And, remaining free of the entanglements of national interest, we must all adopt the boldest possible approach toward it.

Horizons of a New Civilization

A great transformation is now occurring toward the international society of the twenty-first century. In the transnational expansion and intensification of the popular anti-nuclear and anti-war movement, I sense the quickening of a new age of the ordinary people. It is impossible to emphasize too strongly the significance of popular movements that, together with governments and international organizations, strive to eliminate nuclear weapons, erase hunger and poverty from the face of the earth, and protect human rights and the environment. The knowledge that, ultimately, it is the power of the people that moves history is more deeply and more globally realized than ever before.

I am in complete agreement with the world-famous journalist Norman Cousins when, in his recent writings, he says that military might is no longer of much use in guaranteeing the security of a nation. He goes on to say that a new force must be forthcoming if human society is to continue existing and functioning. This new force, which will be expressed in the might of the human will or of a global consensus, will generate the energy and power for the construction of a safe refuge for human society.

The United Nations has designated this year the International Year of Peace. The significance of this designation is to be found in in the way human beings come to manifest and apply the wisdom and ideas needed to stop war and build peace. In a message delivered as the curtain-raiser of the International Year of Peace, United Nations Secretary-General Javier Pérez de Cuéllar said, "It is time to act on behalf of the future well-being of all nations with the vision and forbearance that peace requires." In accord with this sentiment, as it requires no comment, Soka Gakkai International has as its great goal the realization of world peace on the basis of Buddhist teachings. In short, as is firmly established in the basic policies of the organization, SGI strives for lasting world peace and the creation of a flourishing system of culture and education founded on the Buddhism of Nichiren Daishonin and its clearly stated doctrine of respect for the dignity of life force. Moreover, we are resolved to devote our best to the rejection of all violence, including war, and the happiness of humanity and the prosperity of the world. Consequently, we are committed to supporting the spirit of the United Nations Charter and to repeated efforts in the name of world peace. It is highly appropriate that, at this time, the United Nations has set peace and development, and preparation for life in peace as the major dimensions of the program of the year of peace and disarmament. I should like to take this opportunity to restate our determination to play a part in the achievement of these aims.

According to statistics made public by the United Nations last year, about twenty million people have perished in the roughly one hundred fifty wars and other conflicts that have occurred since 1945. The casualty figure is greater than that of the number of military personnel killed in World War II. It is essential to look honestly at the facts; though no global conflict has occurred in the past four decades, virtually incessant local fighting has claimed twenty million victims.

The United Nations report goes on to say that the number of civilian casualties in these large and small conflicts has been extremely high. Furthermore, since recent wars are of an irregular, undeclared kind, combatants feel themselves unbound by laws and treaties. Consequently, in all parts of the world today there are raging conflicts that are truly cruel and tragic in their very lawlessness.

In addition to deliberate belligerence, a number of other problems threaten peace: for instance, violation of human rights, discrimination, famine, and poverty.

Adopting the attitude that today peace and respect for human rights are inseparably linked, our organization supports the refugee assistance program of the Office of the United Nations High Commissioner for Refugees, especially through the efforts of the Soka Gakkai Youth Peace Conference. We are firmly convinced that, since it protects human rights, assistance of this kind is an indispensable condition for the creation of peace. In connection with the International Year of Peace, we are determined to pursue steadfastly, and from various angles, all activities of this kind, since they express respect for the dignity of humanity.

Intensification of interdependence among nations is steadily creating a situation in which large-scale war is becoming impossible. Furthermore, everyone must realize that, because of its adverse influences on the economy, nothing is as wasteful and nothing more destructive of the environment than war.

Of course, it may prove impossible to eradicate all local conflicts. The important thing is to create a framework ensuring regional peace to a maximum extent and then to extend that framework to as much of the world as possible. My examination of the world today leads me to believe that Asia and the Pacific region are the zones in which such a thing is most inherently feasible.

Asia is less harassed than other parts of the world by flames of conflict that could suddenly erupt into a large-scale war. At the present time, in the Middle East and Central America, smoking artillery and showering shells characterize situations so touchy that the slightest misjudgment could detonate them into full destructive force. Furthermore, many of the nations of Africa represent similarly touchy environments owing to so-called structural violence in the form of famines and other kinds of affliction.

Undeniably, we must never take our eyes from these facts for a moment; and Japan must not be remiss in exerting maximum efforts for the sake of peace. But a deeper look at the situation shows that beneath such direct causes as war and famine is an entire complex of other political, economic, cultural, and educational factors that must be taken into consideration. When thought is given to them and when peace is viewed as a lasting condition and not a mere interlude between wars, it becomes clear that hope must be put in Asia and the Pacific region. Obviously, in terms of profound time and space relations, including geopolitical judgments, Japan must play an important role in that region.

The Tide of Nonbelligerence and Peace Arises in Asia

As I said in my proposal last year, unlike Europe, where the members of NATO and the Warsaw Pact oppose each other directly, Asia and the Pacific region are important because of the diversity of their many elements. The multiplicity of interest and activity in the region is immediately apparent when a quick enumeration is made of the nations in the area. The region includes two superpowers—the United States and the Soviet Union—as well as Japan, one of the world's great economic powers and a nation devoted to the preservation of the spirit of its pacifist-oriented constitution. In addition, in it are Canada, with its immense natural resources; China, now eagerly modernizing for the sake of the coming century; the members of the Association of South East Asian Nations (ASEAN), all of whom are steadily becoming stronger; the rapidly growing Newly Industrialized States including Korea, Taiwan, and Hong Kong; and the diverse operations of Australia, New Zealand, and the other nations of the South Pacific.

I put great importance on foreign relations with China and with India as well. In November of last year, during conversations with Prime Minister Rajiv Gandhi of India, who was visiting Japan at the time, I thought constantly of the role of his nation and of all Asia and the Pacific region in the development of global peace. The work of India and of such other nonaligned nations as Sweden, Greece, Mexico, Tanzania, and Argentina in stressing the importance of the experiences of Hiroshima and Nagasaki in their diplomatic efforts to halt the militarization of outer space, strives to produce treaties to forbid nuclear experimentation and to stimulate reduction of nuclear arms, and it deserves the utmost support.

Part of the support our organization can supply takes the form of such activities as sponsoring the exhibition entitled "Nuclear Arms— The Threat to Our World Today," which has already been presented at the United Nations headquarters, in New York, and in twelve cities in ten other nations. In January of this year, the exhibition was held in India and is scheduled to be shown in Canada in April and in China in the fall. Our wish in showing this exhibition in many places is to give added impetus to the anti-war, anti-nuclear sentiment, which must eventually spread throughout Asia, the Pacific region, and the entire world. I intend to devote myself unstintingly to this work in the years to come.

I have already commented on the diversity of peoples and cultures in the Asia-Pacific zone. In many senses, this is a healthy thing. But undeniably, at the present time, this diversity is producing a state of chaos; the very instability of this could prove perilous. Under these chaotic circumstances, aggravation of the current armed tension between the United States and the Soviet Union could trigger a full-scale war. As early as 1974, on an official government visit to Japan, André Malraux made a lasting impression on me when he said that, if it is to occur, the next large-scale war will certainly begin in the Pacific region. Japan must exert an all-out effort to prevent such a dreadful thing from happening.

In spite of the tendency toward chaos prevailing there at present, I believe that the correct way to interpret future historical development involves a keen observation of the energies and possibilities latent in the Asia-Pacific region.

The French poet and essayist Paul Valéry once said that in the final analysis, European civilization is Mediterranean civilization and that it consists of three major elements: Roman law, the Christian religion, and the spirit of Greece. Characterized by the scope of human desire and will power, for better or worse, this civilization has demonstrated a kind of global validity.

Obviously, European civilization has had its good and its bad aspects. Desire and will have pioneered much that is materially beneficial. They have also inspired the cruelties of colonialism and imperialism. I do not believe it is merely an absurd dream to see the civilization of Asia and the Pacific region as ushering in a new dawn with new horizons to be pioneered while sublimated use is made of the best of Euro-Mediterranean culture.

In our dialogue *Choose Life,* the late Arnold J. Toynbee gave the following reasons for the high estimation he made of the role East Asia will play in the coming century. First, he said the experience of the Chinese people in sustaining an empire for twenty-one centuries could serve as a local model for a worldwide state. To this he added the ecumenical spirit with which the Chinese have been imbued during their long history, and the humanism of the Confucian *Weltanschauung.* The rationalism of both Confucianism and Buddhism combined with the sense of the mystery of the universe and the recognition that human attempts to dominate the universe are self-defeating are other characteristics that Mr. Toynbee felt would be valuable. In addition, he mentioned the oriental conviction that, far from trying to dominate it, humanity's aim should be to live in harmony with nature. To these he added the demonstration by the Japanese people of the possibility for East Asians to beat Westerners at their own modern game of applying science to both civilian and military technology and finally the courage demonstrated by the Japanese and the Vietnamese in daring to challenge the West.

While realizing that other interpretations may differ from this profound analysis, I have nothing to add to it except to say that, throughout the great labor of challenging distant problems of the kind Mr. Toynbee envisioned, we must never for an instant lose sight of our basic axis, which must be a new humanism based on the highest human values.

The United Nations and NGOs Must Work Together

As the case of Japan illustrates, most of the interest directed recently toward the Asia-Pacific region has been economic in nature. And this is important in dealing with practical issues. But it is essential to avoid being totally engrossed in matters of economic competition and to take a wider perspective oriented toward global peace. When such a view is taken, for the sake of a new human civilization, Asia-Pacific civilization will be seen to have significance exemplified in the Russell-Einstein manifesto, which says, "I appeal, as a human being to human beings: remember your humanity, and forget the rest."

To assist in adopting this perspective, an organization capable of serving as a center for equal, mutually beneficial cooperation of all the nations of the Asia-Pacific region is necessary. To perform this function, I propose the formation of what can be called the Asia-Pacific Organization for Peace and Culture (APOPAC), which should be loosely, not directly, under the auspices of the United Nations.

Obviously, for the sake of reinforcing its activities such as work for peace, culture, and arms reduction, it would be profitable to think of connections between the APOPCAP and the Economic and Social Commission for Asia and Pacific, which is a suborganization of the United Nations Economics and Social Directorate.

To enable them to protect the peace and work for disarmament and economic development, the nations of this region require a place where they can constantly engage in equitable dialogue on an international level. In conversations I had with Dr. Richard Coudenhove-Kalergi some years ago, to provide such a place, I urged the formation of a United Nations Far East Regional Office in Tokyo. The concept of the APOPAC is a development of the same line of thought in the light of more recent trends in the world situation.

Of course, the headquarters of the United Nations must remain in New York. As a council of one hundred and fifty-nine member nations and the place where all kinds of international problems can be resolved, I place great hopes in that organization and have consistently, if on a modest scale, given it my support. I intend to go on supporting it in the hope that, in the future, the spirit of the United Nations Charter will prove even more fruitful than it has in the past.

Nonetheless, as is widely recognized, the United Nations faces many problems such as the ones related to the Security Council. Furthermore, its global nature hinders the United Nations from dealing effectively with purely regional problems. To rectify these situations, a different structure based on totally new ideas and suited to the nature of the times must now be developed. As one of those new ideas, I propose decentralization.

So-called nongovernmental organizations (NGOs) can serve as a model for the APOPAC. In spite of increases in activity and importance of the private sector in the world today, private and nongovernmental groups cannot be said to participate adequately in the work of the United Nations. I would hope that the APOPAC could operate on the private level in linkage with NGOs, which it should carefully observe for hints and suggestions. As an NGO, our organization should assist in this operation to the maximum possible extent.

The Pacifist Japanese Constitution

A unified global system for the twenty-first century requires the aggregate wisdom of all peoples. But this will be impossible to achieve overnight. The global perspective will, therefore, demand repeated regional, decentralized action.

Discussions of regional cooperation in the Asia-Pacific zone have already produced some concrete ideas, and proposals have been advanced to systematize regional economic necessities and mutual-reliance relations. But the vastness, multiplicity, and diversity of the region that I have already mentioned have hindered the actualization of these ideas and proposals. Differences in social systems, race, religion, culture, and economic-developmental stages obstruct the formation of cooperative relations. As some observers have pointed out, whereas common historical and cultural elements facilitated the formation of the European Community, Asian political, economic, and cultural diversity makes it much harder to bring nations together in a similar organization. It must be remembered that, heretofore, excessive emphasis on politics (security guarantees) and economics have resulted in friction and rejection and have produced only fragile associations.

This is why I feel that peace, disarmament, development, and culture must be the foundation of the APOPAC. In its operations, however, regional traditions and diversity must be afforded the greatest respect. Under no circumstancees should any one culture be given obligatory preference over others for the sake of enforced standardization. The road to mutal understanding will remain blocked unless each culture is given the same respect as all others.

Though a new structure cannot be erected overnight, a start must be made, even though at first all nations may not participate in an ideal form. The work can be initiated in any promising field and then gradually advanced. The important thing is to build a basis of mutual trust through constant dialogue and then to move forward, step by step, in a spirit of resilience. At the first stage, it would be good to form a pliant consulting body.

For instance, though none so far has been held, all top leaders of the related nations could hold an Asia-Pacific summit like the several summit meetings of representatives of industrialized nations that have already taken place. I should like to see the creation of an international organization suited to the needs of the twenty-first century and born of the accumulation of just such achievements and an Asia-Pacific summit meeting.

In neither the APOPAC nor the Asia-Pacific summit should any one powerful nation be permitted to exercise controlling sway, since the peace and prosperity of the world demand the vitalization of all regions.

In the ceremonies admitting Japan into the United Nations in 1956, Foreign Minister Mamoru Shigemitsu said, "The substance of Japan's political, economic, and cultural life is the product of the fusion within the last century of the civilization of the Orient and the Occident. In a way, Japan may well be regarded as a bridge between the East and the West."

Today, in both East and West, one of the most pressing problems facing humanity is how to meld tradition and modernization in a way that makes best use of the good points of both. If it can contribute to the discovery of a way to perform this difficult task, the formation of the APOPAC could represent an updating of the bridge between East and West that Mr. Shigemitsu spoke of three decades ago. To make this possible, a system of cooperation with the United Nations University headquarters in Tokyo is vital.

Melbourne might be selected as a good location for the offices of the APOPAC since, together with Japan, Australia was one of the first nations to recognize the importance of the Pacific region and to sponsor the formation of a collective pan-Pacific organization for it.

I should like Japan to take a leadership role in this concept because of the thoroughgoing rejection of belligerence and dedication to lasting peace expressed in the preamble and in Article Nine of the Japanese constitution. In the preamble of that constitution the following passage occurs: "We, the Japanese people, desire peace for all time and are deeply conscious of the high ideals controlling human relationships, and we have determined to preserve our security and existence, trusting in the justice and faith of the peace-loving peoples of the world."

In other words, the document is a forceful plea for peace based on the "justice and faith" of the peoples of the world and therefore represents a keen perception of the nature of peace in a time like ours, when nuclear weapons threaten the fate of humanity. Some people today would alter this constitution to bring it in line with international political actualities. I, however, feel it is the mission of the people of Japan to do all they can to infuse international politics with the spirit of the pacifist constitution.

I insist that this is the case because distrust, one of the gravest problems facing human society today, can lead to armed conflict and because it is of maximum importance to convince the entire world that such conflicts must be avoided and that problems must be resolved through peaceful negotiations. This is why we must continue to carry the ideals of our epoch-making peace constitution to the whole world.

In this connection, I am greatly encouraged by the prevalence among sensitive people the world over of the sentiments expressed in the following words of Javier Pérez de Cuéllar, the secretary-general of the United Nations: "I think you are setting, or have already set, an interesting example which could be followed by the whole international community. You have dedicated your efforts to your own development, and you have refrained from the production of arms. You have limited your military activities to what is required for your own security. If this example could be followed, we can really think in terms of a very reasonably developed world" (*Mainichi Daily News,* January 4, 1986).

Today, as a major economic power, Japan must both withstand great pressure and live up to increasing expectations. And it is possible to do both without resort to arms. Indeed to give weight to military matters would fundamentally thwart the course of development Japan has followed since the end of World War II and, at the same time, would call down concentrated revulsion on the part of the other Asian nations. Instead of doing this, Japan can assuredly win more approval from the rest of the world by making bold financial contributions to the creation of such peace-preserving bodies as the APOPAC. In this way, it would be possible to create in the Asia-Pacific region a new Geneva or Vienna to serve as a peaceful center for work in the name of disarmament, aid, and development that could have repercussions throughout the world.

Reuniting the Two Koreas

I have spoken of the possibilities and the perils existing in the virtually chaotic diversity of the Asia Pacific region. One of those perils is the division of the Korean peninsula—a close neighbor to Japan geographically and culturally—into North and South Korea. Should the present state of armistice between them be broken, the resulting conflict not only would involve sacrifice for the sixty million inhabitants of the nations, but also would influence neighboring nations because of their strategic locations and could even spark nuclear war. In other words, it is impossible to discuss peace in this region without taking a direct look at the tragic history of a people divided for the past forty years.

The reasons for the division are profoundly related to enforced annexation by the Japanese militarists and Japanese colonial rule. Swept up against their will by the orders of Japanese rulers, the Koreans suffered unspeakable misery. Then, after the Japanese defeat in World War II and the subsequent disarmament of Japanese troops, the United States and the Soviet Union divided Korea into two zones of responsibility along the thirty-eighth parallel. The Soviets controlled Korea north of that line, and the Americans controlled the remainder south of it. Thereafter, the nations of North and South

Korea were proclaimed; then, with the Korean War, which began in June 1950, the military demarcation line was definitely fixed.

Basically this is a matter that the two Koreas should deal with on their own without external interference of any kind. And such recent developments in this direction as Red Cross talks between them deserve special note.

Past events and the existence of many problems demanding immediate solutions greatly complicate the issue of the extent to which Japan is qualified to mediate between the two nations. One of those problems entails the ignorance of the Japanese people. In spite of physical proximity, the Japanese are astoundingly ill-informed about the history of the peoples of North and South Korea. To a large extent, this ignorance results from the wish for disassociation from Asia and association with the industrialized nations of the West that has prevailed in Japan since the latter part of the nineteenth century. Nor can it be said that the unwarranted errors and prejudices born of that ignorance have been eradicated even today.

A second problem is the roughly seven hundred thousand North and South Koreans residing in Japan and forced to deal with errors, prejudices, and discrimination deeply rooted in Japanese society.

Unhappy accounts from the past remain unsettled between Japan and the two Koreas. Attempting to deal with the problems of the two nations without taking those accounts into consideration can bring censure down on us for partiality and for injuring the feelings of the Korean people. Since many of the problems are intricately involved with politics, our statesmen must address themselves to the solutions with a positive, forward-looking attitude.

I am compelled to speak on these matters as the person primarily responsibile for SGI and, from the global standpoint, as a person who longs for lasting peace, the attainment of which is deeply related to the continued division of these two nations. The importance of this issue is illustrated by the invitations issued to both North and South Korea to address the fortieth-anniversary general assembly of the United Nations. I believe that, without tranquility and prosperity in these nations, the peace of Asia and the Pacific—and perhaps of the entire world—will be unattainable. But the light of peace in the Koreas could penetrate the pall of gloom now hanging over the whole world.

The issue of United Nations representation for North and South Korea remains unsettled. Whereas China and the Soviet Union recognize North Korea, the United States, Japan, and the Western nations recognize South Korea. Recognition of North Korea by the Western bloc and South Korea by the Eastern bloc would break the deadlock, but, feeling that simultaneous representation of both would finalize the existing division, North Korea shows no signs of willingness to compromise.

Nonetheless, in the past the two nations have reached agreement on a number of issues. The most important of these was the joint declaration on unification issued on July 4, 1972. The following are the major points of the agreement: (1) the problem of unification must be solved independently by the two Koreas without reliance on or interference from outside powers; (2) unification is to be achieved peacefully without the use of armed force by one party against the wishes of the other; (3) unification should aim for the joining of one single people and therefore must transcend philosophy, ideology, and political system. Though much has taken place since the declaration was made, apparently the main insistence that unification be carried out independently and peacefully remains unchanged.

But forty years of division and different social systems constitute a great barrier to the attainment of this aim. In my proposals last year I welcomed the repeated dialogues that were then taking place between North and South Korea and emphasized the importance of a summit meeting between their leaders. A year has passed, and I feel that the time is all the more ripe for their top leaders to come together at the same table and examine proposals evolved over the past forty years and to give thought to events of the future. In speaking of the summit meeting between the leaders of the United States and the Soviet Union, I said that the act of coming together itself is of the greatest importance. In connection with a Korean summit meeting the same thing is true because it is essential to eliminate the deep-rooted distrust that has been a major factor separating the two nations over the past four decades.

Creating Values That Strengthen Trust

George Kennan, former United States ambassador to the Soviet Union and well-known controversialist on the subject of disarmament, considers this distrust to be a fixation composed of a number of factors. "This is a species of fixation, brewed of many components. There are fears, resentments, national pride. There are misreadings of the adversary's intentions—sometimes even the refusal to consider them at all. There is the tendency of national communities to idealize themselves and to dehumanize the opponent. There is the blinkered, narrow vision of the professional military planner, and his tendency to make war inevitable by assuming its inevitability." Obsession with this kind of fixation is a horrendous thing.

Though my strength is limited, I have traveled to all parts of the world in a search for a road to peace through dialogues with leaders in the United States, the Soviet Union, China, and many other countries. These meetings have impressed on me an important point. Much of a person's image of another person is preconceived before the two encounter each other. The meeting itself, however, often makes apparent totally different aspects of the partner's personality. This is why actual dialogue generates bold decisions and eliminates the kind of fixation George Kennan describes.

Once established, relations of trust lead to agreements connected with the creation of value. The indispensability of a meeting between the top leaders of North and South Korea, in spite of their differing social systems, is perfectly obvious. Since it will be unprecedented, the realization of such a meeting will no doubt entail many twistings and turnings. But the people responsible for it must persevere.

On the basis of an examination of the points on which the two nations have reached agreement in the past, it would seem likely that a summit meeting might produce a pact of mutual nonaggression and noninvasion. Both nations have already denied all intentions of invading. Their top leaders could provide a new starting point for further progress by clearly restating these intentions for domestic and foreign audiences alike.

After three years of war, North and South signed an armistice agreement. But armistice is far from true peace. Since in the state of armistice there is no telling when the flames of war might flare up again, the involved parties must devote a larger part of their national budgets to military expenditures than is the case with other nations.

The Korean peoples long for not armistice, but a lasting cessation to war; a mutual agreement never to invade each other and never to war with each other again might be a historical turning point after forty years of division. I fundamentally believe that a treaty of non-aggression and nonbelligerence should be the premise for all other agreements and that no premises preceding it should be established. If the United States, the Soviet Union, China, and Japan recognize this agreement, tensions between North and South Korea would be greatly relaxed.

The dialogue at a summit meeting between North and South Korean leaders could be a starting point from which could evolve, one by one, other feasible points of agreement that would both facilitate the realization of peace, for which the people long, and admit a ray of sunlight into the gloom that has long hung over northeast Asia. All related parties must exert maximum efforts to this end.

The long military demarcation line (armistice line) that now forms the boundary between the two Koreas extends roughly along the thirty-eighth parallel for 248 kilometers from the mouth of the Han River in the west toward the eastern shore of the peninsula. A demilitarized zone, intended as a buffer region, extends for two kilometers northward and for another two kilometers southward from the line. The sole authorized road running north-and-south through the demilitarized zone passes Panmunjom. Last year, on television, I watched as members of families that have been split for forty years, at last permitted to visit each other, traveled through that city on the way southward from Pyongyang, the capital of North Korea, and northward from Seoul, the capital of South Korea. As I observed this historic event, I was more deeply convinced than ever of the need to work to bring peace to this country so that the barren demilitarized zone can be opened to the people and so that more and more of them may travel through Panmunjom, the sole connecting point between the two, along this north-south road.

The Future is in the Hands of the Young

Perhaps it would be possible to think of establishing a center of peace and cultural revival in either Panmunjom or the demilitarized zone. If the top leaders of the two nations concluded a pact of mutual non-aggression and nonbelligerence, the demilitarized zone would assume new creative significance as a region for the maintenance of peace. In other words, instead of its negative function as a place for the evasion of armed conflicts, it could serve as a place for activities oriented toward the active creation of peace. The process by means of which this could evolve would move from armistice to nonbelligerence and then to creative acts designed to bring the blessings of peace and culture to the people.

At present, South Korea has no relations with China or the Soviet Union at all. But, once a breakthrough with North Korea has been made, it would be highly practical for South Korea to engage in nonpolitical exchanges with those nations in such fields as learning and sports.

Upon viewing the bleak, cold, demilitarized zone as it is now, some people might regard my proposal as no more than a dream. But it must be remembered that, at one time, no military demarcation line divided Korea. People came and went freely from one part of the country to the other. Had it not been for Japanese colonial annexation, war, and antagonism between the Soviet Union and the United States, the Korean people would be leading normal lives in what is now the demilitarized zone, which must be opened to the people again once true peace has been achieved.

As a first step in achieving this, I suggest the possibility of joint research and international exchanges in learning and sports, which are universal fields transcending barriers of national state, race, and ideology. Instead of being reserved for one people alone, the fruits of such research should be turned to the good of all humanity. Accumulated products of study in many fields of endeavor become part of the common human heritage.

I further suggest that this zone be converted into a place of research and discussion open to other countries. This would establish relations between not only North and South Korea, but also between them and those nations of the world with which they have no connections at all at present. Participation in such research and discussions by scholars from the United States, Japan, and the Western nations, with which North Korea has no relations, and by others from China and the Soviet Union, with which South Korea has none, would make possible the correct transmission of new information for application in various fields, including technological ones. I am certain that this, in turn, would make great contributions to the solution of the problem of discrepancy between industrialized and developing nations throughout the Asia-Pacific region.

The demilitarized zone, which international politics once turned into a blood-drenched battlefield, can thus be converted into a region where peace and learning flourish. And this will at last liberate the people of North and South Korea from the fear of war. It is my heartfelt wish that the sunlight of tranquility and prosperity will soon pour down with full strength on a people who have suffered as a result of invasion, wept because of the flames of war, and sighed through years of division.

My desire, as a follower of Buddhist teachings, for world peace and my hope, as a fellow world citizen, that peace will come to the people of the Korean peninsula have inspired me to express my ideas—oriented toward the twenty-first century—on this topic. There can be no doubt that pioneering the way to true peace for the Koreans will give hope and courage to the peoples of other nations.

In a sense, the people of Korea symbolize the kinds of suffering characteristic of the twentieth century. Their revival will long shine as a dazzling model showing all people how wisdom can overcome difficulty.

In all these proposals for the Asia-Pacific region, the most important point is the connection among the minds of all peace-loving peoples. With an eye to the future, in September 1968, at the eleventh general conference of the Soka Gakkai Student Division, I urged friendly relations with the youth of China. At the time, Japan had no diplomatic relations with China, and, as the Vietnam War grew more violent, many people were concerned about a possible armed conflict between China and the United States.

For the sake of altering the situation, which as anyone could see, was very grave, I boldly urged China's reinstatement in the United Nations and normalization of relations between China and Japan.

One reason for making such a proposal was the hope that young Chinese and Japanese who had no direct experience of the war between their two nations could work together, smiling and hand in hand, for the building of a better world. My wish came true, and today the youth of China and Japan are beginning to share ties of profound amity.

I sincerely hope that, as soon as possible, the youth of North and South Korea will enjoy the same kind of peace and friendship. It is my hope that amity will spread as far as possible, inspiring the younger generations who have never tasted the bitterness many of their seniors have known, and who will, in a mood of mutual respect and assistance, cooperate for the sake of the brighter future of their homelands. I further hope that this kind of amity will spread beyond boundaries to reach the nations of Europe, North and South America, Africa—the continent of the twenty-first century—and all other regions, bathing the whole world in the strong light of peace.

The new century draws near. And it is the energy of the young who must challenge its trials and bear its responsibilities. I entrust the realization of my vision to the hands of the young. My heartfelt hope is that they will do their utmost for the future of Asia, the Pacific region, and the world.

Glossary

The purpose of this glossary is to explain and supply further information concerning Buddhist terms, figures, texts, and concepts mentioned, often only in passing, in the text. Glossary entries derive from *A Dictionary of Buddhist Terms and Concepts* (Nichiren Shoshu International Center, 1983), but they have been abridged and, when necessary, adapted. Readers with an interest in pursuing these subjects further should refer to that work. Some terms that appear in standard dictionaries, such as Buddha, have been included to provide a broader context and a deeper understanding. As a rule, the writings of Nichiren Daishonin are not listed. The reader interested in his writings should refer to *The Major Writings of Nichiren Daishonin*, vols. 1–4 (Nichiren Shoshu International Center), in which many appear in English translation. The pinyin system of romanization has been used for Chinese words, and a chart of their Wade-Giles equivalents can be found on page 298.

Abutsu-bō (d. 1279): Abutsu-bō Nittoku, a lay follower of Nichiren Daishonin. Nittoku is his Buddhist name, but he was commonly called Abutsu-bō. His secular name was Endō Tamemori. Tradition has it that he was originally a samurai who served the retired emperor Juntoku in Kyoto, and accompanied Juntoku to Sado Island when the emperor was banished there immediately following the Jōkyū disturbance in 1221 on charges of rebellion against the Kamakura shogunate. However, it seems more probable that he was actually a native of Sado. When Nichiren Daishonin was exiled to Sado, Abutsu-bō visited him at Tsukahara to confront him in debate, but was himself converted. He and his wife Sennichi-ama earnestly served the Daishonin during his exile, supplying him with food and other necessities for more than two years until he was pardoned and left the island in 1274. In recognition of Abutsu-bō's pure faith, the Daishonin inscribed a Gohonzon for him. Abutsu-bō is said to have died on March 21, 1279, at ninety-one.

Aeon of growth: Also, kalpa of formation. The period corresponding to the first stage in the cycle of formation, continuance, decline and disintegration which a world is said to undergo. One of the four aeons, or kalpas. In this kalpa, a world takes shape and living beings appear in it.

Aeon of stability: Also, kalpa of continuance. The period corresponding to the second stage of the four-stage cycle described by the four kalpas of formation, continuance, decline and disintegration, which a world is said to repeatedly undergo. During this period a world and its inhabitants continue to exist.

Amida: (Skt Amitāyus or Amitābha) The Buddha of the Pure Land of Perfect Bliss in the western region of the universe. Amida is the Japanese transliteration of both Amitāyus and Amitābha, which mean "infinite life" and "infinite light," respectively. According to the Muryōju Sutra, immeasurable aeons ago, a certain king was delighted with the preaching of a Buddha called Sejizaiō and renounced his throne to follow him. He took the name Hōzō and began to practice Buddhist austerities under the guidance of the Buddha. After examining an infinite number of Buddha lands and pondering for five aeons, Bodhisattva Hōzō made forty-eight vows in which he pledged to create his own Buddha land which would combine the most outstanding features of all those he had seen. In the eighteenth vow he pledged to bring all sentient beings who put their hopes of salvation in him to his Buddha land, which he named Perfect Bliss. Hōzō completed his practice, becoming the Buddha Amida, and his Pure Land was established in a part of the universe located ten billion Buddha lands to the west. Belief in Amida Buddha spread from India to China, and in Japan prevailed widely.

Amrita: (Skt) Ambrosia. In ancient India it was regarded as the sweet-tasting beverage of the gods. In China it was thought to rain down from heaven when the world became peaceful. *Amrita* is said to remove one's sufferings and make one immortal. The word *amrita* means immortality.

Anger, state of. *See* Asura.

Anryūgyō: (Skt Supratishthitachāritra) One of the four bodhisattvas who are the leaders of the Bodhisattvas of the Earth. He appears in the *Yujutsu* (fifteenth) chapter of the Lotus Sutra. The four bodhisattvas are said to represent the four virtues of the Buddha: true self, eternity, purity and happiness. Bodhisattva Anryūgyō represents happiness.

Arhat: (Skt) One who has attained the highest of the four stages which the men of Learning (Skt *shrāvakas*) aim to achieve through the practice of Hinayana teachings, that is, the highest stage of Hinayana enlightenment. Arhat means one worthy of respect. Arhat was originally synonymous with Buddha. With the rise of Mahayana Buddhism, however, the term came to refer exclusively to the saints of Hinayana Buddhism.

Ashoka (r.c. 268–232 B.C.): The third ruler of the Indian Maurya dynasty and the first king to unify India. He was the grandson of Chandragupta, the founder of the Maurya dynasty, and the son of Bindusāra, the second in the dynastic succession. He began as a tyrant but later governed compassionately in keeping with the ideals of Buddhism. His achievements and views are recorded not only in Buddhist scriptures but also in many edicts inscribed on rocks and pillars which have been discovered throughout his former kingdom.

Asura: (Skt)(Jap *ashura*) A class of contentious demons in Indian mythology who fight continually with the god Indra (Jap Taishaku). They are said to live at the bottom of the ocean surrounding Mount Sumeru. In Buddhism they constitute one of the eight kinds of lowly beings and represent the world of Anger among the Ten Worlds. *See also* Ten Worlds.

Bian Que: A famous physician of ancient Chinese history.

Bodhisattva: One who aspires to Buddhahood. In Hinayana Buddhism the term is used almost exclusively to indicate Shakyamuni in his previous lifetimes. The *Jātaka* or birth stories often refer to him as "the bodhisattva." After the rise of Mahayana, bodhisattva came to mean anyone who aspires to enlightenment and carries out altruistic practice. Mahayana practitioners used it to refer to themselves, thus expressing the conviction that they would one day attain Buddhahood. In contrast to the Hinayana ideal embodied by the men of Learning and Realization who direct their efforts solely toward personal salvation, Mahayana sets forth the ideal of the bodhisattva who seeks enlightenment both for himself and others. Compassion is the bodhisattva's greatest characteristic; he is said to postpone his own entry into nirvana in order to save others. According to the traditional Mahayana concept, all bodhisattvas make the four universal vows when they commence their practice and carry out the six *paramitas* in order to attain Buddhahood. Some sutras divide bodhisattva practice into fifty-two stages, from initial resolution to the time of enlightenment. Bodhisattva practice was generally thought to require successive lifetimes of practice spanning many aeons to complete. However, from the standpoint of the Lotus Sutra, the bodhisattva practice can be completed in a single lifetime.

Bodhisattva Fukyō. *See* Fukyō.

Bodhisattvas of the Earth: The bodhisattvas entrusted by Shakyamuni with the mission of propagating the Mystic Law in the Latter Day. They appear in the *Yujutsu* (fifteenth) chapter of the Lotus Sutra at the beginning of the essential teaching. In this chapter, countless bodhisattvas from other worlds ask for permission to propagate the Lotus Sutra in the *saha* world after the Buddha's death, but Shakyamuni refuses, saying that the *saha* world already has bodhisattvas who will carry out this task. At this point the earth trembles and a host of bodhisattvas equal in number to the sands of sixty thousand Ganges Rivers emerge, each with his own retinue of followers. Their bodies are golden and possess the thirty-two features. They are led by the four bodhisattvas—Jōgyō, Muhengyō, Jyōgyō and Anryūgyō—and Jōgyō is the leader of them all. In the *Jinriki* (twenty-first) chapter, Shakyamuni transfers the essence of the Lotus Sutra to the Bodhisattvas of the Earth, entrusting them with the mission of propagating it in the Latter Day. *See also* Latter Day of the Law; *Yujutsu* chapter; individual bodhisattva's names.

Buddha: One who perceives the true entity of all phenomena, and who leads others to attain the same enlightenment. In India the word *buddha* was originally a common noun meaning "awakened one," but in Buddhism it is used to mean one who has become awakened to the ultimate truth of life.

Buddhahood: The state which a Buddha has attained. The ultimate goal of Buddhist practice. The highest of the Ten Worlds. The word enlightenment is often used as synonymous with Buddhahood. Buddhahood is thought of as a state of perfect freedom, in which one is awakened to the eternal and ultimate truth that is the reality of all things. It is characterized by boundless wisdom and infinite compassion. *See also* Ten Worlds.

Buddha land. *See* Pure land.

Buddha nature: (Skt Buddhadhatu or Buddhatā) The internal cause or potential for attaining Buddhahood. Also called the seed of Buddhahood or Matrix of the Tathāgata (Skt *tathāgata-garbha*, Jap *nyoraizō*). Mahayana generally holds that all people possess the Buddha nature inherently, though it may be obscured by illusions and evil karma. Throughout the history of Buddhism there have been numerous explanations and arguments concerning the Buddha nature and whether or not all people possess it. Nichiren Daishonin's Buddhism teaches that all people can manifest their inherent Buddha nature through faith in the Gohonzon.

Dai-Gohonzon: The object of worship which Nichiren Daishonin inscribed on October 12, 1279, as the ultimate purpose of his advent in this world. Also called the Dai-Gohonzon of the high sanctuary of true Buddhism. It is enshrined at Taiseki-ji, the head temple of Nichiren Shoshu. The Daishonin defines the True Law in the Latter Day as the Three Great Secret Laws—the object of worship, the high sanctuary, and the invocation or the Daimoku, of true Buddhism. The object of worship of true Buddhism is the basis of the Three Great Secret Laws. The Daimoku is the chanting of Nam-myoho-renge-kyo with faith in the object of worship, and the high sanctuary is the place where the object of worship is enshrined and the Daimoku is chanted to it. Thus the inscription of the object of worship essentially includes all three aspects: the object of worship, Daimoku, and the high sanctuary. The object of worship, therefore, encompasses all Three Great Secret Laws within itself, and is called the One Great Secret Law, which indicates the Dai-Gohonzon. *See also* Three Great Secret Laws.

Dependent origination: (Skt *pratītya-samutpāda*) Also dependent causation, conditioned co-arising or co-production. A fundamental Buddhist doctrine of the interdependence of things. It teaches that all beings and phenomena exist or occur only because of their relationship with other beings or phenomena. Therefore, nothing can exist in absolute independence of other things or arise of its own accord. The doctrine of the twelve-linked chain of causation is a well-known illustration.

Eight Hindering Winds: Eight conditions which prevent people from advancing along the right path to enlightenment. They are: prosperity, decline, disgrace, honor, praise, censure, suffering, and pleasure. People are often swayed either by their attachment to prosperity, honor, praise, and pleasure, or by their aversion to decline, disgrace, censure, and suffering.

Eshō funi: Oneness of life and its environment. A principle stating that the self and its environment are two integral phases of the same entity. *Eshō* is a contraction of *ehō*, the insentient environment or objective world, and *shōhō*, the living self or subjective world. *Shō* of *shōhō* means subject and *e* of *ehō*, to depend, meaning that life is dependent on its environment for survival. *Hō* in both words means manifest effect, indicating that an individual's karmic reward appears in both his subjective and objective reality. *Funi* is an abbreviation of *nini-funi* (two but not two) and *funi-nini* (not two but two). These expressions mean that life and its environment are two independent phenomena but one in their fundamental essence.

Fahua Wenju: Full title, *Miaofa Lianhua Jing Wenju* (Jap *Hokke Mongu* or *Myōhō-renge-kyō Mongu*), "Words and Phrases of the Lotus Sutra." A ten-fascicle commentary on the Lotus Sutra expounded by Tiantai and recorded by Changan during the Sui dynasty. *See also* Tiantai, Great Master.

Five components of life: Also five Skandhas. Form, perception, conception, volition and consciousness. These five components unite temporarily to form an individual living being. Form (Jap *shiki*) means the physical aspect of life and includes the five sense organs—eyes, ears, nose, tongue and body—through which one perceives the external world. Perception *(ju)* is the function of receiving external information through the six sense organs (the five sense organs plus the "mind," which integrates the impressions of the five senses). Conception (*sō*) is the function of creating mental ideas or conceptions about what has been perceived. Volition (*gyō*) is the will which acts on the conception and motivates action toward what has been perceived. Consciousness (*shiki*) is the function of discernment, and gives rise to the components of perception, conception, and volition. Form represents the physical aspect of life, and perception, conception, volition, and consciousness represent the spiritual aspect. Because the physical and spiritual properties of life are inseparable, there can be no form without perception, conception, volition, and consciousness, and no consciousness without form, perception, conception, and volition. All life carries on its activities through the interaction of these five components. Their workings are colored by the karma one has formed in successive lifetimes, and so function to create future karma.

Five Skandhas. *See* Five components of life.

Four devils. *See* Three obstacles and four devils.

Fukyō: (Skt Sadāparibhūta) Full name Jōfukyō, but often shortened to Fukyō. A bodhisattva described in the *Fukyō* (twentieth) chapter of the Lotus Sutra who appeared during the Middle Day of a Buddha called Ionnō when Buddhism was in decline and arrogant monks held great authority. This bodhisattva held everyone he met in reverence, speaking words of praise (later called the twenty-four-character Lotus Sutra) which read, "I deeply respect you. I would not dare despise you or be arrogant, for you will all practice the bodhisattva way and surely attain Buddhahood." Therefore he was dubbed Bodhisattva Jōfukyō (Never Despising). People ridiculed him and attacked him with sticks and rocks. Toward the end of his life he heard about the Lotus Sutra which had been expounded by Ionnō Buddha, and was able to embrace it fully, thus purifying his six senses and extending his life span by two hundred, ten thousand, a hundred thousand nayuta years, and preached the Lotus Sutra to countless millions of people. Those people who had slandered Fukyō now followed him and took faith in the sutra, but due to their past offenses of harboring anger and grudges against him, they languished in the hell of incessant suffering for one thousand kalpas. For twenty million kalpas they never encountered a Buddha, heard of the Law, or saw any monk. Eventually, however, they were reborn with Bodhisattva Fukyō and were converted by him to the Lotus Sutra. In the *Fukyō* chapter, Shakyamuni identifies Bodhisattva Fukyō as himself in a previous lifetime. Nichiren Daishonin often cites the story of Bodhisattva Fukyō to illustrate the principle of attaining enlightenment through reverse relationship (Jap *gyakuen*).

Gohonzon. *See* Dai-Gohonzon.

Gohyaku-jintengō: Also pronounced *gohyaku-jindengō*. An incredibly long period of time described in the *Juryō* (sixteenth) chapter of the Lotus Sutra which indicates how much time has elapsed since Shakyamuni's original enlightenment. Up until the *Juryō* chapter Shakyamuni taught that he had first attained Buddhahood at the age of thirty in India. In the *Juryō* chapter, however, he reveals that he actually attained enlightenment in the inconceivably remote past. He explains *gohyaku-jintengō* in this chapter as follows: "Suppose there is one who reduces five hundred, thousand, ten thousand, hundred thousand, nayuta(10^{11}), asōgi(10^{51}) major world systems into particles of dust, and then takes them all toward the east, dropping one particle each time he traverses five hundred, thousand, ten thousand, hundred thousand, nayuta, asōgi worlds. Suppose that he continues traveling eastward in this way, until he has finished dropping all the particles. . . . Suppose all these worlds, whether they received a particle or not, are once more reduced to dust. Let one particle represent one aeon. Then the time which has passed since I attained Buddhahood surpasses this by one hundred, thousand, ten thousand, hundred thousand, nayuta, asōgi aeons." *Gohyaku* (five hundred) stands for the five hundred, thousand, ten thousand, hundred thousand, nayuta, asōgi major world systems which one reduces to dust in beginning this calculation. *Jinten* means placing all the reduced dust particles side by side, and *gō* means kalpa, or aeon.

Gongyo: Literally, "assiduous practice." Generally speaking, gongyo means to recite Buddhist sutras in front of an object of worship, though the exact ritual and method of practice differ according to the sect of Buddhism. In Nichiren Shoshu, gongyo means to chant Nam-myoho-renge-kyo and recite part of the *Hōben* (second) chapter and the entire *Juryō* (sixteenth) chapter of the Lotus Sutra in front of the Gohonzon. This is the most fundamental practice of Nichiren Shoshu and is performed each morning and evening. The gongyo of Nichiren Shoshu consists of two parts: the primary practice, or chanting Nam-myoho-renge-kyo, and the supplementary practice, or reciting the *Hōben* and *Juryō* chapters.

Great Teacher Miaoluo. *See* Miaoluo, Great Teacher.

Great Teacher Tiantai. *See* Tiantai, Great Teacher.

Hokke Mongu. See *Fahua Wenju.*

House Afire: This refers to the parable of the three carts and the burning house, one of the seven parables in the Lotus Sutra, which appears in the *Hiyu* (third) chapter. Also called the parable of the burning house. Shakyamuni relates this parable to illustrate his statement in the *Hōben* (second) chapter that the sole purpose of the Buddha's advent is to enable all people to attain Buddhahood, and that the three vehicles of Learning, Realization and Bodhisattva are simply means to lead people to the one Buddha vehicle. Suppose, he says, there is an extremely wealthy man who has innumerable children. One day a fire suddenly breaks out in his spacious but decaying mansion, and his children, totally absorbed in their playing, do not realize that the house is in flames and ignore his cries of warning. He therefore resorts to an expedient device to induce them to come out of the house. He shouts to them that outside he has three kinds of carts which they have long wanted: one kind pulled by a sheep, one by a deer, and one by an ox. Immediately they race each other out the door. Having coaxed them to safety in this way, the wealthy man gives each of his children a cart not of three kinds that he had promised but a much finer kind, adorned with jewels and drawn by a great white ox. In this parable, the burning house represents the threefold world, and the flames are the sufferings of birth and death. The rich man is the Buddha, who appears in this troubled world to save the people, the children are all living beings, and the games in which they are so absorbed are worldly pleasures. The three kinds of carts originally promised represent the three provisional vehicles of Learning, Realization, and Bodhisattva, and the great white ox cart symbolizes the supreme vehicle of Buddhahood, that is, the Lotus Sutra.

Huang Di: A legendary sage-king of ancient China.

Ichinen sanzen: "A single life-moment possesses three thousand realms." A philosophical system set forth by Tiantai in the *Moho Zhiguan* on the basis of the Lotus Sutra, clarifying the mutually inclusive relationship of the ultimate truth and the phenomenal world. *Ichinen* (one mind, life moment or life essence) is the life that is manifest at each moment within common mortals, and *sanzen* (three thousand), the varying aspects and phases it assumes. In terms of the "true entity of all phenomena" (Jap *shohō jissō*), *ichinen* corresponds to "true entity"—life's true nature or ultimate reality—and *sanzen* to "all phenomena." The expression "three thousand" is an integration of the Ten Worlds, their mutual possession, the ten factors and the three realms of existence. These figures multiplied $(10 \times 10 \times 10 \times 3)$ yield three thousand. These component principles may be thought of as the three thousand conditions according to which the life essence manifests itself as phenomena. With this principle, Tiantai showed that all phenomena—body and mind, self and environment, sentient and insentient, cause and effect—are integrated in the life moment of the common mortal. The pre-Lotus Sutra teachings generally hold that the mind is the basis of all phenomena and that all phenomena arise from the mind, but the *ichinen sanzen* principle, based on the Lotus Sutra, teaches that the mind and all phenomena are "two but not two," and neither can be independent of the other.

Jisui: A renowned physician appearing in the Konkōmyō Sutra. According to that sutra, he lived countless aeons ago in the Middle Day of the Law of a Buddha called Hōshō, during the reign of King Tenjizaikō who was a believer in the Buddha's teaching. Jisui was well versed in medicine and healed innumerable people. At one time, an epidemic swept through the country, but Jisui was by then too old to exercise his skill. However, he taught secret medical arts to his son Rusui, who then saved the people in Jisui's stead.

Jīvaka: A skilled physician of Magadha in ancient India and a devout Buddhist. He treated King Bimbisāra and Shakyamuni himself and thus won renown. He served as minister to King Ajātashatru, and when Ajātashatru killed his father, King Bimbisāra, and was about to kill his mother, Vaidehi, Jīvaka dissuaded him. Later, when King Ajātashatru broke out in malignant sores all over his body, Jīvaka succeeded in persuading him to reflect on his past conduct and to seek the Buddha's teaching.

Jōbutsu. *See* Buddhahood.

Jōgyō: (Skt Vishishtachāritra) One of the four bodhisattvas and the leader of the Bodhisattvas of the Earth. He appears in the *Yujutsu* (fifteenth) chapter of the Lotus Sutra. The four bodhisattvas are said to represent the four virtues of the Buddha's life: true self, eternity, purity, and happiness. Among these, Jōgyō represents the virtue of true self.

Juryō chapter: "The Life Span of the Tathāgata." The sixteenth chapter of the Lotus Sutra, in which Shakyamuni reveals his original enlightenment in the distant past. Its full title is the *Nyorai Juryō* chapter. It opens with a ritual exchange called the three exhortations and four entreaties, in which the Buddha three times admonishes the multitude to believe and understand his words, and the assembly four times begs him to preach. "Listen well," Shakyamuni then says, "to the Tathāgata's secret and his mystic power." He proceeds to explain that while all heavenly gods, men, asuras and other beings think that he first attained enlightenment in that lifetime under the Bodhi tree, it has actually been an incalculable length of time since he attained enlightenment. To indicate how immeasurably long ago it was, he explains the concept of *gohyaku-jintengō*. He refutes the view that he attained enlightenment for the first time in India and reveals his original enlightenment in the remote past. This is called "opening the near and revealing the distant" (Jap *kaigon kennon*). "Life span" in the title of the chapter means the duration of Shakyamuni's life as the Buddha, i.e., how long he has been enlightened. Ever since that time, he continues, he has been here in this world preaching the Law, appearing as many different Buddhas and using various means. Though he says that he enters nirvana, he merely uses his death as a means to arouse in the people the desire to seek a Buddha. He then illustrates this idea with the parable of the excellent physician and his sick children. The chapter concludes with a verse section which restates the important teachings of the preceding prose section.

Jyōgyō (Skt Vishuddhachāritra) One of the four leaders of the Bodhisattvas of the Earth. He appears in the *Yujutsu (fifteenth)* chapter of the Lotus Sutra. The four bodhisattvas are regarded as representing the four virtues of the Buddha's life—true self, eternity, purity, and happiness. Of these, Bodhisattva Jyōgyō represents purity.

Kanishka: The third king of the Kushāna dynasty in northern India. He is said to have lived during the first half of the second century, though there are differing views and some scholars place him at the end of the first century. He was the most outstanding monarch of the Kushāna dynasty and is famous as a great patron of Buddhism, together with King Ashoka. He was converted to Buddhism by Ashvaghosha. The

Fourth Buddhist Council was held in Kashmir under his patronage. He also built a great stupa in his capital at Purushapura, the modern Peshawar. The flowering of Gandhara culture reached its peak under Kanishka's rule.

Kōsen-rufu: Literally, to "widely declare and spread [Buddhism]." The term appears in the *Yakuō* (twenty-third) chapter of the Lotus Sutra, which states, "In the fifth five hundred years after my death, accomplish worldwide *kōsen-rufu* and never allow its flow to cease." Nichiren Daishonin defines Nam-myoho-renge-kyo of the Three Great Secret Laws as the Law to be declared and spread widely during the Latter Day. Nichiren Shoshu identifies two aspects of *kōsen-rufu:* the *kōsen-rufu* of the entity of the Law (Jap *kehō no kōsen-rufu* or *hottai no kōsen-rufu*), or the establishment of the Dai-Gohonzon which is the basis of the Three Great Secret Laws, and the *kōsen-rufu* of substantiation *(kegi no kōsen-rufu* , or the widespread acceptance of faith in the Dai-Gohonzon among the people. On October 12, 1279, the Daishonin established the Dai-Gohonzon of the high sanctuary of true Buddhism as the object of worship for attaining Buddhahood. Thereby the object or the entity of the Law, which all people should worship, was established. This is called the *kōsen-rufu* of the entity of the Law. Through propagation of the Daishonin's teaching, many people will come to recognize this Dai-Gohonzon as their object of worship. This constitutes the *kōsen-rufu* of substantiation, and the Daishonin entrusted this task to his disciples.

Kuon ganjo. See Original Buddha.

Latter Day of the Law: The last of the three periods following Shakyamuni Buddha's death when Buddhism falls into confusion and Shakyamuni's teachings lose the power to lead people to enlightenment. It is said to last for ten thousand years and more. The beginning of the Latter Day of the Law also corresponds to the fifth of the five five-hundred-year periods following Shakyamuni's death. This fifth period was widely expected to be an "age of conflict," when monks will disregard the precepts and feud constantly among themselves, heretical views will prevail, and Shakyamuni's Buddhism will perish. In contrast, the Lotus Sutra views the Latter Day, when Shakyamuni's teachings lose their power of redemption, as the time when the essence of the Lotus Sutra will be propagated. Though modern research tends to place Shakyamuni's death around 500 B.C. Asian Buddhist tradition holds that he passed away in 949 B.C.

Calculating from this date, Japanese Buddhists believed that the Latter Day of the Law had begun in 1052.

Lay Priest Takahashi. *See* Takahashi, Lay Priest.

Lotus Sutra: (Skt *Saddharma-pundarīka-sūtra*) One of the Mahayana sutras. There are a few Sanskrit texts, including fragments, which were discovered in Nepal, Kashmir, and Central Asia. There is also a Tibetan version. Six Chinese translations of the Lotus Sutra were made, of which three are extant. The Lotus Sutra is the most widely revered Buddhist scripture in Chinese and Japanese Buddhism, and it is the base upon which Nichiren Daishonin built his life and teachings. The main doctrines of the Lotus Sutra are: (1) that the Buddha employs many different skillful means to lead all sentient beings to enlightenment, but the Lotus Sutra is the only way for all; and (2) that the Buddha is eternal and universal. In addition, the theme of the bodhisattva and his compassionate practice is strongly emphasized in the sutra.

Miaoluo, Great Teacher (711–82): The sixth patriarch of the Tiantai school in China, counting from Great Teacher Tiantai. Since he lived at Miaoluosi temple, he is called Great Teacher Miaoluo. At the age of twenty Miaoluo studied the doctrine of the Tiantai school under Xuanlang, the fifth patriarch, and at the age of thirty-eight he entered the priesthood. At that time, the Chan (Jap Zen), Huayan (Kegon), Faxiang (Hosso), and other schools were flourishing while the Tiantai school was in decline. Miaoluo reasserted the supremacy of the Lotus Sutra and wrote commentaries on Tiantai's three major works, thus bringing about a revival of interest in Tiantai Buddhism. He is revered as the restorer of the school. In his later years he lived at Guoqingsi temple on Mount Tiantai and devoted his efforts to propagating the Tiantai doctrine. He died at Folong Monastery on Mount Tiantai. His commentaries on Tiantai's three major works are entitled (in Japanese) *Hokke Gengi Shakusen, Hokke Mongu Ki,* and *Maka Shikan Bugyōden Guketsu.*

Middle Way: The way which transcends the extremes of two one-sided and opposing views. Interpretations of the term Middle Way vary considerably from one text or school to another. Among them are: (1) In Shakyamuni's teaching, the rejection of the two extremes of self-indulgence and self-mortification. While still a prince, Shakyamuni lived in luxury in his father's palace and gave himself to the pleasures of life, but after renouncing the world, he abandoned these diversions and subjected himself to years of harsh austerities. Eventually he rejected asceticism as well, and after attaining enlightenment he preached a way of life that avoids both extremes. The Pali text *Majjhima-nikāya* terms this path the Middle Way. It is exemplified by the eightfold path. (2) According to Nāgārjuna's *Chū Ron,* the true nature of all things which neither is born nor dies, and which cannot be defined by either of the two extremes, existence or nonexistence. This true nature of things is non-substantiality or *kū,* and is called the Middle Way. (3) In terms of Tiantai's doctrine of the three truths, the truth of the Middle Way (Jap *chū* or *chūtai*), which means that the true nature of all things is neither non-substantiality (*kū*) nor temporary existence (*ke*), but manifests the characteristics of both. (4) In Nichiren Daishonin's Buddhism, Nam-myoho-renge-kyo, the ultimate truth of things that is at the same time the entity of the body and mind of common mortals. The Gosho "Isshō Jōbutsu Shō" (On Attaining Buddhahood) states, "Life is indeed an elusive reality that transcends both the words and concepts of existence and nonexistence. It is neither existence nor nonexistence, yet exhibits the qualities of both. It is the mystic entity of the Middle Way that is the reality of all things."

Moho Zhiguan: (Jap *Maka Shikan*), "Great Concentration and Insight." One of Great Teacher Tiantai's three major works, along with the *Fahua Xuanyi* and the *Fahua Wenju.* The *Moho Zhiguan* is actually a compilation of lectures delivered by Tiantai in 594, compiled in ten volumes by his disciple Changan. It elucidates the principle of *ichinen sanzen* based on the Lotus Sutra and teaches the method of practice for observing one's mind in order to realize this truth within oneself. The *Moho Zhiguan* consists of ten chapters; the seventh chapter, entitled "The Chapter on the Correct Practice" (Jap *Shōshu Shō*), is regarded as the core of the *Moho Zhiguan* and reveals the practice of concentration and insight. This work is regarded as Tiantai's ultimate teaching.

Muhengyō: (Skt Anantachāritra) One of the four bodhisattvas who lead the Bodhisattvas of the Earth. Muhengyō literally means no boundary and represents eternity, one of the four virtues of the Buddha's life.

Mystic Law: The ultimate Law of life and the universe. The Law of Nam-myoho-renge-kyo. *See also* Nam-myoho-renge-kyo.

Nam-myoho-renge-kyo: The ultimate Law or true entity of life permeating all phenomena in the universe. Also, the invocation of Nam-myoho-renge-kyo or Daimoku of true Buddhism, one of the Three Great Secret Laws. The invocation of Nam-myoho-renge-kyo was established by Nichiren Daishonin, who first chanted it aloud on April 28, 1253, at Seichō-ji temple in the province of Awa. *Namu* or *nam* derives from the Sanskrit word *namas* and is translated as devotion (Jap *kimyō*, literally, "to dedicate one's life"). *Myōhō* is the Mystic Law. *Renge* means the lotus flower. The lotus blooms and seeds at the same time, and thus represents the simultaneity of cause and effect, which is one expression of the Mystic Law. In addition, the lotus grows and blooms in a muddy pond, which symbolizes the emergence of Buddhahood from within the life of a common mortal. *Kyō* literally means sutra, the voice or teaching of a Buddha. The character for *kyō* originally meant the warp of cloth, and later came to have the additional meanings of thread of logic, reason, way, or law. It was therefore also used in the sense of a teaching to be preserved. The *kyō* of *Myōhō-renge-kyō* indicates that Myōhō-renge-kyō itself is the eternal and unchanging truth. Nichiren Daishonin teaches that the Mystic Law encompasses all laws and teachings within itself, and that the benefit of chanting Nam-myoho-renge-kyo includes the benefit of conducting all virtuous practices.

Nichimoku (1260–1333): The third high priest of Nichiren Shoshu, also called Niidakyō Ajari Nichimoku. He was born in Hatake Village of Nitta District of Izu Province. At the age of thirteen he entered a temple called Izu-san, and in 1274 he witnessed a religious debate between Shikibu Sōzu, a priest of that temple, and Nikkō Shonin. On the spot he resolved to become Nikkō Shonin's disciple. In 1276 he went to Minobu, where he took the tonsure and was ordained by Nichiren Daishonin. For the next six years until the Daishonin's death, Nichimoku Shonin served him. After the Daishonin passed away, Nichimoku Shonin served Nikkō Shonin, and took part in the rotation system for attending the Daishonin's tomb. He also devoted himself to propagation activity in Izu Province and in the Ōshū area in the north, converting many people and building a number of temples. In 1332 Nikkō Shonin officially transferred the Dai-Gohonzon to Nichimoku and charged him with the administration of Taiseki-ji and the observance of daily worship for *kōsen-rufu*. At this time Nichimoku Shonin became the third high priest. On behalf of Nichiren Daishonin and Nikkō Shonin, he remonstrated with the Kamakura government, the imperial court, court nobles, and leading samurai on dozens of occasions, urging them to take faith in the Daishonin's Buddhism. In May of 1333, the Kamakura government fell and power reverted to the imperial court in Kyoto. Nichimoku Shonin resolved to remonstrate again with the new authorities and urge them to accept the Daishonin's teachings. In November of that year, having transferred the office of high priest to Nichidō Shonin, he set out for Kyoto, accompanied by his disciples Nichizon and Nichigō. It was a cold, grueling journey, and Nichimoku Shonin died en route at Tarui in Mino Province. His two disciples went on to Kyoto to remonstrate in his stead; Nichizon remained there and Nichigō returned to Taiseki-ji with his ashes.

Nichiren Daishonin (1222–82): The founder of all Nichiren sects, and, from the standpoint of Soka Gakkai, the founder of true Buddhism. Nichiren entered a local temple as a boy, and as a young man studied at Mount Hiei and many other major centers of Japanese Buddhism. He returned to his place of birth, the fishing village of Kominato in the province of Awa (modern Chiba Prefecture) in 1253 to lecture on the results of his studies. During that lecture, at Seichō-ji, he refuted the Pure Land sect, which infuriated the local steward, who was one of its followers. He was forced to flee and took up residence in Kamakura. There he preached to the people and gained faithful followers. He also composed *Risshō Ankoku Ron,* which stated that the calamities Japan had suffered recently were due to the belief in false teachings of Buddhism that were rampant in Japan. His insistence that the government withdraw support from those sects created for Nichiren many enemies, who attacked and burned his hut in 1260; eventually, in 1261, he was exiled to Izu. He was pardoned in 1263 and returned to Kamakura. He continued to proselytize in Kamakura and in the northern Kanto provinces of Awa, Kazusa, Shimosa, and Hitachi. He also continued to remonstrate the government for its failure to recognize true Buddhism, and his activities led, in 1271, to his second banishment, this time to the island of Sado in the Japan Sea. Life there was very hard, but eventually Nichiren won over local supporters, and it was during this period that he composed several of his major writings. Nichiren was finally pardoned in 1274. He returned to Kamakura and reiterated his criticism of the government, pointing out that the impending attack of Mongol forces was a calamity that he had predicted, and was due to the nation's failure to recognize the true Law. With this last remonstrance, Nichiren withdrew to Mount Minobu, where, in his final years he gathered his disciples around him, wrote, taught, and built the base for what is now Nichiren Shoshu by inscribing the Dai-Gohonzon.

Nichiren Shoshu: "Orthodox Nichiren sect." A sect of Buddhism which regards Nichiren Daishonin as its founder and Nikkō Shonin as his immediate successor. Its head temple is Taiseki-ji in Shizuoka Prefecture. Nichiren Shoshu holds that all people possess the Buddha nature and can attain enlightenment in this present world by believing in the Dai-Gohonzon. Moreover, because the self and its objective world are essentially one, the individual attaining Buddhahood simultaneously transforms his environment into the Buddha land. Nichiren Shoshu therefore upholds "the practice for self and others" (Jap *jigyō keta*), aiming at personal enlightenment and also the salvation of others, society, and the world itself through the process of *kōsen-rufu*, or widespread propagation of the Mystic Law. In contrast to the other Nichiren sects which regard Shakyamuni as the object of worship and Nichiren Daishonin as a great bodhisattva, Nichiren Shoshu reveres the Daishonin as the embodiment of the original Buddha who appears in the Latter Day of the Law, and the mandala (Gohonzon) which he inscribed as the correct object of worship for all people in the Latter Day to attain Buddhahood.

Nichiren Shū: "Nichiren sect." In a strict sense, that sect of Nichiren Buddhism that has its head temple at Kuon-ji temple in Minobu. Broadly speaking, however, Nichiren Shū is a generic term for all those sects which regard Nichiren Daishonin as their founder. In this sense, the name Hokke Shū (Hokke sect) is also used. Nichiren Daishonin himself used the name Hokke Shū. Nichiren Daishonin had six senior disciples: Nisshō, Nichirō, Nikkō, Nikō, Nitchō, and Nichiji. Among them, he chose Nikkō Shonin as his successor. After the Daishonin died, however, the other five did not follow Nikkō Shonin but maintained their own interpretations of the teaching. This was the origin of the various Nichiren schools.

Nikkō Shonin (1246–1333): Byakuren Ajari Nikkō, Nichiren Daishonin's successor. The second high priest of Nichiren Shoshu and the founder of its head temple, Taiseki-ji. He was born at Kajikazawa in Koma District of Kai Province. In 1258 Nichiren Daishonin visited Jissō-ji to do research in its sutra library in preparation for the writing of his *Risshō Ankoku Ron*. Nikkō had an opportunity to serve him there, and was

moved to become the Daishonin's disciple, receiving the name Hōki-bō
Nikkō. He was then thirteen. From that time on, he devotedly served
the Daishonin. Nikkō Shonin recorded the lectures on the Lotus Sutra
which the Daishonin gave to his disciples at Minobu and compiled them
as the *Ongi Kuden* (Record of the Orally Transmitted Teachings) in
January 1278. He also carried out a great propagation effort centered in
Kai, Suruga, and Izu, which spread to other provinces as well. Shortly
before his death he wrote an admonishment to priests and lay believers
to maintain the purity of Nichiren Daishonin's teachings. He transferred
the entirety of the Daishonin's Buddhism to the third high priest, Nichimoku Shonin, and died at the age of eighty-eight.

Nittatsu Shonin (1902–79): The sixty-sixth high priest of Nichiren Shoshu.

Original Buddha: Also, the Buddha of *kuon ganjo*. The Buddha from time
without beginning. The Buddha who has been enlightened since the
infinite past to the ultimate truth or the Law of Nam-myoho-renge-kyo.
According to the Nichiren Shoshu doctrine, the Buddha of *kuon ganjo*
appeared in the Latter Day of the Law as Nichiren Daishonin, in order
to save all people. In the *Juryō* (sixteenth) chapter of the essential
teaching of the Lotus Sutra, Shakyamuni revealed his attainment of Buddhahood at a specific point in time called *gohyaku-jintengō*. However,
he did not clarify the Law or cause that enabled him to attain that original
enlightenment. Nichiren Daishonin, as the manifestation of the Buddha
of *kuon ganjo,* revealed Nam-myoho-renge-kyo as the ultimate Law of
life and identified it as the original cause for Shakyamuni's enlightenment
and for the enlightenment of all people.

Paradise in the West. *See* Pure Land.

Perfect teaching: Sometimes called the round teaching. The supreme
teaching of Buddhism. In China, scholars made numerous attempts to
organize the vast array of sutras which had been introduced at random
from India into coherent systems. In these systems of comparative classification (Jap *kyōsō-hanjaku*), as they were called, the sutra which was
ranked highest was called the perfect teaching. For example, Huiguang
(468–537) divided the Buddhist teachings into three categories—gradual,
abrupt, and perfect—and designated the Kegon Sutra as the perfect teaching. Tiantai declared the doctrine of the mutually inclusive relationship
of ultimate reality and all phenomena to be the perfect teaching. He

defines two categories of perfect teaching: that expounded in the pre-Lotus Sutra teachings (*nizen no en*) and that taught in the Lotus Sutra itself (*hokke no en*). Both teach the concept of attaining Buddhahood as a common mortal, but the former teaches it in name only with no example of it ever having occurred, or else draws various distinctions and exceptions. The latter teaches that all people can without exception attain enlightenment, illustrating it with examples. The term "perfect teaching" is often used synonymously with the Lotus Sutra.

Pure land: The land where a Buddha dwells. The term is used in contrast to "impure land," meaning the present *sahā* world defiled by suffering and desire. Since the Buddha land is free from the five impurities, it is called the pure land. Broadly speaking, there are two views concerning the relationship of the *sahā* world and the pure land. The first is that the pure land is another realm entirely, physically removed from the *sahā* world. Examples of this view are the Emerald Land of Yakushi Buddha in the east and Amida Buddha's Pure Land of Perfect Bliss in the west. (The term Pure Land in capitals is often used to mean Amida's land.) The second view as represented in the Lotus Sutra or the Vimalakīrti Sutra is that there can be no pure land apart from the *sahā* world. It is a matter of one's state of life; when one purifies his heart, the world he lives in becomes a pure land.

Risshō Ankoku Ron: "On Securing the Peace of the Land through the Propagation of True Buddhism." One of Nichiren Daishonin's major writings, which he submitted to Hōjō Tokiyori—at that time the retired regent but still the most influential member of the ruling Hōjō clan—on July 16, 1260, when the Daishonin was thirty-nine years old. The *Risshō Ankoku Ron* begins by depicting the misery caused by the frequent disasters ravaging Japan in those days. It regards people's slanderous acts against the True Law as a major factor responsible for undermining the country as a whole. In this treatise, the Daishonin teaches that the people should abandon their faith in erroneous teachings and embrace the True Law, which is the basis for establishing a peaceful land.

Rusui: A legendary physician said to have lived countless aeons ago in the Middle Day of the Law of Hōshō Buddha. He is described in the Konkōmyō Sutra. According to that sutra, an epidemic broke out in his country, and Rusui asked his aged father Jisui, also a skilled physician, to teach him secret medical practices. Thus he was able to save the population from the epidemic.

Saichō (767–822): The founder of the Tendai sect in Japan. His honorific name and title is Dengyō Daishi (Great Teacher Dengyō). In 1804 Dengyō went to Tang China accompanied by his disciple, Gishin. In 805 he returned to Japan and the next year established the Tendai sect. At that time, all priests were ordained exclusively in the Hinayana precepts. Dengyō made continuing efforts to secure imperial permission for the building of a Mahayana ordination center on Mount Hiei, despite concentrated opposition from the older sects of Nara. Permission was finally granted a week after his death, and in 827, the ordination center was completed by his successor, Gishin. In addition to this project, after his return to Japan, Dengyō concentrated his efforts on refuting the interpretations of the older Buddhist sects. His works include the *Hokke Shūku, Kenkai Ron, Shugo Kokkai Shō* and *Sange Gakushō Shiki.*

Seven Bells: The name of the program dividing Soka Gakkai activities into seven periods of seven years each, from the time of the organization's foundation in 1930 to 1979. Each of the seven-year stages had a specific goal. Soka Gakkai is now in the second of its Seven Bell programs.

Seven disasters: Disasters said to be caused by slander of the True Law. In the Ninnō Sutra they are listed as (1) extraordinary changes of the sun and moon, (2) extraordinary changes of the stars and planets, (3) fires, (4) unseasonable floods, (5) storms, (6) drought, and (7) war, including enemy attacks from without and rebellion from within. The Yakushi Sutra defines the seven disasters as (1) pestilence, (2) foreign invasion, (3) internal strife, (4) extraordinary changes in the heavens, (5) solar and lunar eclipses, (6) unseasonable storms and typhoons, and (7) unseasonable drought. The *Kannon* (twenty-fifth) chapter of the Lotus Sutra also lists seven disasters from which one can be saved by the power of Bodhisattva Kannon: (1) fire, (2) flood, (3) *rakshasa* (Jap *rasetsu*) demons, (4) attack by swords and staves, (5) attack by *yaksha* (*yasha*) and other demons, (6) imprisonment, and (7) attack by bandits.

Shakubuku: A method of propagating Buddhism by refuting another's attachment to heretical views and thus leading him to the correct Buddhist teaching. The term is used in contrast to *shōju,* or leading another to the true teaching gradually without refuting his misconceptions. The two methods of propagation are described in the Shrīmālā Sutra, *Moho Zhiguan,* and elsewhere. In the *Nyosetsu Shugyō Shō* (On Practicing the Buddha's Teachings) and other writings, Nichiren Daishonin states that the method of *shakubuku* should be used in the Latter Day of the Law. In the *Kaimoku Shō* (The Opening of the Eyes), he clarifies that even in the Latter Day of the Law both *shōju* and *shakubuku* should be used, because there are two kinds of countries, those whose people are ignorant of Buddhism, and those where people willfully go against the Law. It is necessary to consider carefully, he adds, to which category one's country belongs.

Shen Nong: A legendary sage-king of ancient China.

Shoho. See *Esho funi.*

Taiseki-ji: The head temple of Nichiren Shoshu, located in Fujinomiya City in Shizuoka Prefecture at the foot of Mount Fuji. It was founded by Nikkō Shonin, Nichiren Daishonin's successor and the second high priest of Nichiren Shoshu.

Takahashi, Lay Priest: Jap Takahashi Nyūdō. A follower of Nichiren Daishonin, also known as Takahashi Rokurō Hyōe Nyūdō. He lived in Kajima in Fuji District of Suruga Province. His wife was Nikkō Shonin's aunt, and he was converted to Nichiren Daishonin's teachings by Nikkō Shonin. A letter sent to him from the Daishonin entrusts him with the responsibility of propagation in the area where he was living, which would indicate that he enjoyed the Daishonin's trust and was a leading figure among the lay believers in Fuji District.

Ten Worlds: Ten life-conditions which a single entity of life manifests. Originally the Ten Worlds were viewed as distinct physical places each with its own particular inhabitants. In light of the Lotus Sutra, they are interpreted as potential conditions of life inherent in each individual. The ten are: (1) The state of Hell (Jap *jigoku*). Hell indicates a condition in which one is dominated by the impulse of rage to destroy oneself and everything else. (2) The state of Hunger (*gaki*). Hunger is a condition characterized by insatiable desire for food, clothes, wealth, pleasure, fame, power and so forth. One in this state is tormented by relentless craving and by his inability to assuage it. (3) The state of Animality (*chikusho*). It is a condition governed by instincts, in which one has no sense of reason or morality. One in the state of Animality stands in fear of the strong but despises and preys upon those weaker than himself. (4) The state of Anger (*shura*). It is a condition dominated by a selfish ego. One in this state is compelled by the need to be superior to others in all things, despising them and valuing himself alone. (5) The state of Humanity or Tranquillity (*nin*). In this state, one can pass fair judgment, control his instinctive desires with reason, and act in harmony with his environment. (6) The state of Heaven or Rapture (*ten*). This state indicates the sense of pleasure which one experiences when his desire is fulfilled. However, the joy in the state of Heaven is temporary, and disappears with the passage of time or with even a slight change in circumstances. (7) The state of Learning (*shōmon*), a condition in which one awakens to the impermanence of all things and the instability of the six paths, and seeks some lasting truth and aims at self-reformation through the teachings of others. (8) The state of Realization (*engaku*), a condition in which one perceives the impermanence of all phenomena and strives to free himself from the sufferings of the six paths by seeking some lasting truth through his own observations and effort. (9) The state of Bodhisattva (*bosatsu*). In this state, one not only aspires for enlightenment himself but also devotes himself to compassionate actions. The characteristic of Bodhisattva lies in this dedication to altruism. (10) The state of Buddhahood (*butsu*). This is a condition of perfect and absolute freedom, in which one enjoys boundless wisdom and compassion, and is filled with the courage and power to surmount all hardships. A Buddha understands all phenomena and realizes the Middle Way.

Three bodies: (Skt *trikāya*) Also called the three properties or three enlightened properties. Three kinds of body which a Buddha may possess. A concept adopted in Mahayana to organize different concepts of the Buddha appearing in the sutras. The three bodies are: (1) The Dharma body or body of the Law (Skt *dharma-kāya*, Jap *hosshin*). The fundamental truth or Law to which the Buddha is enlightened. (2) The bliss body (*sambhoga-kāya*, *hōshin*), sometimes called the reward body, which is obtained as the reward of completing bodhisattva practice and having understood the Buddha wisdom. Unlike the Dharma body, which is immaterial, the bliss body is conceived of as an actual body, although one that is transcendent and imperceptible to common mortals. (3) The manifested body (*nirmāna-kāya, ōjin*), or the physical form in which the Buddha appears in this world in order to save the people.

Three calamities: Disasters said to occur at the end of a kalpa. There are two sets of three calamities—lesser and greater. They are explained in the *Kusha Ron*. (1) Three lesser calamities—warfare, pestilence, and famine. The calamity of famine is also called the calamity of high grain prices or inflation, because inflation was caused by a shortage of grain. These calamities are said to occur at the end of each kalpa of decrease in the Kalpa of Continuance, that is, whenever the human life span diminishes to ten years. According to one explanation, all three occur at the end of each kalpa of decrease; first, war rages for seven days, then epidemics prevail for seven months, and finally famine sets in for seven years. According to another, they occur alternately, pestilence at the end of the first kalpa of decrease, war at the end of the second, famine at the end of the third, and so on, each calamity lasting for seven days. (2) Three greater calamities—fire, water, and wind. These are said to occur at the end of the Kalpa of Decline and to destroy the world. In the calamity of fire, seven suns appear at the same time and burn up the world. The flames reach from the hell of incessant suffering to the first meditation heaven in the world of form. In the calamity of water, flood sweeps away everything from the hell of incessant suffering up to the second meditation heaven. In the calamity of wind, a great storm demolishes everything from the hell of incessant suffering up through the third meditation heaven. It is said that these calamities occur in a fixed pattern over a cycle of sixty-four major kalpas. In the first seven major kalpas, the world is destroyed by fire. In the eighth, it ends in flood. This pattern repeats itself seven times in all. Then the world ends in fire for seven successive major kalpas, and in the next, sixty-fourth major kalpa, the world is destroyed by wind. In a cycle of sixty-four major kalpas, the disaster of fire occurs fifty-six times, water seven times, and wind one time. Nichiren Daishonin defines the cause of the three lesser calamities to be the three poisons of greed, anger and stupidity which are the fundamental evils inherent in life: greed brings about famine, anger incites war and stupidity leads to pestilence. Furthermore, the Daishonin attributes the most fundamental cause of these calamities to ignorance of the Law of Nam-myoho-renge-kyo, which gives rise to the impurity of life, that is, the three poisons.

Three disasters. *See* Three calamities.

Three Great Secret Laws: The object of worship of true Buddhism (Jap *hommon no honzon*), the invocation or Daimoku of true Buddhism (*hommon no daimoku*) and the high sanctuary of true Buddhism (*hommon no kaidan*). These three constitute the core of Nichiren Daishonin's Buddhism. The object of worship of true Buddhism is the Dai-Gohonzon which the Daishonin inscribed on October 12, 1279, to enable all people to attain Buddhahood. The invocation or Daimoku of true Buddhism is the Daimoku of Nam-myoho-renge-kyo which one chants with faith in the object of worship, and the high sanctuary of true Buddhism is the place where one chants the daimoku to the object of worship. Since the invocation of Nam-myoho-renge-kyo is directed toward the object of worship, and the high sanctuary is built to enshrine the object of worship, the object of worship ultimately encompasses all Three Great Secret Laws within itself, and is also called the One Great Secret Law. The Daishonin himself established the Daimoku and the object of worship of true Buddhism. He entrusted his disciples with the mission of attaining *kōsen-rufu* and establishing the high sanctuary for all humanity to come and worship.

Three obstacles and four devils: A categorization of the various obstacles and hindrances which trouble one's practice of Buddhism. The three obstacles are: (1) The obstacle of earthly desires (Jap *bonnō-shō*), or obstacles arising from the three poisons of greed, anger, and stupidity. (2) The obstacle of karma (*gō-shō*), or obstacles due to bad karma created by committing any of the five cardinal sins or ten evil acts. This category is also interpreted as opposition from one's wife or chidren. (3) The obstacle of retribution (*hō-shō*), or obstacles due to painful retribution for actions in the three evil paths. This category also indicates obstacles caused by one's sovereign, parents, or other persons who carry some sort of secular authority. The four devils are: (1) The hindrance of the five components (*on-ma*), that is, those obstructions caused by one's physical and mental functions. (2) The hindrance of earthly desires (*bonnō-ma*), or obstructions arising from the three poisons. (3) The hindrance of death (*shi-ma*), because the fear and suffering that death entails obstruct one's practice of Buddhism. (4) The hindrance of the Devil of the Sixth Heaven (*tenji-ma*). This obstruction is usually said to take the form of oppression by men of power.

Three poisons: Greed, anger, and stupidity. Sometimes translated as avarice, anger, and ignorance, etc. The fundamental evils inherent in life which give rise to human suffering. The three poisons are so called because they pollute people's lives. The three poisons are also said to be the underlying cause of the three calamities: greed brings about famine, anger gives rise to war, and stupidity leads to pestilence.

Three powerful enemies: Three groups of people who persecute the votaries of the Lotus Sutra in the evil age after Shakyamuni Buddha's passing. They were defined by Miaoluo on the basis of descriptions in the twenty-line verse which concludes the *Kanji* (thirteenth) chapter of the Lotus Sutra. They are: (1) lay people ignorant of Buddhism who denounce the votaries of the Lotus Sutra and attack them with swords or staves; (2) arrogant and cunning priests who think they have attained what they have not yet attained and slander the votaries; and (3) priests revered as saints and respected by the general public who, in fear of losing fame or profit, induce the secular authorities to persecute the votaries of the Lotus Sutra.

Three truths: The truth of non-substantiality (Jap *kūtai*), the truth of temporary existence (*ketai*) and the truth of the Middle Way (*chūtai*). Because they are not separate but indicate three phases of the one truth, they are sometimes translated as the threefold truth, triple truth, or three perceptions of the truth. The truth of non-substantiality means that phenomena have no absolute or fixed existence of their own; their true nature is *kū*, the potential state that cannot be defined as either existence or nonexistence. The truth of temporary existence means that while all things are *kū* or nonsubstantial in nature, they nevertheless possess a provisional or temporary reality which is in constant flux. The truth of the Middle Way is that all phenomena are characterized by both non-substantiality and temporary existence yet are in essence neither non-substantiality nor temporary existence. The true nature of all phenomena is beyond the limitations of words or conception.

Tiantai, Great Teacher (538–597): Also called Zhiyi. The founder of the Chinese Tiantai school. His name and title were taken from Mount Tiantai where he lived. He lived during the Northern and Southern Dynasties period and the Sui dynasty. Tiantai refuted the scriptural classifications formulated by the ten major Buddhist schools of his day, which based themselves either on the Kegon Sutra or Nirvana Sutra, and devised the classification of the five periods and eight teachings, thereby establishing the supremacy of the Lotus Sutra. He also expounded the theory of *ichinen sanzen*. Because he systematized both its doctrine and method of practice, he is revered as the founder of the school. Tiantai's lectures were recorded by his disciple and successor Changan. His most important teachings were compiled as the three major works of the Tiantai school—the *Fahua Xuanyi*, the *Fahua Wenju*, and the *Moho Zhiguan*.

Time without beginning: (Jap *kuon ganjo*) Also called the infinite past. The term *kuon ganjo* is used to indicate an eternity without beginning, as opposed to the specific point in time called *gohyaku-jintengo*, which is expounded in the *Juryō* (sixteenth) chapter of the Lotus Sutra. *Kuon ganjo* suggests a past far older than even the inconceivably distant *gohyaku-jintengō*, but philosophically speaking, it indicates that dimension which is outside the temporal framework, having neither beginning nor end.

Treasure Tower: The tower of Tahō Buddha which emerges from below the earth in the *Hōtō* (eleventh) chapter of the Lotus Sutra. According to the sutra, it measures 250 *yojana* wide and 500 *yojana* high, and is adorned with the seven kinds of gems: gold, silver, lapis lazuli, giant clam shell, coral, pearl, and carnelian. Seated inside the tower is Tahō Buddha. Concerning the question as to what the Treasure Tower symbolizes, Nichiren Daishonin stated that it is Nam-myoho-renge-kyo, or the life of those who manifest their inherent Buddhahood by chanting Nam-myoho-renge-kyo. The *Abutsu-bō Gosho* (On the Treasure Tower) states, "In the Latter Day of the Law, there is no Treasure Tower other than the figures of the men and women who embrace the Lotus Sutra. It follows, therefore, that those who chant Nam-myoho-renge-kyo, irrespective of social status, are themselves the Treasure Tower and likewise they themselves are Tahō Buddha. There is no Treasure Tower other than Myoho-renge-kyo. The Daimoku of the Lotus Sutra is the Treasure Tower, that is to say, the Treasure Tower is Nam-myoho-renge-kyo."

Vulture Peak: (Skt Gridhrakūta) Sometimes called Eagle Peak. A mountain located to the northeast of Rājagriha, the capital of Magadha in ancient India, where Shakyamuni is said to have expounded the Lotus Sutra and other teachings. Vulture Peak was so called because its summit is shaped like a vulture and because it was inhabited by many vultures. The expression Vulture Peak is also used to symbolize the Buddha land or the state of Buddhahood.

Yakushi Sutra: "Sutra of Yakushi Buddha." A sutra which emphasizes the blessings of the Buddha Yakushi, or Buddha of Medicine. The Yakushi Sutra is a general term for any of the four extant Chinese translations of this scripture, though it usually refers to the Yakushi Rurikō Nyorai Hongan Kudoku Sutra (Sutra of the Blessings of the Original Vows of Yakushi Buddha), a translation made by Xuanzang of the Tang dynasty. In it Shakyamuni expounds the blessings of the Buddha Yakushi to Bodhisattva Monju. First the sutra recounts a previous life of Yakushi Buddha in which, as a bodhisattva, he made twelve great vows to benefit the people. The great benefit of invoking his name is then described. The sutra also explains the seven disasters and asserts that making offerings to Yakushi can avert them and restore peace to the land.

Yujutsu chapter: "Emerging from the Earth." The fifteenth chapter of the Lotus Sutra and the beginning of the essential teaching. Its full title is *Jūji Yujutsu* chapter. At the beginning of this chapter, the innumerable great bodhisattvas who have assembled from other worlds vow to propagate the Lotus Sutra in the *saha* world after Shakyamuni's death. Shakyamuni stops them, however, saying that there is no need; the *saha* world already has great bodhisattvas who will carry out this task. With this, the earth trembles and splits open, and a host of bodhisattvas emerge, equal in number to the sands of sixty thousand Ganges Rivers, each with his own retinue (Jap *kenzoku*). They are headed by the four bodhisattvas, the leader of whom is Bodhisattva Jōgyō. Bodhisattva Miroku, astounded at this sight, asks the Buddha on behalf of the assembly who these bodhisattvas are, where they came from, for what purpose, what Buddha they follow and what teaching they practice. Shakyamuni Buddha replies that they are his original disciples whom he has been teaching since long ago. Miroku again asks to know how, in the mere forty-odd years since his awakening, Shakyamuni has managed to teach so many countless bodhisattvas. He beseeches Shakyamuni to explain further, for the sake of people in the future who may have doubts about this point. The *Yujutsu* chapter ends here. To answer Miroku's question, the Buddha reveals in the *Juryō* (sixteenth) chapter that in reality countless aeons have passed since he first attained enlightenment.

Zhiguan Fuxing: In full, *Moho Zhiguan Fuxingzhuan Hongiue* (Jap *Maka Shikan Bugyoden Guketsu*), "Annotations on the *Moho Zhiguan*." Usually abbreviated as *Hongjue* (Jap *Guketsu*). A very detailed commentary on Tiantai's *Moho Zhiguan* written by Miaoluo. After Tiantai's death, a number of differing interpretations of the *Moho Zhiguan* began to appear both from other schools and from within the Tiantai school itself. Miaoluo wrote the *Hongjue* to refute mistaken interpretations and clarify the correct doctrines of the Tiantai school. *See also* Miaoluo, Great Teacher; *Moho Zhiguan*

Zhiyi. *See* Tiantai, Great Teacher.

Wade-Giles Romanizations for Chinese Words

PINYIN	WADE-GILES
Bian Que	Pien Ch'üeh
Changan	Ch'ang-an
Fahua Wenju	Fa-hua Wen-chü
Fahua Xuanyi	Fa-hua Hsüan-i
Faxiang	Fa-hsiang
Folong	Fo-lung
Guoqingsi	Kuo-ch'ing-ssu
Huang Di	Huang Ti
Huayan	Huayen
Miaofa Lianhua Jing Wenju	Miao-fa Lien-hua Ching Wen-chü
Miaoluo	Miao-lo
Miaoluosi	Miao-lo-ssu
Moho Zhiguan	Mo-ho Chih-kuan
Moho Zhiguan Fuxingzhuan Hongjue	Mo-ho Chih-kuan Fu-hsing-chuan Hung-chüeh
Shen Nong	Shen Nung
Tang	T'ang
Tiantai	T'ien-t'ai
Xuanlang	Hsüan-lang
Xuanzang	Hsüan-tsang
Zhiguan Fuxing	Chih-kuan Fu-hsing
Zhiyi	Chih-i

The "Weathermark" identifies this book as a production of John Weatherhill, Inc., publishers of fine books on Asia and the Pacific. Book design and typography: Miriam F. Yamaguchi. Photo layout: Yutaka Shimoji. Production supervision: Mitsuo Okado. Composition: Samhwa Printing Co., Seoul. Printing: Shobundo Printing Co., Tokyo. Binding: Makoto Binderies, Tokyo. The typeface used is Monotype Bembo.